NEGOTIATING THE POSTCOLONIAL

NEGOTIATING THE POSTCOLONIAL:

EMERGING PERSPECTIVES ON
TSTSI DANGAREMBGA

EDITED BY
ANN ELIZABETH WILLEY
&
JEANETTE TREIBER

Africa World Press, Inc.

P.O. Box 1892
Trenton, NJ 08607

P.O. Box 48
Asmara, ERITREA

Africa World Press, Inc.

P.O. Box 1892
Trenton, NJ 08607

P.O. Box 48
Asmara, ERITREA

Cover design: Ashraful Haque

Library of Congress Cataloging-in-Publication Data

Emerging Perspectives on Tsitsi Dangarembga : negotiating the postcolonial / [edited by] Ann Elizabeth Willey and Jeanette Treiber.
    p. cm.
Includes bibliographical references and index.
ISBN 0-86543-932-X -- ISBN 0-86543-933-8 (pbk.)
    1. Dangarembga, Tstsi--Criticism and interpretation. 2. Women and literature--Zimbabwe--History--20th century. 3. Postcolonialism--Zimbabwe. 4. Zimbabwe--In literature. I. Willey, Ann Elizabeth. II. Treiber, Jeanette.

PR9390.9.D36 Z66 2001
823'.914--dc2

                     2001022097

Contents

I Critiques of Postcolonial Rhetoric

II Material Culture

III Postcolonial Subjectivities

Introduction

Ann Elizabeth Willey and Jeanette Treiber

For decades, Chinua Achebe's *Things Fall Apart* was the primary novel that introduced Americans to African literature. It was used in universities across the country in a wide variety of disciplines, from Anthropology to History, to give Western audiences an insight into African culture. In the last ten years, however, Achebe's novel has increasingly been replaced by a newcomer: Tsitsi Dangarembga's *Nervous Conditions*. In high schools and universities, from Women's Studies to literature courses, students read and discuss *Nervous Conditions* as representative of African literature, culture, and history. This coming of age story of a young Zimbabwean girl asks readers to engage the history of colonialism, cultural roles for women, the impact of education, the importance of community, and the act of writing in their importance for the formation of an African woman's identity. But *Nervous Conditions* is only part of the thought-provoking body of works by Tsitsi Dangarembga. Before the 1988 publication of her novel, Dangarembga had produced plays for a university theater group and published short stories; in 1996, she directed the film "Everyone's Child." This collection of essays seeks to bring together the widely varied strands of conversation that Dangarembga's work continues to engender. Though most of the essays in this collection concentrate on her novel, we have specifically included essays that look at her short stories and film in order to better assess Dangarembga's impact on the field of Postcolonial Studies.

The subtitle, "Negotiating the Postcolonial," reflects several points of emphasis that we had in mind as this collection came together. First, it emphasizes the important time period in which Dangarembga's work is set: the era immediately preceding and following independence for the majority of the African continent. Authors and scholars of African literature are increasingly drawn to the problematic of representing an African engagement with modernity that accompanied these struggles for national liberation. While Achebe's *Things Fall Apart* depicts African social disruption in the first moments of colonial contact, *Nervous Conditions* looks at a more recent past to diagnose the social dis-ease that haunts its characters. Dangarembga's other works similarly situate their characters in a recent past or immediate present. Secondly, the title, with its admittedly trendy overtones, signals our commitment to a theoretical engagement with Dangarembga's work. As African literature becomes more and more prevalent in American and European academic curricula, it is increasingly in dialogue with formal academic modes of reading. This collection contains readings influenced by Freudian, Jungian, Narratological, Feminist, Marxist, and other schools of literary analysis. While we leave it to the reader to judge the usefulness of any given approach, we hope that the variety present here suggests the rich possibilities of studying African literature. Finally, we hope that the reader takes to heart the suggestion that reading Dangarembga's work draws us into the postcolonial discussion. As twentieth and twenty-first century people, we are all implicated in the negotiations of an increasingly global, if uneven, modernity. It is not surprising that most of the essays in this collection address the very notion of modernity itself.

An engagement with global modernity is indicated by the trajectory of Dangarembga's life. Born in Rhodesia in 1959, Dangarembga left for England at the age of two. After four years (1965), she returned to Rhodesia, only to voyage once again to England in 1977 to pursue a degree in medicine. Profoundly discouraged by the implicit and explicit racism at Cambridge and concerned for the well-being of her family and country during the armed struggle for independence, Dangarembga returned to Zimbabwe in 1980 where she continued her studies. At the University of Harare while studying psychology, she began publishing plays and short stories. In the early 1990s, following the success of her first novel, *Nervous Conditions*, Dangarembga moved to Berlin to study film.

It is the 1988 novel, *Nervous Conditions,* that perhaps paradoxically first gave Tsitsi Dangarembga wide recognition. While the story of Tambudzai Sigauke's pursuit of an education is firmly grounded in local Zimbabwean realities, Dangarembga had to look to London to find its first publisher. Her U.S. Publisher, Seal Press, features *Nervous Conditions* prominently in their catalogue, claiming that to date 80,000 copies of the novel have been sold in the U.S. As a text that raises crucial questions of how identities are formed in the crucible of African nations in search of independence, *Nervous Conditions* broaches several of the topics that have come to occupy the forefront of Postcolonial Studies in general. The main character, Tambudzai Sigauke, struggles to define a place for herself in a society that is imbricated with both patriarchal and colonial epistemes. In the process of telling her story, the narrative tackles issues such as colonial education, traditional versus "modern" or western modes of living, gender relations, and the role of writing itself. Dangarembga's latest film, "Everyone's Child," similarly examines the trials of growing up in a Zimbabwe ravaged by AIDS and uneven development, exacerbated by unequal gender relations that leave young men with little hope and young women with even less. Because of their often subtle but always gripping portrayal of these complex dynamics of development, gender difference, and the development of an identity in a postcolonial context, these texts have gained a wide audience in American academies. And yet, her work often challenges our understandings of the common tropes of postcolonial studies. Both from a feminist and a culturally particular point of view, Dangarembga's work invites the reader to rethink categories often used to analyze postcolonial African literature.

Dangarembga's reference to Fanon in the title and epigraph of *Nervous Conditions* has inspired many critics to explore the relationship between the Fanonian discourse of colonial nervousness and Dangarembga's response. Are we to read the reference as an interpretive framework or as a starting point from which to reinterpret Fanon's diagnosis of colonial and anticolonial mentality? Many of the essays in this collection give partial or comprehensive answers to this question. Generally there is an agreement among contributors that Dangarembga's main concern is to address the formation of national consciousness much in the same way as Fanon did, but that she adds a factor to the discussion that Fanon had not considered: gender. Heather Zwicker's essay illustrates most extensively in this collection that Dangarembga's representation of Rhodesia is in line with Fanon's theory, but that the theory is incomplete if it fails to acknowledge that colonial and patriarchal structures are intertwined. Her paper argues that the trope of anorexia becomes most intelligible when read through a revisionary use of Fanon, and that it is only through understanding this revisionary nationalism that the implications of *Nervous Conditions* as a *Bildungsroman* become clear. In "On Violence," Fanon argues that colonialism is inherently violent, but that its destructive violence produces a creative counter-violence that leads to a consciousness of national identity. Zwicker argues that Nyasha's anorexia–set up from the novel's opening as one mode of rebellion—is a consequence of the violence of colonialism, of patriarchy, and of cultural hybridity. But insofar as it brings Tambudzai to a revolutionary national consciousness that enables her to write, Nyasha's eating disorder turns destructive violence into constructive violence. The body of Nyasha in effect becomes an allegory for Zimbabwe; although Nyasha, like Zimbabwe, is torn apart by internal violence, this violence produces another enabling story. In using anorexia for this trope, Dangarembga not only demonstrates that nationalism and colonialism collude with patriarchy in particularly damaging ways for women, but also insists that African theories of nationalism need to be rethought from the perspective of gender. Susan Andrade is much more skeptical. She takes up the question of politics and nationalism with the understanding that, especially for women, politics has both a public and a domestic dimension. It is women's relationship to the nationalist imaginary as both figures and actors that concerns her. She points out the explicitly anticolonial politics in the novel, as voiced by the Fanonian reference in the title, coupled with a refusal to engage—or even depict—the nationalist guerrilla struggles taking place at the time during which the novel is set. The text insists on claiming a girl's right to a formal education along with the entrance to modernity this presumes and insists on positioning itself as anti-colonial. In contrast to the male-authored literary texts of the time, however, it does this without also celebrating (or even acknowledging) the nationalist struggles for decolonization. Andrade insists that Dangarembga's narrative takes seriously the axiom that nationalism subsumes feminism. In fact, *Nervous Conditions* appears to enact the opposite: the telling of a domestic (and gendered) political tale which subsumes and metaphorizes nationalism in the interests of feminism. Ann Elizabeth Willey shows how this novel brings together three terms that have been central to discussions of

African literature: modernity, alienation, and development. For in this novel, Dangarembga challenges our definitions of alienation by linking the question of development as implication in the modern world to the process of a young girl developing into an adult voice. In this, Dangarembga challenges our usually male defined sense of alienation and modernity to suggest a female paradigm for the understanding of the processes of alienation and development in relation to modernity. Through the modern technology of writing, Tambu struggles to represent her own development into an educated woman and the various efforts that she and the women around her have used to make a space for themselves in the rapidly developing world of 1960s Rhodesia. Equally concerned with the question of gender, colonialism, and modernity, Jeanette Treiber shows how *Nervous Conditions* dismantles gender and cultural essentialism by studying the way in which the text diffuses the geographies of home and "not home," tradition and modernity, essential purity versus contaminated fusions. Evoking and reversing images of dirt, cleanliness, and cleansing, the text examines their manipulative power within the colonial and postcolonial context. Refusing to submit to the restrictive discourses surrounding these images, the female protagonist of *Nervous Conditions* develops mental strategies that help her assert herself against the negative odds created by her predicament of being female and colonized in Rhodesia. The novel itself is read as a strategy to dismantle disabling essentialisms on a number of fronts.

Illness has long been a central trope in European discourse on Africa. The representation of anorexia nervosa, a predominantly Western feminine illness, in *Nervous Conditions* is widely discussed among scholars. Brendon Nicholls argues that while scholars of Dangarembga's text have generally acknowledged a correspondence between the socio-cultural setting of the novel and the emergence of Nyasha's illness, their descriptions of this illness as "anorexia" or "bulimia" amount to a failure by these scholars to heed the most astute insights advanced in their work. Quite clearly, if anorexia and bulimia are usually prevalent in Western contexts, he

argues, then their application to Nyasha's predicament risks eliding her specifically African context. He understands the symptom
to be the product of both Nyasha's Anglicization and her selective
re-assimilation into her effaced Shona mother-culture. His article
offers "boulimia" as an interim designation for Nyasha's nervous
condition. He then proceeds to discuss one particular Southern
African understanding of illness, *amafufunyane*, which appears to
highlight many of the concerns raised in Dangarembga's novel and
speaks towards the argument for entertaining the term "boulimia"
in relation to Nyasha. The theme of illness and decay also features
in Jeffery Geller's essay on "Cultural Autopsy." As coroners are
charged to determine whether suspicious deaths are the result of
natural causes or foul play, according to Geller, *Nervous Conditions* investigates the question of whether the survival of the
narrator's culture is threatened by internal disintegration, external
assault, or a combination of both. By comparing *Nervous Conditions* to Achebe's *Things Fall Apart* and Fanon's *Wretched of the
Earth*, two texts that also fall into the genre of cultural autopsy, his
essay traces Dangarembga's complex treatment of the process of
cultural change. He shows how, unlike the other two texts,
Dangarembga's future-oriented narrative demonstrates the advantage of putting autopsy to work, of harnessing death as a resource
for the living. Throughout the process of obtaining her western
style education, the narrator Tambu develops the two imperatives
that allow her to avoid the death by assimilation that consumed her
brother: to avoid undervaluing indigenous culture and to avoid overvaluing exogenous culture. For the narrative shows how the imperative to maintain pride of original affiliation and remain critical
of the new are linked: failure to achieve the second predisposes
one to fail at the first. Guiliana Lund's essay traces the history of
medical discourse in colonial and postcolonial literature in order
to illuminate the transformations wrought in this discourse by Tsitsi
Dangarembga in her novel *Nervous Conditions* and the movie
"Everyone's Child." Dangarembga not only undermines the colonial stereotype of the African woman as a source of contagion, but

also challenges the propensity of male writers to critique the corruption of the postcolonial state through an abstract language of pathology that takes woman as a symbol, rather than a participant, in national struggles.

Several essays seek to explore how the material culture of Southern Africa and 1960's Rhodesia form an interpretive framework for situating the novel and the film in contemporaneous discourses of cultural change and adaptation. Sally Ann Murray takes a closer look at the representation (or not) of commodity relations as they bear upon the identities evolved by Dangarembga's characters. Her paper outlines a reading which moves beyond the obvious neuroses depicted in the book, allowing into the mix Dangarembga's struggles to express the awkward intersections of cultural institutions such as colonial education, liberal enlightenment, traditional patriarchy, modernity, and consumer culture. Murray argues that the ambivalence in the novel towards consumer culture comprises Dangarembga's authorial "nervous condition" and, importantly, that this is a condition of the global modernities which we are likely to call our own. Kelli Wixson focuses on one particular consumer item and its real and metaphorical implications: food. Her essay explores how women in Dangarembga's novel use food as a means to assert their individuality and agency. She claims that as the women in the novel are doubly removed from access to power--once by the traditional Shona patriarchy, and again by the English colonial system which reinforced that patriarchy even as it subjugated the country to colonial rule--they use the only resource at their disposal, food, to exert control over their bodies. Food becomes the focus of the women's self-assertion because of its importance in the oppressive colonial and patriarchal systems depicted in the novel. The essay draws on Fanon's "Algeria Unveiled" and "On National Culture" in conjunction with other theories of eating disorders to contextualize how a specific material item can become the site of contested cultural meanings and how resistance works to redefine such meanings.

The postcolonial African subject and its definition and redefinition has long been a central point of discussion in the criticism of African literature. The essays presented on the subject here
reflect the diversity of that discussion. Linda Chown's reading of
the novel uncovers a plethora of foregrounded tensions between
"two disconnected entities," between Western, thoroughly psychologized manners of understanding and a less self-conscious,
pre-Cartesian epistemology. *Nervous Conditions*, according to
Chown, sinuously shifts between two perspectives—that of auto-
diagetic and homodiagetic narrative positions--using the paradigms
suggested in the work of the linguist Lev Vygotsky. In its complex
narrative presentation, *Nervous Conditions* affirms the nexus between individual consciousness and social conditions. There is also
the development of a new kind of individualism based on a way of
knowing which moves through spiraling indecision into rich affiliated certainty. Biman Basu reminds us that postcolonial intellectuals inhabit the structures of violence which define their situatedness
and serve as the site of production for this discourse. In such a
position, these intellectuals are particularly susceptible to the possibilities of resolution offered at the level of transcendent categories. They shift grounds and refer themselves to the category of
consciousness and subjectivity, even if consciousness of the material conditions that structure their existence does not necessarily
alter those conditions and in fact may serve to elide the materiality
of this contradictory position. Basu claims that *Nervous Conditions* relentlessly details the process of enculturation as a material
process. Yet, equally insistently, it deploys the category of a transcendent consciousness and refers to a liberated subjectivity. He
reads the novel as a textual transaction, a cultural document that
maps the institutional spaces through which the shifting positions
of the transnational intellectual may be plotted. Starting from Frantz
Fanon's description of the materiality of the spaces that intellectuals occupy, this essay argues that texts like Tsitsi Dangarembga's
Nervous Conditions need to be read not as instances of postmodern
auto-referentiality in their figuring of the intellectual, but instead
as texts whose narrative and critical difficulties arise from within a

specific historical circumstance. Mary Jane Androne's essay argues that this novel is best understood as belonging to the "outlaw genres" or "literature of revolt," testimonio, temoinage, renegade autobiography, and resistance literature. What Dangarembga's novel has in common with these other genres which resist formal classification is an underlying ideology that questions the validity of liberal humanist concepts of self-discovery revealed in a linear plot which records the triumphs and victories of an individual woman struggling against impossible odds. *Nervous Conditions* is a text which destabilizes the idea of progress and individual achievement in political regimes which are oppressively sexist as well as elitist. In demonstrating the deformation and truncation of women's lives, Dangarembga's narrator Tambu subverts the very notion of "development" as she acknowledges how the generations of threat, assault, and neglect batter the negative myths of women into beliefs about themselves that African women internalize. Jacqueline Wigfall examines the short story "The Letter," or more specifically, its narrative strategies such as authenticating African detail and the feminist impact of first person perspective. This short fiction uncovers the effect of (neo)colonialism on a South African woman political prisoner. Her body becomes a site of representation for the multiple experiences of colonized women. This multiplicity is one aspect of her potentially universal appeal for a variety of readers. The narrator mediates several ideological realms ushered into the text by way of letters and shifting geographies, tropes that consistently circulate in postcolonial and postmodern literatures. "The Letter" invites readers to "role play," particularly readers who meet Dangarembga's text outside of South Africa and have much to learn, from many vantages, about resistance, complicity, and apartheid. The text negotiates binaries of public/private and domestic/political in constructing female subjectivity. The shifting identity of the detainee from memoir narrator to letter writer (and from free, to detained) also parallels the multiplication of audience perspective(s). These tactics, integral to the detainee's strategic narration, reflect the ultimate political strength of

Dangarembga's project. Kgomotso Masemola's essay seeks to locate the interstitial spaces within which *Nervous Conditions'* characters have to operate due to the necessarily hybridized space of colonial and postcolonial societies. By looking at Dangarembga's use of the Jungian archetype of the shadow, this essay traces how various characters in the novel struggle within the colonial discourse of cultural difference and how Tambu in particular achieves a sense of her persona through an acceptance of the radical undecidability of the subjectivities presented by modernity.

While the essays collected here suggest the multivalence of Dangarembga's work in their wide range of interests and approaches, we acknowledge that they only begin to explore the full import of the novel, stories, plays, and movies that Dangarembga has produced. While we look forward to seeing the results of Dangarembga's continuing artistic endeavors, we encourage all those who are interested in African literature, African culture, and Postcolonial Studies in general to join in and continue the discussions circling around the increasingly prevalent and uneven modernity that we hope to have given voice to here.

I

CRITIQUES OF POSTCOLONIAL RHETORIC

Chapter 1:
The Nervous Collusions of Nation and Gender: Tsitsi Dangarembga's Challenge to Fanon[1]

Heather Zwicker

In one of her interviews, Tsitsi Dangarembga discusses the trouble she had getting her novel *Nervous Conditions* published in Zimbabwe. Noting that Zimbabwean people do not have a "habit of reading," she goes on to detail the difficulties entailed in writing:

> [W]ith all the things you read, with everything that you're taught, you construct a kind of cognitive map for yourself that is comfortable. I feel that for the people who grew up during my parents' time and my own time this was some-

thing that was denied to us, absolutely and completely. And this was done knowingly. People were not encouraged to write. We had what was called the Literature Bureau and they published all the African writing. And they would only allow tales of traditional witchcraft, wives poisoning their husbands, you know, that kind of thing. And of course my parents wouldn't let us read them, because they *were* destructive. And yet, that was the only cognitive map that the forces in power then were allowing us to construct. (George and H. Scott 311-12)

There is much to note in this short statement: Dangarembga asserts that literacy—reading and writing—produce a sense of identity, that such a sense of identity was forcibly withheld from black Rhodesians during the years leading up to independence, and that the Literature Bureau, one of the "forces in power," deliberately trained the minds of would-be Zimbabweans in particular ways. Dangarembga also suggests, in her comment that "they would only allow tales of traditional witchcraft, wives poisoning their husbands, . . . that kind of thing," that this curtailing of identity was directed against women in specific ways, entraining them to become or stay "traditional" at the very moment that a rising nationalist movement was holding out alternative ways of being. Dangarembga highlights a familiar yet still disheartening example of how feminism gets hived off from nationalism in the process of decolonization.

It is well known that Dangarembga was not able to publish her 1988 novel *Nervous Conditions* in Zimbabwe. In several interviews she has told the story of how the manuscript languished in a publishing house until she asked for its return (see especially Wilkinson, 1992). The London-based Women's Press first picked up the novel, which was reprinted in North America by Seal Press. Although Dangarembga is careful not to blame the Literature Bureau directly for the fact that her novel was not published in Zimbabwe, Dangarembga's interviews and essays paint a picture of a Zimbabwean publishing industry that discriminates against writing by women and actively discourages realistic representations of the lives of actual Zimbabwean girls and women. About the reason why her early plays were not published, for instance, Dangarembga says, "I had the distinct impression that the sympathetic young male editor found these women [characters] too nasty to be allowed to exist"; in discussing her novel, she comments that, "[i]t seems to be very difficult for men to accept the things that women write and want to write about and the men are the publishers" ("This Year" 43, George and H. Scott 311). The subtitle of Chigango Musandireve's review of *Nervous Conditions* in *Moto Magazine*, a popular Zimbabwean forum for current events, may speak for itself: "Woe unto bossy man!" it warns.[2]

And yet Dangarembga is not unaware of the dangers of international feminism either. While obviously glad to have her novel published by an international feminist press, she draws her interviewers' attention repeatedly to the limitations of white Western feminism for articulating or explaining her experiences (see Veit-Wild 106, Petersen 345 and 347, George and H. Scott 316). The material conditions under which *Nervous Conditions* was published chart out for the novel an explicitly feminist, liminal space between indigineity and internationalism. The novel—famous for being the first novel in English to be written by a black Zimbabwean woman—stands to be regulated by either the Literature Bureau within Zimbabwe or the international women's press and its attendant feminist vision. In this essay, I read the liminal space between the nation and the international as an important site of feminist agency, arguing that *Nervous Conditions* intervenes in institutionalized understandings of national literacy in order to model a nationalist feminism that resists both the pieties of the category "gender" as it is commonly used in a Western context as well as the platitudes of a patriarchal pan-African nationalism that refuses to take account of the lives of women. In my view, the trope of anorexia—signal concern of feminism—becomes most intelligible when read through Dangarembga's revisionary use of Fanon, and it is only through such a revisionary nationalism that the implications of *Nervous Condition* as a *bildungsroman* become clear.

A brief perusal of the Literature Bureau's mandate suggests that Dangarembga's assessment of its mission—explicit and implicit—is correct. Ellen Ellerman's research documents Literature Bureaus as widespread phenomena in former colonies. She argues that they serve contradictory purposes: conceived as tools of decolonization that would shore up indigenous languages and cultures, they nonetheless perpetuate colonial mechanisms and betray their indebtedness to an Arnoldian sense of education as social pacifier (Ellerman 207). To speak more practically, Literature Bureaus were designed as temporary institutions "to serve the literary and educational needs of the newly literate" by "facilitat[ing] the transfer of a viable literary system to the colony" (206, 208). Literature Bureaus preserved and codified indigenous languages, eventually translating them from orature to literature. In addition, they provide reading material other than the prayer books, Bibles, and catechisms dispensed by Christian missionaries. While such techniques of "decolonizing the mind" might remain constant across different colonial locations, it is important to note that Literature Bureaus take different forms in different colonial and postcolonial locations and that their functions change over time.[3]

As Ellerman puts it, the Literature Bureau "took on a wide range of shapes in different colonies as it responded to local needs"; often, in spite of its putative anti-colonial origins, the Bureau would "shift away from the traditional decolonizing role it had first adopted and move into another, more permanent manifestation" that involved "demonstrating, or transferring, a Western-style cultural system to colonized people" (209, 211, 213). The cultural effects of the Literature Bureau are often ambivalent, but it is clear that its machinations are inextricably wrapped up in the transmission of cultural values.

As the status of the Bureau as government branch suggests, the specific cultural values espoused in postcolonial locations are often explicitly nationalist. This is certainly the case with Zimbabwe's Bureau. In a 1992 *Editor's Manual*, the Literature Bureau of Zimbabwe describes its history, lays out its current purpose, and explains its procedures. [4] Like Bureaus elsewhere in the colonial world, the Literature Bureau of Zimbabwe was established (in 1954) for the ostensibly anti-colonial purpose of preserving the Ndebele and Shona languages and of producing thereby a meaningfully literate populace: as one contributor to the *Editor's Manual* puts it, "there was literacy without literature" in the absence of published Shona and Ndebele works (51). As did Bureaus in other colonial locations, the Literature Bureau of Zimbabwe eventually branched into English writing as well. Today the Bureau has two main roles, economic and cultural. The Literature Bureau solicits and assesses manuscripts, acting as guarantor of their literary value so as to encourage their publication. The Literature Bureau itself is not a publisher. The cultural role of the Bureau is to encourage literacy, to make reading and writing everyday habits of the people of Zimbabwe, a goal it meets through subsidiary objectives such as providing reading materials to schools, setting and judging writing contests, standardizing orthography, commissioning authors, participating in cultural exchanges, and so on. Such endeavors are explicitly nationalist—they constitute what I term "national literacy," a program designed not just to foster the technical skills of reading and writing, but also to school citizens in the language of nationalism. Here is how the Literature Bureau describes the material it promotes:

> The material we write must not be geared at imparting the 3 Rs only but also at skills to deal with the readers' immediate problems and the creation of awareness. The objectives of the material should be knowledge acquisition, skills development and attitudinal change. Material for new literates should, additionally, reflect Zimbabwe's national goals and priorities. They should act as a vehicle for the social, economic, cultural and political transformation of the nation. (16)

At first glance, such objectives are unimpeachable: every successful nationalist movement requires a cultural wing. But Dangarembga's comment about the strictures imposed on women's narratives, combined with other restrictive elements of post-revolutionary Zimbabwean society (Mugabe's virulent homophobia comes to mind particularly quickly, although there is much to criticize in post-independence Zimbabwe's record on women), suggest that the aims of the Literature Bureau are somewhat more sinister.[5]

Statements that might initially appear to be value-free, such as "New literates want to read about issues that are relevant and related to their life experiences. They do not want to read about what is offensive to them" start to sound suspicious once it becomes clear that there is a governmental bureau overseeing the definition of what is offensive (3). Likewise, a feminist critic must ask what the Literature Bureau might mean by stating that one of its roles is to "prepare children's and women's reading material to meet their reading needs" (2). What "needs" do traditional stories about witchcraft and wives poisoning their husbands (to use Dangarembga's description again) serve? Perhaps more importantly, *whose* needs do they serve? Rhetorical questions like these give a hollow ring to the self-congratulatory tone of the assertion later on in the *Editor's Manual* that "[t]he Literature Bureau has played a significant role in encouraging women to write. To date there are 20 women who have written in either Shona or Ndebele" (52). National literacy, overseen by such government branches as the Literature Bureau, involves the cultivation of particular kinds of national subjects, both writers and readers.[6]

This is the field Dangarembga's writing enters: a field in which literacy is shot through with conservative nationalist ideology and in which the written word carries huge cultural force. Understanding that Zimbabwean nationalism is articulated in such a field starts to explain why Dangarembga has repeatedly and explicitly stated that she sees her novel as a contribution to the nationalist struggle. Her life story is familiar to readers of her interviews: although she began studying medicine at Cambridge in the late 1970s, she grew increasingly frustrated by the willful ignorance and indifference of her British colleagues to Zimbabwe's independence struggle. Returning home to write, Dangarembga says, was not only necessary for her personal well-being, but was also a matter of national service (see Whyte 12) brought about by being "conscientized" (Veit-Wild 104). Clear that her writing has a political purpose, Dangarembga is always aware of speaking to an audience of Zimbabwean girls and women (see Wilkinson, 1992). Although Dangarembga herself did not participate actively in the independence struggle—indeed, by the time she returned to Zimbabwe in 1980 the most intense moments of the war were over, and the post-revolutionary moment had begun—she very carefully sets *Nervous Conditions* in the context of the Zimbabwean independence movement. The novel opens in the early 1960s, at the important if also inadequate nationalist stage at which Rhodesia's white minority government was negotiating, and then demanding, independence from Britain. *Nervous Conditions* follows its main character and narrator, Tambudzai, until 1971, when she enters Sacred Heart, the exclusive school administered by the nuns. For Tambudzai that moment is one of revolutionary consciousness and literary awareness; for Rhodesia as a whole, it ushers in a near-decade of civil war that led, ultimately, to Mugabe's nationalist win and the establishment of Zimbabwe as such. Tambudzai's growing self-consciousness coincides with Zimbabwe's emergent national awareness.

In spite of the close parallels between Tambudzai and Zimbabwe *per se*, to read the novel as an allegory is too simplistic. For one thing, to read so-called "third world" texts as national allegories is to retreat to a much earlier moment of postcolonial criticism (Jameson, 1996), one which insists on a clear distinction between first- and third-world texts and assigns distinct roles to each. Such a position is untenable in a text with a feminist vision that is irreducible to either national or international spaces. Secondly, the novel is not organized around a single protagonist: the figure of Nyasha is at least as important as that of Tambudzai, and the story unfolds primarily in the relationship between the two of them. Finally, Dangarembga is not interested in allegorizing the nation, freezing it as an abstraction, but, rather, in exploring the work of identity-building done in the name of nationalism. If the novel is a *bildungsroman* for a nation, it works by carefully orchestrating the role each main character plays in consolidating personal and national consciousness.

While *Nervous Conditions* may not be an allegory of nationalism, it must be read as both exemplification of and also as corrective to Frantz Fanon's key 1963 treatise on pan-African nationalism, *The Wretched of the Earth*. As is well known, *Nervous Conditions* is explicitly indebted to Fanon: the title of the novel comes from a line in Jean-Paul Sartre's preface which states that "the condition of native is a nervous condition" (Fanon, 1963, 20). While Dangarembga apparently came to Fanon only after she had drafted the manuscript of her novel, her admission that she wanted through her writing "to examine [colonialism's] effects upon the psyche of the individual" uncannily mirrors Fanon's life-long investigation into the psychological effects of domination (Whyte 13). Furthermore, in the sense that it tells its story against the backdrop of growing nationalist sentiment, *Nervous Conditions* mirrors *The Wretched of the Earth*, written in the midst of the Algerian war of independence.

Fanon's text, a collection of essays including "Concerning Violence," "The Pitfalls of National Consciousness," and "On National Culture," seeks to explain the relationship between colonial and anti-colonial violence, while it examines "the legitimacy of the claims of a nation" (207). I will briefly review Fanon's main ideas. In "On Violence," Fanon argues that colonialism is inherently violent, that it is, in fact, "violence in its natural state": "colonialism is not a thinking machine," he asserts, "nor a body endowed with reasoning facilities. It is violence in its natural state, and it will only yield when confronted with greater violence" (Fanon 61). Because colonialism is violent, it breeds a violent response. This violence is not only destructive, but also creative; it's the second term in the dialectic that produces national identity. In other words, colonialism's destructive violence calls for a creative violence that will produce national identity.

As for what Fanon means by "national identity," the definitions are multiple and sometimes contradictory. Certainly he is dismissive of a national bourgeoisie, which he regards as merely a comprador class which is as inexcusable as the settler class—criticizing comprador nationalism is one of the main burdens of his essay "The Pitfalls of National Consciousness." But as Neil Lazarus has most clearly (and most passionately) pointed out in his essay "Disavowing Decolonization," Fanon by no means does away with the idea of nation as a progressive organizing principle (see also Mowitt). Rather, he argues against bourgeois nationalism "from an *alternative nationalist standpoint*" (Lazarus 71-72, emphasis original). What Fanon has in mind is a nationalism that works from the bottom up, one that is progressive and deeply anti-colonial. He chooses to organize this around the nation despite the colonial origins of the concept because he believes that colonialism can be successfully fought only on its own ground. Given that colonialism has produced nations, they are the most useful ground for anti-colonial struggle. According to Fanon, a national culture is "the whole body of efforts made by a people in the sphere of thought to describe, justify, and praise the action through which that people has created itself and keeps itself in existence" ("On National Culture" 233). Fanon makes no distinction between the nation as an ideological construct and the nation as a material entity, between the nation and the state, or between cultural production and political action: "The living expression of the nation is the moving consciousness of the whole of the people; it is the coherent, enlightened action of men and women . . .. The national government, if it wants to be national, ought to govern by the people and for the people, for the outcasts and by the outcasts" ("Pitfalls" 204-05). A national struggle is the liberatory fight by which a people *will* themselves into being.

If the fight for liberation and the struggle for national culture are the same, it follows that a national literature is a "literature of combat" that "calls on the whole people to fight for their existence as a nation . . . because it molds the national consciousness, giving it form and contours and flinging open before it new and boundless horizons . . . because it assumes responsibility, and because it is the will to liberty expressed in terms of time and space" ("On National Culture" 239-40). The job of such a literature is to awaken national revolutionary consciousness in people, and Fanon's prescription depends on both a revolutionary class and, at least equally important, an intellectual vanguard (see Lazarus, again—and, for an alternative point of view, Mowitt). This intellectual vanguard works by instilling an education that is progressive because it addresses the masses and encourages them to imagine themselves as members of the national body. As Fanon puts it, "[t]o educate the masses politically is to make the totality of the nation a reality to each citizen. It is to make the history of the nation part of the personal experience of each of its citizens" ("Pitfalls" 200). The revolutionary consciousness Fanon has in mind begins emphatically with the people themselves:

> To educate the masses politically does not mean, cannot mean, making a political speech. What it means is to try, relentlessly and passionately, to teach the masses that everything depends on them; that if we stagnate it is their responsibility, and that if we go forward it is due to them too, that there is no such thing as a demiurge, that there is no famous man who will take the responsibility for everything, but that the demiurge is the people themselves and the magic hands are finally only the hands of the people. ("Pitfalls" 197-98)

It is my argument that we can understand Dangarembga's *Nervous Conditions* as a work of national literature in the terms Fanon sets out—with the significant difference that "the people" be understood as gendered, not just gender-neutral, as Fanon assumes.[7]

Like Fanon, Dangarembga insists on the indivisibility of colonialism and violence, and she approaches concepts like nation, citizen and agency as problems to be explored rather than stable ideas with predictable meanings. *Nervous Conditions* announces itself as a "problem novel" from its very opening paragraph:

> I was not sorry when my brother died. Nor am I apologising for my callousness, as you may define it, my lack of feeling. For it is not that at all. I feel many things these days, much more than I was able to feel in the days when I was young and my brother died, and there are reasons for this more than the mere consequence of age. Therefore I shall not apologise but begin by recalling the facts as I remember them that led up to my brother's death, the events that put me in a position to write this account. For though the event of my brother's passing and the events of my story cannot be separated, my story is not after all about death, but about my escape and Lucia's; about my mother's and Maiguru's entrapment; and about Nyasha's rebellion— Nyasha, far-minded and isolated, my uncle's daughter, whose rebellion may not in the end have been successful. (1)

The problems introduced by this opening paragraph are many: gender discrimination against girls and the systematic disenfranchisement of women; the question of experience, its rendering by memory and its translation into writing; agency, especially women's; the difficulty of evaluating the effectiveness of different modes of resistance; the value and meaning of self-determination, history, independence, and violence. These are issues faced by women struggling to navigate both colonial and patriarchal authority, and they are heightened by being contextualized in a nationalist struggle. *Nervous Conditions* insists on the materiality of bodies as sites for the articulation of both political problems and political solutions. As students of the novel are quick to grasp, the body becomes the ground on which violent struggles over identity take place and through which resistance is articulated. Hence the novel opens with Nhamo's death and ends with Nyasha's near-death. Both incidents keep violence in the forefront of our minds: Nhamo's death because it is the indirect result of a poverty produced and maintained by colonial underdevelopment, Nyasha's because it is so self-destructive.[8] The novel is framed, then, by the violent destruction of the bodies of black Africans, lining up Dangarembga's concerns even more closely with Fanon's.

Nyasha's eating disorder has several meanings in the text. Most immediately and literally, it is a response to her father's authority. The two of them fight throughout the novel, not least over Nyasha's body: Babamukuru wants to control how she uses it, how she trades it, and how she feeds it, prompting Nyasha to respond by controlling her food consumption. More figuratively, Nyasha's anorexia is a response to the collusion of patriarchal and colonial domination. As several critics of the novel have persuasively argued (see Bahri, Creamer, Sugnet, Uwakweh, Wright), Babamukuru stands in for colonial and patriarchal authority, and Nyasha's eating disorder represents her response to that dual domination. Nyasha in this reading has the status of "hybrid" caught between two cultures, and anorexia is seen as a deeply compromised attempt to control body and life in the face of colonial and patriarchal authority. This figurative reading of Nyasha's eating disorder is intuitively compelling to a certain degree: certainly, as I argued at the beginning of this essay, women are disadvantaged in specific ways by colonial relations of power, and these relations of power often descend on women's bodies. Intuitively compelling, too, is the view, that sees eating as a powerful way of reclaiming control of the body. But there is a limit to the usefulness of such a reading. First, it relies on a conception of power as repressive, not productive, which would seem to give away too much of the ground colonial discourse theory has claimed by taking its cue from Foucault's important point that power produces subjects. Second, the reading of anorexia as battleground for control relies on an individuation of power's effects, with the consequence that it seems as though any woman, anywhere, might respond in the same way to patterns of domination. This gives away important ground in postcolonial feminist theory, which insists on seeing women embedded in and arising out of precise and local contexts. Third, although this reading accords the anorexic *some* agency, it seems to curtail what that agency might look like (i.e., it's always self-destructive) from the outset.[9]

Some of the most interesting research emerging on eating disorders argues that, among other things, anorexia and bulimia function as symptoms of deeper social upheaval and as such are not restricted to western contexts. Theorists who make these arguments contest the longstanding feminist view that anorexia or bulimia nervosa is a disease that middle class white women "catch" from mass media (see especially Bray, Probyn, Thompson). While there are fewer cases of eating disorders among non-white women, their incidence appears to be on the rise, and observers suggest that this increase results from complex cultural causes, including poverty, racism, trauma, heterosexism—the leap to colonialism is not hard to make here. In an essay entitled "'A Way Outa No Way': Eating Problems Among African-American, Latina, and White Women," Becky Wangsgaard Thompson "establishes bulimia and anorexia as serious responses to injustices" (558). Closer to the novel, insofar as their subjects are Zimbabwean girls, scientists Malcolm Hooper and David Garner suggest that eating disorders might be less common among black than white or mixed-race schoolgirls, but nonetheless their incidence is on the rise. My point here is that it is dangerous to continue to regard eating disorders solely as a western phenomenon, not only because it contradicts the evidence of scientific researchers and of the novel, but also because it appears to reinscribe a strict "west/the rest" demarcation at precisely the point that postcolonial feminist scholars have been pointing to the inter-imbrication of women in various postcolonial locations (see C. Mohanty, 1991).

Like Thompson, Hooper and Garner cite western ideals of female beauty as one possible cause of eating disorders (cf. Tambudzai's somewhat incredulous observation that Nyasha "preferred angles to curves" [135]) but they point more insistently to the role of social change:

Rapid change brings with it a breakdown in traditional, protective, religious, and social standards previously bound together by a strong extended family system that provided support and succor. Further, following in the wake of so called "liberation" is a wider range of choices, which may provide personal freedom for those who are psychologically robust but may be overwhelming for the field-dependent adolescent who lacks internal structure. (Garner, Garfinkel, & Olmstead, 1983, 7). (167-68)

Hooper and Garner's conclusions reiterate those of Susan Bordo, who insistently reads anorexia less as the extreme expression of a character structure than as "a remarkably overdetermined *symptom* of some of the multifaceted and heterogeneous distresses of our age" (141, emphasis original). Taken together and applied to the novel, these conclusions suggest that Nyasha's eating disorder is a response not just to her father's patriarchal authority and colonial relations in general, but also to the specific nationalist struggle going on during her childhood years. As Bahri succinctly puts it, "[w]hat ails Nyasha, then, is not simply an eating problem but a rampant disorder in the socio-cultural complex that determines her fate as woman and native on the eve of the birth of a new nation" (para 6).

The novel suggests that the causes of anorexia are multiple and cannot necessarily be distinguished from one another. During the catastrophic scene that immediately precedes Nyasha's actual diagnosis and treatment, causality slides all over the place:

"They've done it to me," she accused, whispering still. "Really, they have." And then she became stern. "It's not their fault. They did it to them too. You know they did," she whispered. "To both of them, but especially to him. They put him through it all. But it's not his fault, he's good." Her voice took on a Rhodesian accent. "He's a good boy, a good munt. A bloody good kaffir," she informed in sneering sarcastic tones. Then she was whispering again. "Why do they do it, Tambu," she hissed bitterly, her face contorting with rage, "to me and to you and to him?" (200)

The referent for "they" and "them" in this passage is constantly shifting, and Nyasha speaks in several different voices, alternately angry, rational, sarcastic, bitter, angry, and, later in the passage, wheedling.[10] It is as if she channels the languages of colonialism and decolonization at once, becoming a cipher for the confusion of ideologies and locations marked out in a period of intense social destabilization. The violence she voices is not just physical at this point, but mental, too: Nyasha embodies and voices profound literal and figurative disorder. Indeed, I would go so far as to argue that she figures the very dialectic of colonial and anti-colonial violence that Fanon suggests in *The Wretched of the Earth*.

Insofar as she literally embodies the dialectic of violence, Nyasha is the clearest object of the warning implied in the novel's title and epigraph. Not only does her eating disorder, anorexia or bulimia *nervosa*, echo the "nervous condition" of the title, but her very character seems to realize the perils of disregarding Sartre's caution. I want to repeat that statement here, in its entirety, because unlike several other commentators on the novel, I think that the ending of Sartre's sentence matters.[11] Sartre writes, "the condition of native is a nervous condition introduced and maintained by the settler among colonized peoples *with their consent*" (Fanon 20, emphasis original). What is significant about Sartre's statement is that it points to the complicity of the colonized in their colonization; he gives us a way of thinking colonialism as hegemony (that is, domination by consent, in the common Gramscian tag) rather than simply monolithic oppression. Nyasha, it would seem, is a subject colonized by hegemony and who therefore necessarily bears its ambivalent effects. This is not to say that Nyasha is simply colonized, nor to belittle the degree of her suffering—in fact, I wish to suggest the precise opposite. (As Bahri reminds us, there is a difference between saying that someone has been victimized and calling someone a victim.) Since eating disorders require a high degree of self-regulation, Nyasha's anorexia suggests a degree of agency in the form of consent (she chooses, after all, what she consumes and what she rejects), but insofar as she ends up weakened and sick, the agency may not take Nyasha very far.[12] And Bordo suggests that this paradox is not unusual: "Paradoxically . . . pathologies of female protest . . . actually function as if in collusion with the cultural conditions that produced them" (159). If Nyasha literalizes Fanon's arguments as read by Sartre, we have to see her anti-colonial, violent response to literal and figurative domination as a willed act that is excruciatingly self-destructive. Tambudzai is right to say at the outset of the novel that Nyasha's rebellion "may not in the end have been successful" (1).

And yet Tambudzai's statement holds out the possibility of *some* success for Nyasha's rebellion: the sentence she utters is carefully open-ended. At the end of the novel we do not know what will become of Nyasha: she has received some medical attention although the doctors refuse to diagnose her as anorexic (see Creamer). The last word our narrator gives us on Nyasha is that "progress was still in the balance" (*NC* 202). But to focus on Nyasha alone is, I think, inadequate. What is most significant about Nyasha's near-death is not its effect on her, but its effect on Tambudzai. At the end of *Nervous Conditions*, Nyasha's eating disorder—her *rebellion*—has served to bring Tambudzai to the sort of *revolutionary* consciousness that Fanon calls for throughout *The Wretched of the Earth*. Hence we have the arresting final paragraph of the novel:

> I was young then and able to banish things, but seeds do grow. Although I was not aware of it then, no longer could I accept Sacred Heart and what it represented as a sunrise on my horizon. Quietly, unobtrusively and extremely fitfully, something in my mind began to assert itself, to question things and refuse to be brainwashed, bringing me to this time when I can set down this story. It was a long and painful process for me, that process of expansion. It was a process whose events stretched over many years and would fill another volume, but the story I have told here, is my own story, the story of four women whom I loved, and our men, this story is how it all began. (203-04)

The passage is rife with possibilities for the future, seeds that will grow through a "process of expansion" into, presumably, a woman who thinks and acts for herself, a woman whose consent is informed and meaningful. The novel closes on the moment at which Tambudzai, the black African girl, put in her place as such by the nuns, arrives at a sense of her own agency. Significantly, this agency is realized through writing—through the novel we have just read and, presumably, in the story that is to come. At this final moment in the text, the *bildungsroman*, or novel of development, and the *künstlerroman*, or novel of artistic awakening, come together in the narrative of a woman who has learned how to tell "[her] own story."

The importance of the fact that it is Nyasha's eating disorder that brings Tambudzai to this state of revolutionary consciousness can be extrapolated from Fanon's insistence on thinking revolutionary national thoughts in material terms. Remember that Fanon's nation requires not just the masses, but also an intellectual component. We may be encouraged to see Nyasha as an intellectual (at least this is one way of explaining the correlation between her increased studying and her intensified eating disorder), but her usefulness can only be measured by the degree to which she, in Fanon's words again, "teach[es] the masses that everything depends on them; that if we stagnate it is their responsibility, and that if we go forward it is due to them too" ("Pitfalls" 197-98). This is the lesson that Tambudzai learns from her cousin. Nyasha's intellectual understanding on its own is inadequate, since the gendered oppression she endures from her father cuts her off from maintaining meaningful relationships with the rest of her family. Although she "had taken seriously the lessons about oppression and discrimination that she had learnt first-hand in England," Nyasha's relationship to Shona culture has been formalized into an almost anthropological interest in traditional crafts like basket-making (63). Reading Nyasha through Fanon, we are given to understand that an intellectual vanguard cut off from the people will only ever be self-destructive.

Tambudzai, however, has learned her revolutionary lessons well. In the final sentence of the novel, Tambudzai's story is indivisible from the story of "four women whom I loved, and our men." The collectivity implied by this last sentence gives us cause for hope—not least because just as Tambudzai discovers her own form of agency in the course of the novel, so do the other women she brings to life. In their own ways, each of them manifests an agency that fleshes out—quite literally—what Fanon leaves implicit in his text. While Tambudzai finds self and communal articulation through writing, her Aunt Lucia occupies the interstices of the web of power that constructs Babamukuru's home. She parrots, parodically, exactly what is expected of her as a woman in order to get what she wants. When Nyasha disapproves of her ingratiating praise of Babamukuru, Lucia responds, "'But you, Nyasha, are you mad! . . . Babamukuru wanted to be asked, so I asked'" (160). In this way, Lucia gets a home, an education, and a job, all the while maintaining her freedom of sexual choice. Tambudzai's Aunt Maiguru, simultaneously the best educated and least enlightened woman in the novel, does not remain wholly circumscribed by the role of patriarchal wife demanded by her well-educated husband: her five-day hiatus from Babamukuru's house may not amount to the "escape" Tambudzai effects in her own life, but it does have some important ramifications for family dynamics at the mission. Tambudzai's mother, Mainini, manifests perhaps the most interesting form of agency. Given to us at the beginning of the novel as the most oppressed character, dominated, as she puts it, by "the poverty of blackness on one side and the weight of womanhood on the other" (16), Mainini sees things more clearly than do other characters in the text. Hence she is the first to actually recognize Nyasha's eating disorder, and to diagnose it: "It's the Englishness," she says, shortly (202). Mainini demonstrates an extraordinary self-consciousness throughout the novel.

That the novel closes with a look to the future matters for a text that takes as its subject revisionist national struggle. By pairing Nyasha's ambivalent embodiment of colonial violence with

Tambudzai's revolutionary consciousness, and embedding the two of them in the midst of various feminist strategies of resistance, Dangarembga suggests that the somewhat formulaic pronouncements of Fanon, useful in outline, need to be grounded in specific material contexts—especially *gendered* contexts—that make visible a range of responses to oppressive situations. At the same time as the novel criticizes Fanon, the specificity of its Zimbabwean referents (an entire paper remains to be written on the importance of rural and urban spaces in *Nervous Conditions*) and its incorporation of a trope long taken to be singularly western (anorexia) means that Dangarembga's vision cannot be easily co-opted into western feminism, either. In positioning her novel between the nation of Zimbabwe and the international feminist community, and drawing on each for problems and solutions, Dangarembga self-consciously crafts a national literature for the new Zimbabwe—a national literature that puts young women first.

Notes

1. Many people collaborated to make this essay possible: Rick Lee provided superb research assistance, and librarians at the School of African and Oriental Studies in London helped locate information on The Literature Bureau, while Mary Chapman, Mo Engel, Mark Simpson, Debby Thompson and Teresa Zackodnik offered close critical readings of this essay in its early stages. My thanks to all.

2. The tone of Musandireve's review is, overall, sympathetic and warm, but it clearly assumes that its readers will need to be convinced of the value of the novel's feminist implications.

3. The phrase "decolonizing the mind" is Ngugi's. I use it, like Ngugi does, to signal the relevance of one African country's independence struggle to that of another.

4. The 1992 *Editor's Manual* consolidates policy determined during a two-week conference in early 1988, and I assume that the policies were debated for some time before 1988 as well. For these reasons, I do not

believe it anachronistic to rely on a 1992 publication to explain publishing decisions made during the previous decade. Although some of the pieces in the *Editor's Manual* are attributed to particular writers, I will treat the text as an anonymous whole, since its main purpose is to articulate institutional policy.

5. In 1995 Zimbabwean president Robert Mugabe evoked international outrage after disallowing the organization Gays and Lesbians of Zimbabwe from participating in the Zimbabwe International Book Fair in Harare. His homophobic comments on this occasion (among them that lesbian women and gay men were "worse than dogs and pigs" and deserved "no rights at all") sought to solidify a narrow view of nationalism: he framed his remarks as "a question of protecting and guaranteeing the cultural health of Zimbabwe" and insisted that homosexuality represents a form of western decadence that has no historical basis in "authentic" Zimbabwean culture. For research on the status of post-independence women in Zimbabwe, see Seidman and Sylvester (who use the telling phrase "official ambiguity about women's position in Zimbabwe)" (42).

6. The *Editor's Manual* is canny about the function of literacy in the international marketplace, too. A section explaining the relationship between The Literature Bureau, Author, Publisher, Public and International Audience ends by stating, "In a nutshell you can see that when an author has a published work, he ceases to be an individual but a man of the people and of the world" (26).

7. A thoroughgoing critique of Fanon's misogyny is long overdue, although I haven't space in this essay to do it. Bart Moore-Gilbert's essay is a good first pass at such a project.

8. The doctor cautiously diagnoses Nhamo with mumps, a disease that—tellingly, given other events in the narrative—can produce sterility in adult males if untreated.

9. An important refrain in the research on eating disorders holds that the girls who suffer from anorexia or bulimia are not helpless. See especially Bray and Probyn.

10. Most critics read this passage progressively, as evidence of Nyasha's growing sense of how Babamukuru's patriarchal authority is embedded in colonial relations (see Sugnet, Bahri, etc.). However, I think that reading the passage symptomatically is at least as important.

11. Sugnet's essay is an important exception to this trend: he reads the entire Sartre quotation against the novel quite compellingly.

12. It goes without saying that this reading of eating disorders also goes against biomedical explanations.

Chapter 2:
Tradition, Modernity, and the Family: Reading the *Chimurenga* struggle into and out of *Nervous Conditions*

Susan Z. Andrade

In its apparent silence on the question of the black independence struggle, *Nervous Conditions* by Tsitsi Dangarembga differs sharply from the two best-known and most celebrated Zimbabwean novels in English published at about the same time, both by men of Dangarembga's generation. *Bones* (1988) by Chenjerai Hove and *Harvest of Thorns* (1989) by Shimmer Chinodya are dissimilar from each other in form and subject matter; nevertheless, both represent and engage the Zimbabwean struggle for national liberation in a direct manner. In contrast, *Nervous Conditions* appears to efface the story of Zimbabwean nationalism entirely, emphasizing instead the personal travails of two black Rhodesian girls as they arrive into womanhood. For all the formal innovativeness that garnered it the Noma award in 1989, at the level of theme, *Bones* simply rewrites the clichéd figure of Mother Africa through its violated heroine, Marita. *Harvest of Thorns* resembles *Nervous Conditions* more closely in its realist form and in that at least one section conforms to the genre of the *Bildungsroman* in its exploration of the disorientation of its narrator-cum-freedom-fighter. Part of this novel's interest is to narrate the impossibility of objectively recounting war experiences. Self-consciously problematized though *Harvest of Thorns* makes that representation, it exists. The war can be, and is, represented directly in language. Published in 1988, *Nervous Conditions* is set a couple of decades earlier, opening in 1968 and continuing into the 1970s, yet the novel makes almost no reference to the *Chimurenga*, or guerrilla war, which would have been gathering steam at the time and in the location of the story. Rather, *Nervous Conditions* charts a less direct and much more conflicted route of narrative and characterological development. Part of that conflict stems from the novel's critical attention to gender, one that appears to authorize the notion that decolonizing nationalism subsumes feminism into its over-arching, totalizing agenda. I will argue that one might see this novel as responding to this problematic.

In my reading, *Nervous Condition*s' dense interplay of structures between family and nation, between domestic and public spheres, even between the discursive constructs of tradition and modernity, becomes legible only through a corresponding legibility of history and literary history. Following Pierre Macherey's notion of the "non-said" I suggest that the nationalist story of *Nervous Conditions* remains invisible, obscured by the feminist, until the facts of Zimbabwean history and theories of decolonizing nationalism are juxtaposed against it. These discourses bring to light what the text cannot speak about itself: the "discontinuity," in

Macherey's terms, is an investment in national decolonization.[1] After outlining some of Rhodesia/Zimbabwe's history, I will consider the novel's deployment and revision of generic conventions. The genre of the *Bildungsroman* comes in for particular scrutiny, as I read it in relation to literary theories of realism as well as to the political theory of Frantz Fanon. Attention to both structure and theme unearths a more complex narrative, illustrating how the micro- and macro-political spheres are allegorically represented. The public political import of Dangarembga's text becomes legible only when the critical apparatus for interpreting it is revised or reconsidered.

Like South Africa, Rhodesia, renamed Zimbabwe after independence, was dominated by an intransigent white settler colony. Rhodesia came about after the breakup of the Federation of Rhodesia and Nyasaland in 1963, wherein Northern Rhodesia and Nyasaland became the independent states of Zambia and Malawi. Southern Rhodesia, known now as Rhodesia, declared independence from England in 1965. The misleadingly named Unilateral Declaration of Independence (UDI) was synonymous neither with black access to national economic power nor with black enfranchisement and, in fact, represents one of the bleakest periods in Rhodesia/Zimbabwe's cultural history. Not until 1980, after the *Chimurenga*, a protracted guerrilla struggle fought by the Zimbabwean liberation movement, was suffrage extended to the majority black population.

In many respects, *Nervous Conditions* is a conventional *Bildungsroman* and seems to exist in marginal relation to fictions of the nation as told by Hove and Chinodya. This novel tells in straightforwardly realist terms the story of a black Rhodesian girl whose quest for an education takes her to the home of her more urbanized and westernized cousin and from there to an elite convent boarding school. Recounted at a moment of thoughtful reflection after Tambudzai Sigauke's successful integration into the socius, it exemplifies many aspects of the typical *Bildungsroman* as the genre has evolved from its eighteenth-century German origin, narrating the unfolding of an individual in all his (or her) complexity and richness. Reading *Nervous Conditions* formally makes visible a classical realism that both conforms to the genre's basic outlines and yet highlights the limitations of the earlier and important critique of this narrative as advanced by Roland Barthes, Colin MacCabe and others. The novel's focus on the burgeoning strength of its female protagonists troubles its form and brings it up against the limits of its own theoretical project.

    The conventional understanding of realism is that it presents concrete, individualized figures embedded in the context of particular places at particular times, its impression of fidelity to life stemming from figural individualization and particularization. The epitome of the classical realist form is the *Bildungsroman*, which, in psychological terms, represents the development of an interiorized subjectivity and, in social terms, the consolidation of the lone, bourgeois, and usually male, subject who takes up a place in (or outside) society. Tambudzai appears to be the traditional protagonist, who, in a manner consonant with the European tradition, develops during the course of the novel into an individualized and bourgeois subject. By illustrating the values of thrift and hard work, her story charts a course comparable to that of the masculine *Bildungsroman*, which illustrates the self-discovery and consolidation of a subjectivity that also poses as seamless and universal. Though the fact of her gender powerfully determines the content of narration (the desire for a poor girl to acquire an education, which, as a girl, she would not otherwise have), in structural terms Tambu's personal story reaffirms the *Bildungsroman* as a narrative of uplift. Her quest for advancement is preceded a generation earlier by that of her uncle, Babamukuru. Early on, the novel establishes Babamukuru's journey as the paradigmatic story of advancement through merit, scholarship, and hard work. This is the story Tambu prepares herself to emulate: "It was truly a romantic story to my ears, a fairy-tale of reward and punishment, of cause and effect. It had a moral too, a tantalizing moral that increased your aspirations, but not beyond a manageable level" (19).

By dint of her own industriousness, Taml
for the school fees her parents cannot afford, tak'
tional task of growing mealies, or maize, for s....
tuckshops. Though almost thwarted by her brother in this enterprise, she continues undaunted, and with the help of a kindly teacher,
takes her mealies to Umtali, a nearby city, and earns enough money
to secure Babamukuru's notice and ultimately her much-prized education at his mission school.[2] Her real path towards maturation
begins with her move to the mission school and to the home of
Babamukuru and Maiguru, a move which, not coincidentally, cor-
responds with the generic convention of a move from country to
city. Under the watchful eyes of her uncle and aunt, she is afforded
a more rigorous formal education as well as the material means
(books, time, and artificial light) by which to acquire it, and she is
exposed to Western or European ways such as eating with a knife
and fork and the sampling of non-Shona foods. Above all, as she
assures us, she begins to examine social values. In particular, her
cousin, Nyasha, encourages her to think critically about the books
she reads as well as about the means by which her education is
made available. At the novel's end, having completed her schooling at Sacred Heart convent and having grown into an adult, Tambu
stands poised to enter the sphere of the Zimbabwean elite.[3]

Nyasha, on the other hand, incarnates all the problems with
women's access to development: She is the exceptional woman,
or, in this case, girl, doomed either to transgress and be punished,
or to suffer a life in which she does not believe. Tending towards
the former path, Nyasha frequently challenges her parents' authority, especially that of her father, Babamukuru. She pays the price
for open defiance with her mental and physical health and even at
the novel's end persists in an unstable, uncertain psychological state.
The social constraints on female maturation produce conflicts,
which, while not unique to female characters, are more relentlessly
explored there, say Elizabeth Abel, Marianne Hirsch, and Elizabeth Langland in their path-breaking collection on the female
Bildungsroman: "Repeatedly, the female protagonist or

Bildungsheld must chart a treacherous course between the penalties of expressing sexuality and suppressing it, between the costs of inner concentration and of direct confrontation with society, between the price of succumbing to madness and of grasping a repressive 'normality'" (12-13). Feminine sexuality, female engagement with dominant structures of power, and the looming specter of psychological instability are the three primary motifs by which the girls engage the world and enter adulthood. By applying pressure to these sites of narrative tension we can make visible the novel's expression of divergent positions, which ultimately form the basis for Tambu's developmental success and Nyasha's undoing.

Tambu and Nyasha's parallel stories illustrate the argument advanced by Abel, Hirsch, and Langland that feminine fictions of development reflect tensions between the assumptions of a genre which evolved representing the growth of male characters on the one hand and the often conflicting aspirations of female ones on the other. By reading gender and genre as intertwined, they make visible the *Bildungsroman*'s legacy of representing woman as sign of the sexual for male protagonists, and they highlight the fraught terrain of sexuality for female protagonists. Indeed, that women-authored novels have tended to represent narrative resolution for female protagonists as a choice between marriage (success) or death (failure) has become axiomatic within feminist criticism. Rachel Blau Du Plessis, Penny Boumhela, and Rita Felski all agree that romance usually complicates and sometimes co-opts the *Bildungsroman*'s quest course with the marriage plot in order to inhibit or contain the aspirations of their female characters. Consequently, some feminist critics have asserted that, unlike in the process of masculine development, sexuality in and for itself rarely plays a central role in women's processes of self discovery.[4] Felski claims that "Erotic passion, by its very intensity, can sabotage the protagonist's struggle to strengthen an often precarious sense of independent identity . . . ." (132). And Du Plessis, to whose exposition of romance I am much indebted, begins her book with "[o]nce upon a time, the end, the rightful end, of women in novels was social—successful courtship, marriage—or judgmental of her sexual and social failure—death" (1). In the case of *Nervous Conditions*, romance and its avatar, the marriage plot, are juxtaposed against sexual self-expression uninhibited by wedlock and its goal of procreation. Instead of inverting the conventional logic of Woman as a sign of the sexual by representing a male figure as sexuality incarnate, as, for example, does Sembene in *Xala*, this female-authored novel displaces sexuality from the female body into one of two feminine discourses. In the prototypical *Bildungsroman*, the male hero negotiates his path to adulthood by— and through—at least one debased and one exalted female character. *Nervous Conditions* rewrites the cliché of the sexualized woman by using its two main characters to explore two stances on sexuality, all the while refraining from depicting actual objects of interest on the part of either female character.[5] Tambu, the successful *Bilgen*, has faith in the romance plot, and Nyasha, her resisting counterpart, issues challenges to it.

Given my earlier claim that Tambu's narrative exemplifies *Bildungsroman* as a story of uplift, it is noteworthy that romance is the single major aspect of the "masculine" *Bildungsroman* that remains undeveloped in Tambu's narrative. Sexuality, even curiosity about sexuality, is absent from Tambu's maturation, having been quashed early on the homestead, as this description of her love of dancing illustrates:

> My early childhood had been a prime time for dancing. As I had grown older and the music had begun to speak to me more clearly, my movements had grown stronger, more rhythmical and luxuriant; but people had not found it amusing anymore, so that in the end I realised that there were bad implications in the way I enjoyed the rhythm. My dancing compressed itself into rigid, tentative gestures. I did not stop completely, but [family] gatherings were much less fun after that and made me feel terribly self-conscious. (42)

Later, when at the mission school, Tambu admits to being thrilled when male preceptors dress formally, and even considers Nyasha's brother, Chido, handsome and dashing. None of these potential objects of desire ever seriously engages her attention, however, and her libido is represented as diffuse and unformed. Unlike Nyasha, she does not question the institution of marriage and, indeed, apparently continues to believe in its value even in her older and wiser narrating voice. Not coincidentally, the primary difference between Tambu's story and that of the prototypical male is that this novel specifies that here the female hero is desexualized, partaking neither of the Scylla of the romance narrative nor of the Charybdis of unsanctioned sexual desire for its own sake.[6]

Tambu's hazy vision of romantic love throws into sharp relief her cousin's open curiosity about sexuality for its own sake, especially sexuality that is unsanctioned or transgressive. Nyasha shocks her parents by reading *Lady Chatterley's Lover* and by even unselfconsciously bringing it to the dining table.[7] Later she proclaims to Tambu that she would rather give up her virginity to a tampon than a womanizing man. In fact, when Tambu begins to menstruate, Nyasha teaches her slightly scandalized cousin how to use tampons and assures her that Maiguru would supply them with the expensive products: "Although Maiguru knew that tampons were offensive, that nice girls did not use them, she would be pleased enough to know we were not pregnant to be persuaded to provide. [Nyasha] chuckled. 'No, really,' she conceded. 'Mum's quite sensible underneath all the feathers.' That cousin of mine! Shocking and funny; disrespectful and irrepressible" (96). Because she continually challenges the authority of the conjugal love plot for herself, for Tambu, and, perhaps most importantly, for her own mother, Nyasha runs the risk of becoming a "bad girl," the youthful equivalent of a "fallen woman," a conceit which the narrative deploys to illustrate the function of gendered relations of power and simultaneously exposes as false.

This setting frames the tumultuous events of the night of the school dance. Most commentators rightfully interpret Nyasha and Babamukuru's battle as one about power and patriarchy; however, few acknowledge that it takes place on the field of sexual expression. The miniskirt Nyasha wears, one which has been approved by her mother, rankles her father when he sees her in it before the dance. Afterwards, her tarrying behind Chido and Tambu with one of the Baker boys in order to learn new dance steps provokes the notorious fight:

> "No decent girl would stay out alone, with a boy, at that time of the night," Babamukuru was insisting in a quavering tenor. "But you did it. I saw you. Do you think that I am lying, that these eyes of mine lie?"

> Nyasha, unfortunately, was still unrepentant. "What do you want me to say?" she asked. "You want me to admit that I'm guilty, don't you. All right then. I was doing it, whatever you're talking about. There. I've confessed."

> "Do not talk to me like that, child," warned Babamukuru. "You must respect me. I am your father. And in that capacity I am telling you, I-am-telling-you, that I do not like the way you are always walking about with these—er—these young men. Today this one, tomorrow that one. What's the matter with you, girl? Why can't you behave like a young woman from a decent home? What will people say when they see Sigauke's daughter carrying on like that?"

> I like to think that Nyasha really believed that the confrontation had taken a conciliatory turn. She smiled that the number of her male acquaintances was the one thing that should put her father at ease.

> "You know me," she told him, but of course she was mistaken. "You've taught me how I should behave. I don't worry about what people think so there's no need for you to." She did not know her father either, because anyone who did would have retreated at that stage . . . .

> "You, Chido, keep quiet" Babamukuru snapped. "You let
> your sister behave like a whore without saying anything . .
> . ."
>
> Nyasha grew uncharacteristically calm at times like this.
> "Now why," she enquired of no particular person, "should
> I worry about what people say when my own father calls
> me a whore?" She looked at him with murder in her eyes .
> . . .
>
> "Chido, I have told you to keep out of this," reminded
> Babamukuru, gathering himself within himself so that his
> whole weight was behind the blow he dealt Nyasha's face.
> "Never," he hissed. "Never," he repeated, striking her other
> cheek with the back of his hand, "speak to me like that."
> (113-14)

Though mere steps behind her companions, Nyasha's actions are
interpreted by her father as a breach of propriety, and his response
quickly escalates from verbal to physical retribution. Instead of
accepting the name-calling and blows, Nyasha fights back and even
punches him once in retaliation for his three strikes, a response to
paternal violence I have never before encountered in African fiction.
That it comes from a daughter is even more shocking. Babamukuru
pummels her fiercely for this. The altercation marks the beginning
of Nyasha's mental and emotional decline; though her analysis
remains sharp through the remainder of the novel, she does not
emerge from the decline even at its end.

In the passage above the novel blurs the distinction between discipline and punishment, between Babamukuru's benevolent paternalism and the malevolent consequences of sexual per-
missiveness against which Babamukuru positions himself. That is
to say, the father's desire to protect himself from shame becomes
inseparable from his anxiety about protecting his daughter from
public sexual mistreatment and thereby takes the form of the violence and humiliation he enacts on her. And the passage above
echoes an earlier one: As a youthful narrator welcoming her then

seven-year-old cousin Nyasha, Chido, and their parents back from England, Tambu quietly disapproves of Nyasha because she wears a short skirt. That some years later, in the fight after the dance, Babamukuru begins his repudiation of Nyasha with an objection to the length of her skirt is not narratively coincidental. Skirt length, then, is just one of the many circuits through which sexual control is exercised, and not only by men or by those in the previous generation, though, to be sure, they have greater power and are represented as blinded by it. The novel alleges that by Babamukuru's own standards of moral virtue, the fears he harbors about his daughter's sexual expression prove groundless. Fourteen-year-old Nyasha's chastity is secure; no particular boy even claims her interest. Tambu understands that the regulation of sexuality constitutes one form of control, and sometime in the brief interval between the child-narrator and adult-narrator she recognizes that such regulation focuses on women's bodies; but by then it is too late to intervene on behalf of her cousin. In direct contrast to the policing of Nyasha's friendships, Chido experiences many fewer restrictions and enjoys greater freedom of association outside the home.[8]

Desire itself is never narratively represented; sexuality functions as a metaphor.[9] As vehicle, sexuality illustrates women's engagement with dominant structures of power, illustrating the risks of openly challenging patriarchy, and, as tenor, it serves to catalyze the moment of Nyasha's psychological instability. Nyasha and Tambu occupy structurally divergent narrative positions which should be understood as investment in or refusal of the romance narrative: Tambu maintains an ideological commitment to romance while she refuses to partake of it herself while Nyasha demonstrates curiosity about one transgressive aspect of romance, sexuality, which in all its menacing aspects, becomes the sign of and catalyst for her undoing.

Because the analysis of Abel, Hirsch, and Langland is conducted at the level of individual psychology rather than at that of a dialogue between the psychological and the social, it tends to represent gender as fixed, largely unaffected by history, class, or culture. Their advocacy of the simple inclusion of gender and sexuality as categories of literary analysis unintentionally occludes a more complex understanding of narrative mechanisms. I wish to be clear about the limits of my literary assertions: *Nervous Conditions* neither constitutes a radically new genre nor does it lay claim to the conscious resistance to "a humanist ideology of the literary" that John Beverley declares on behalf of the Latin American *testimonio* narrative (96). This Zimbabwean novel stretches the boundaries of this conservative genre which delineates the making of bourgeois individualism, and it thereby articulates a different literary politics. That the novel renders two female protagonists in lieu of the typical, lone male serves to unsettle the genre's celebration of individualism. It functions instead as a refusal to narrate in the unproblematized terms of autonomous selfhood. In both formal and thematic terms it rewrites the *Bildungsroman*'s extreme emphasis on self-creation, and it downplays what Fredric Jameson has called the genre's "overripe subjectivity" in favor of a mode that underscores the role of the collective in producing the individual (Beverley 96). On the one hand, *Nervous Conditions* modifies convention by affirming Tambu's identity; through Nyasha's unmaking it also exposes the genre's avowal of a seamless and unified construction of identity. On the other, the very manner of and reasons for Nyasha's unmaking link the critique of bourgeois consolidation with a critique of the imperialist enterprise in Africa, a point to which I will later return.

One important difference between *Nervous Conditions* and the more conventional *Bildungsroman*'s assumption of autonomous and heroic self-making can be seen in the relationship between individuality and collectivity. The novel tells the story of the formation and dissolution of subjectivity through Tambu and Nyasha. At the primary level of explication of the feminine conflict between the desire for self-realization versus the virtually universal understanding of womanhood as living for others, this novel endorses the former position through its assertion and celebration of Tambu's arrival into adulthood. At a secondary level, however, the older Tambu perceives her psychological development and social success to have been made possible through the community of women in whose company she comes of age; she says so explicitly on the novel's first page. The myth of the exceptional woman is therefore undermined, first by the open acknowledgment that she was produced by a collective, and secondly by the parallel unraveling of her narrative counterpart. Nyasha, the unmade girl, is herself instrumental to Tambu's formation, helping to shape her cousin's social and critical acumen. She exposes Tambu to a library beyond the limited one of the Mission School and frequently prods along her cousin's increasing awareness of patriarchy and colonialism.[10] Felski contends that in general the female community serves a mediating function which shapes the cautiously positive conclusion of the feminist *Bildungsroman*. The female community "functions as a barrier against and a refuge from the worst effects of a potentially threatening social order by opening up a space for nonexploitative relationships grounded in common goals and interests. The feminist *Bildungsroman* thus combines the exploration of subjectivity with a dimension of group solidarity which inspires activism and resistance rather than private resignation, and makes it possible to project a visionary hope of a future change . . ." (139).

Several women contribute to the making of Tambu, both directly and indirectly. Despite her constant weariness, Tambu's mother, Ma'Shingayi, quietly encourages her eldest daughter to pursue her scholarly ambitions by persuading her husband, Jeremiah, to allow their daughter to use maize seeds to grow crops for sale.[11] Ma'Shingayi, more than any other character, is obscured in individual personality, taste, and habits by the oppressive burdens of her maternal and wifely status. Tambu succeeds in school both because of her mother's encouragement and out of fear of becoming like her. However, as if taking a leaf from her own text as example, Ma'Shingayi also warns her daughter not to expect too much from life, lest she be disappointed.[12] Tambu's grandmother contributes the land and agricultural skills which equip Tambu to

grow maize for sale towards her school fees, but her most important legacy is that of providing, and, indeed, embodying, a different history. It is from her, with Nyasha's later and next-generational
reinforcement, that Tambu learns a counterdiscourse to the colonial history taught in school. Tambu's aunt, Maiguru, of course,
exemplifies the kind of woman Tambu would like to become. However, Tambu's growing realization of the nature and number of sacrifices her aunt makes prompts a reconsideration of this path from
the perspective of the older narrator, and, for the reader, prompts a
reconsideration of modernity as the corrective to feminine ills: "I
felt sorry for Maiguru because she could not use the money she
earned for her own purposes and had been prevented by marriage
from doing the things she wanted to do. But it was not so simple,
because she had been married by my Babamukuru, which defined
her situation as good. If it was necessary to efface yourself, as
Maiguru did so well that you couldn't be sure that she didn't enjoy
it, if it was necessary to efface yourself in order to preserve his
sense of identity and value, then, I was sure, Maiguru had taken
the correct decision" (102).

Illiteracy and the lack of training virtually ensure servitude for a woman in postcolonial times. The squalid conditions
under which Tambu's mother lives testify to this. But education
does not necessarily liberate women, as the example of Maiguru
indicates. Though, like her husband, she has a Master's degree and
is a teacher, the text offers no information at all about Maiguru's
accomplishments outside of her home or the domestic world she
supervises at the homestead. Her educational achievements are
unknown to most. She gives her money to her husband to spend on
his extended family. Her personal narrative centers around her
worries about Babamukuru's eating and on the Herculean task of
food preparation she undertakes each time she and her family visit
Tambu's nuclear family on the homestead. The only exception takes
place when, towards the novel's end, she leaves Babamukuru and
her household duties for a brief period of time and an unspecified
place. The novel's description of her, as with that of Ma'Shingayi,

is primarily devoted to their performing domestic duties. For "traditional" and "modern" women alike, their role as housewife dominates the narrative horizon. Lucia, the only unmarried adult woman besides the servant, Anna, is free precisely because she is not responsible to a husband and, as a "barren" woman, is not hampered by the burdens of reproduction.[13] These facts, normally considered severe limitations in the African context, enable her to have a sex life based primarily on pleasure, and she is the only woman who does.

The female community provides a mediating force between the female protagonist and the burdens of the society she struggles against; moreover, it offers a communal counter-icon to that of The African Family, emblem of group solidarity and resistance. In the novel's oft-quoted first paragraph, the African Family is dethroned and replaced by a female community:

> I was not sorry when my brother died. Nor am I apologising for my callousness, as you may define it, my lack of feeling. For it is not that at all. I feel many things these days, much more than I was able to feel in the days when I was young and my brother died, and there are reasons for this more than the mere consequence of age. Therefore I shall not apologise but begin by recalling the facts as I remember them that led up to my brother's death, the events that put me in a position to write this account. For though the events of my brother's passing and the events of my story cannot be separated, my story is not after all about death, but about my escape and Lucia's; about my mother's and Maiguru's entrapment; and about Nyasha's rebellion— Nyasha, far-minded and isolated, my uncle's daughter, whose rebellion may not in the end have been successful (1).

Most readers, whether or not they approve of Tambu's outspokenness, would find the thinly veiled hostility striking. Within the context of the europhone African novel, the effect is heightened, for certainly until the 1980s rarely do such novels begin by eschewing all pretense at harmonious tranquillity within family relations. In fact, most novels written by men nostalgically assume the family to be a site of tranquillity and sustenance. The African Family remains a sacralized icon whose representation ranges from the hyper-romanticized, as in Camara Laye's early novel, *L'enfant noir* (1953), to the gently mocked but fundamentally upheld, as in Wole Soyinka's more recent autobiographical novel, *Ake* (1981). Naturally given, biologically determined and timeless in duration, the family is universally assumed to predate and outrank other forms of social organization. Michele Barrett and Mary McIntosh suggest that as an institution the family is imbued with a unique social and moral force, since it is seen as the embodiment of general human values rather than of the conventions of a particular society. Within Africa, even outspoken feminists who trenchantly critique patriarchy in their fiction tend to represent the family as a largely, or at least, potentially supportive structure in which the African subject might find shelter from the ravages of colonialism.

Dangarembga is one of few African novelists who baldly represents the family as coercive and occasionally violent, not just hierarchical but patriarchal and gerontocratic.[14] In the subsequent couple of pages, Nhamo reveals himself to be lazy, as is his masculine due, as well as frequently cruel towards his younger sisters; moreover, he commits the unpardonable sin of trying to foil Tambu's attempt to earn money for school fees, money he does not himself have to earn. The introductory paragraph allows Tambu to protest her brother's privilege and to refuse to feel sad or guilty over his death because, as we later learn, he actively opposed her attempt to acquire an education. Within the first two sentences, in fact, she represents her narration as dependent on—not simply coincident to—his death: "Therefore I shall not apologise but begin by recalling the facts as I remember them that put me in a position to write this account." Though she does not kill Nhamo, she harbors murderous thoughts towards him, as Charles Sugnet points out, and, like Nyokabi of Grace Ogot's *The Graduate*, Tambu is willing to accept his death as the price of her freedom. Perhaps most important is the fact that Nhamo's death serves a rhetorical as well as a structural function. Rhetorically, it captures the reader's attention (Sugnet claims that Dangarembga takes some pains to wrench the narrative around to begin this way); structurally, however, because Tambu's ability to narrate is openly and gratefully predicated on her brother's demise, the novel offers no narrative space for grief, or, in fact, for any response but a certain relief.[15] In form and content, then, Nhamo's death serves as the catalyst to the story of Tambu, and, as she has told us, the story of the women who produced her.

Through its men, the African Family is portrayed in this novel as a network of power relations which almost always works against its most disadvantaged members, children, and, particularly, women. Examples of masculine offenses within this network include Jeremiah's laziness, Nhamo's malicious rivalry, Takesure's philandering, and Babamukuru's benevolent domination. So instead of a domestic collectivity based on biology or kin to nurture her, the text tenders its protagonist one based on women's shared experience of oppression or persecution. The female collective Tambu celebrates in the novel's first paragraph is placed in ideological and functional opposition to and takes the place of the African Family. The family serves to oppress her, Nyasha, Maiguru, Mainini and Lucia. Similarly, if one of the most important moments of ideological negotiation occurs in the way a novel resolves loose ends and achieves closure, then it is remarkable that Tambu ends by repeating her testimony that her own story overlaps with those of these women. The last line, in fact, is: "the story I have told here, is my own story, the story of the four women whom I loved, and our men, this story is how it all began" (204).

Tambu's hunger for education, the discourse that dominates the first part of the novel, is replaced by Nyasha's self-starvation in the second part, as the latter's increasingly precarious state replaces the securely plotted path of Tambu's development. Because Nyasha's eating disorder fuels the narrative trajectory of the second part and looms over the ending, *Nervous Conditions* has frequently been interpreted as a simple parable of deracination and cultural alienation. On the working assumption that the endings of realist novels yield more interesting results for feminist criticism than a simple failure to provide either positive role models or expose the paucity of social opportunities, I suggest that closer inspection of Nyasha's relationship to food reveals that figures of eating and control are everywhere to be found in *Nervous Conditions*. Nyasha is not the only female character to stop eating, nor even the only African. Towards the middle of the novel, Tambu's mother goes on a hunger strike in small part because she becomes fed up with her family's mistreatment and in large part in protest against Tambu's decision to attend Sacred Heart convent. Maiguru refuses both material and symbolic domestic duties and stops cooking for and otherwise caring for her family, even leaving her house in protest against her husband. So, while alienation in the broadest sense is at issue in the depiction of food, simple deracination or cultural purity is not. Eating and education have a complex structural relationship; the novel explores an interrelation between food and instruction that might be read, among other ways, as parallel to the constantly mutating discourses of tradition and modernity.

Eating and education have a metonymic association, which sometimes make them opposed to each other, sometimes make them substitute for one another. On the symbolic level, education is equated with the consumption of strange, new ideas, and with estrangement. It is this logic behind Ma'Shingayi's blaming of Babamukuru and Maiguru for Nhamo's death; she bitterly claims that they exposed him to alien (and poisonous) ways, killing him as a result. And she objects when Tambu decides to attend Sacred Heart and remove herself even more from the world of the homestead. On another level, the relationship between eating and education is straightforwardly material: having an education gives one upward mobility and enables one to eat more and better food. This is why Tambu yearns to attend school in the first place: Maiguru and Babamukuru's education translate for her into the lack of material want and the possession of a certain leisure that only men on the homestead have. Ma'Shingayi understands her daughter's desire, though her chastising of Tambu refers to the material world in symbolic terms:

> If it is meat you want that I cannot provide for you, if you are so greedy you would betray your own mother for meat, then go to your Maiguru. She will give you meat. I will survive on vegetables, as we all used to do. And we have survived, so what more do you want (141).

Mainini believes that the ideas Tambu will consume there will make their shared life on the homestead even more alien to her daughter. Moreover, the quote above precedes Mainini's own hunger strike, a fact which gives the lie to the notion that only the "modern" and overly-educated refuse food in order to control their life circumstances. When, against her mother's will, Tambu decides to attend the elite school, her mother stops eating in protest and withdraws from her family responsibilities. In an insightful reading of the social and symbolic value of food in the novel, Heidi Creamer notes that "Because her family cannot function without her, her resistance is effective, but for the same reason it is shortly recuperated. Lucia brings Mainini back to health . . . [she] also incorporates the symbolic power of food into her healing; she insures that Mainini eats meat and milk which are usually served only to men during holidays" (354). Babamukuru, as we have noted, eats little, especially during times of stress, and Maiguru takes it upon herself to worry about his food consumption.

Eating, or not eating, signifies control over one's limited resources, provoking a response at the sociosymbolic level. Nevertheless, the novel does not lose sight of the brute fact that food cultivation and preparation are women's work. In the case where a woman is unfortunate enough to be with a man who doesn't "provide" food, such as Ma'Shingayi is with Jeremiah, she has the additional burden of making food before making the meal. The novel

offers several accounts of the feminine time and labor required of
the girls and women who feed the rest of the African Family. The
examples of gatherings of the patriarchy at the homestead are particularly appropriate:

> Counting Nyasha, Anna, Netsai, Rambanai and myself,
> there were twenty-four people altogether on the homestead,
> which was twenty-four stomachs to fill three times a day.
> Twenty-four bodies for which water had to be fetched from
> the Nyamarira daily. Twenty-four people's laundry to wash
> as often as possible, and Tete's youngest was still in nap-
> kins. Now, this kind of work was women's work, and of
> the thirteen women there, my mother and Lucia were in-
> capacitated a little, but nevertheless to some extent, by preg-
> nancy. Tete, having patriarchal status, was not expected to
> do much and four of us were only ten years old or younger.
> So Maiguru, Nyasha, the three helping girls and myself
> were on our feet all day. (133)

The relationship of the novel's female community towards food
preparation and consumption is deeply bound up with control over
self as well as with the daily grind of food acquisition and
preparation. In the first part, when Tambu lives on the homestead,
the novel makes endless references to the difficulties of procuring
food as well as to how her father's laziness forces her mother to
both provide and prepare their meals. Moreover, as is made clear,
girls have far less time to study if cooking and clean-up are an
assumed part of their duties.

At the mission school, the physical work load is far less
severe, though women still bear the responsibility for feeding and
nurturing; and as Maiguru illustrates, nurturing is frequently accomplished via food (she ritually feeds and attends to Babamukuru,
makes sadza and other familiar foods to ease Tambu into her new
life, and worries about Nyasha's inadequate eating). Above all,
though she is her husband's equal in educational status, on their
visits to the homestead, it is Maiguru who must bear responsibility

for feeding the entire familial group:

> Maiguru worked harder than anybody else, because as the
> senior wife as well as provider of the food to cook, she
> was expected to oversee all the culinary operations. It was
> ceaseless work and unwise to delegate, because she had to
> make sure that the food lasted until the end of the vaca-
> tion. With thirteen extra people to feed—and the lot of us
> devouring seven loaves of bread and half a pound of mar-
> garine each morning . . . Maiguru had to be strict about
> sharing out the food, and this made my mother irritable . .
> . [Later, some of the side of beef Maiguru brings spoils
> due to lack of adequate refrigeration; the lone woman in
> the patriarchy insinuates that the meat is inedible.] This
> threw my aunt, who was a good woman and a good wife
> and took pride in this identity, into a dreadful panic. She
> took to cooking, twice a day, a special pot of refrigerated
> meat for the patriarchy to eat as they planned and con-
> structed the family's future. (135-36)

Education and food themselves function as signifiers of modernity
and tradition, respectively: as non-fixed symbols of women's (and
men's) status under colonialism, in developing countries, as
signifiers of cultural authenticity and tradition. Education is bound
up with the imperatives of decolonizing nationalism, and, though
one of the promises decolonizing nationalism makes is to create
the New (and educated) Woman, education itself is seen as the
provenance of men. Food, of course, is usually part of the domain
of women; in addition, food, more than other cultural signs, reflects
a tie to "tradition" and to cultural purity, the possible loss of which
haunts women, especially the educated women of the new
nation-state.

Nervous Conditions narrates the struggle for
self-determination of two teenaged girls and yet never risks
trivializing their problems or making either a simple icon of the
nation. I believe that these departures from convention, such as

depicting full and complex female characters against a literary field populated by Mother Africa and prostitute figures, explain why it has not yet been read as a national parable.[16]   Since the political practices of female-authored African novels are not always visible, readers must devise new forms of literacy, new and informed understandings of how these texts represent politics. Tambu and Nyasha function as two aspects of Zimbabwean subjectivity as the new nation emerges from and against Rhodesia. In Tambu, the novel depicts the making of one subject whose evolution is not particularly heroic, and is, in fact, bolstered by that of the female community in whose custody she comes of age. My argument thus far is not much different from Felski's. However, I would like to suggest that *Nervous Conditions* also explicates a decolonizing nationalism that it understands as overlapping with and aided by its feminism, and, moreover, that the textual politics of it become evident only through a thorough reconsideration of Nyasha's place and function.

While Tambu embodies the development of the national bourgeoisie and the hope of the New Woman in particular, Nyasha's tragedy evokes the unfulfilled promise of the persecuted nation. To Tambu's matter-of-fact striving is juxtaposed Nyasha's heroic pathos; to Tambu's repression, Nyasha's frank curiosity about sex. Like Tambu's narrative, Nyasha's is teleological and filled with obstacles. Unlike Tambu's narrative, Nyasha's is, at a certain level at least, a story of miscarriage in that by the novel's end the survival of its protagonist is not at all assured. At the level of surface representation Nyasha's personal struggle against her father's benevolent tyranny might be a failed one. However, closer inspection illustrates that Nyasha's very failure as a coming-of-age subject raises questions about subjectivity, power, and control that go beyond the private domain of home and family to the public one of nation and state. This linking of domains belies the received wisdom, firstly, that decolonizing nationalism only asks questions about the public sphere, and secondly, that female writers usually leave such questions unanswered. As I have argued elsewhere, it is female authors who by and large have illustrated the deep interpenetration of both domains.[17]

Nyasha's unrelenting search for Truth, coupled with the register in which she articulates her objections to her father, moves the novel out of a single-minded feminist politics, such as the exercising of minute control of the body, to suggest a more complex politics of anticolonialism. While the genre of the *Bildungsroman* involves a progression or quest in the development of a self, that quest need not entail only the making of individual subjectivity but might also encompass self-realization in the service of a larger ideology. Nyasha's search for a "higher truth" makes manifest her interpellation in the psychological and physical violence of a triumphant colonialism, and her crusade for self-control serves to expose the self's identity as colonized (as a "mimic," to appropriate Bhabha's appropriation of Fanon). As an undone character in a *Bildungsroman* that thematizes colonialism, Nyasha highlights the novel's powerful, if buried, black nationalist agenda.

In contrast to Tambu, who frequently exhibits uncertainty about her relation to the public political arena, and to Babamukuru and Maiguru, who assume positions of "responsibility" which means dismissing what they consider to be their daughter's foolhardy criticisms, Nyasha is unhesitatingly and passionately interested in politics, both local and global. She frequently pushes Tambu to situate her enthusiastic discoveries about the cultural sphere within a larger geopolitical one. Moreover, with the exception of the girls' shared grandmother—who, early in the novel, recounts to Tambu the history of their family's displacement from its land upon the arrival of the "white wizards"—it is Nyasha who voices the novel's most stringent and consistent critique of colonialism. She responds thusly to her father's forcing of the Christian wedding ceremony onto Tambu's indigenously-married parents: "'It's bad enough,' she said severely, 'when a country gets colonised, but when the people do as well! That's the end, really, that's the end'" (147).[18]

As Sugnet astutely notes, *Nervous Conditions* makes only three "direct references to . . . [national political] events in the novel, and they are brief and passing ones" (34). I am indebted to Sugnet for his cataloguing of these references and for his insightful reading of the novel in general, and I agree that "there may be a complex, partly subterranean relationship between it and the struggles of the young Tambudzai against the immediate manifestations of patriarchy in her life" (34). However, I disagree with his appraisal that "*Nervous Conditions* contains enough chronological specifics so a reader familiar with Zimbabwean history will know that the novel's period encompasses . . . landmark events in the national narrative as the founding of ZANU and ZAPU, the ten-year detention of Robert Mugabe and Joshua Nkomo, Ian Smith's Unilateral Declaration of Independence, and the officially celebrated 'first battle' of the *Chimurenga* war on April 28, 1966" (34). That is to say, a reader already familiar with Zimbabwean history might be aware that a historical narrative undergirds the more literary tale of Tambu and Nyasha. But none of the abovementioned historical or political events arises specifically or obliquely to the novel's surface. The reader has to labor to discover and then trace a relationship between them, so elliptical are the allusions. There is a connection between the shape of the political palimpsests and the individualist narrative, but it requires some elucidation.

Nervous Conditions directly ascribes to Nyasha two of the three national political allusions, and the remaining one appears to be the result of her influence. All three illustrate the novel's assertion that the public and private spheres interpenetrate and are interdependent. In the first instance, Nyasha wants to know "exactly why UDI was declared and what it meant" (93); she refers here to the United Declaration of Independence by which white Rhodesians declared their sovereignty from Britain and enshrined black disenfranchisement. The reference appears in the paragraph immediately following Tambu's elated description of her personal blossoming under the superior educational environment at the Mission School: "'So,' [Nyasha] advised, concerning my fairy-tales and my reincarnation, 'enjoy it while you can. These things don't last'" (93). This admonition functions to temporarily halt the *Bildungsroman*'s normative and near-narcissistic tendency of acclaiming self-development to the exclusion of all else. The second reference, which involves only Tambu and Maiguru, is undoubtedly prompted by Nyasha's influence. Tambu has just discovered that her aunt has a Master's degree, is as equally well-educated as her husband, but does not keep all her money: "'What happens to your money?' I asked. 'The money that you earn. Does the Government take it?' For I was beginning to learn that our Government was not a good one" (101). Though the novel makes plain that Maiguru's money enables Babamukuru's largesse towards his (extended) family, without which Tambu would not have her education, it nevertheless simultaneously compares Maiguru's economic subordination to her husband with that of blacks to the white government. The third and final reference comes towards the end. As in the previous examples, the text places public, national, and "important" concerns against those private, domestic, and mundane ones that shape their everyday lives:

> Beside Nyasha I was a paragon of feminine decorum, principally because I hardly ever talked unless spoken to, and then only to answer with the utmost respect whatever question had been asked. Above all, I did not question things. It did not matter to me why things should be done this way rather than that way . . . . I did not think that my reading was more important than washing the dishes, and I understood that panties should not be hung in the bathroom where everybody could see them . . . . I was not concerned that freedom fighters were referred to as terrorists, did not demand proof of God's existence nor did I think that the missionaries, along with all the other Whites in Rhodesia, ought to have stayed home. (155)

Under the pressure of Nyasha's relentless interrogation, the public and private spheres are again shown to be deeply overlapping and both established as political. The quotation above constitutes the novel's single most powerful challenge to the received understanding of late colonialist politics as explicated in this novel: because Tambu recounts Nyasha's stinging denunciation of colonialism, because the novel makes its most explicit reference to the *Chimurenga* war here and suggests, albeit obliquely, that an end is in sight, and, above all, because missionary work, from which Babamukuru has benefited and which he promotes, is represented as part and parcel of the colonialist enterprise. This textual moment occurs shortly before Nyasha becomes manifestly unstable.

If Tambu's developmental success can be read as an example of a successful *Bildungsroman*, an understanding of Nyasha benefits from an intertextual reading of the anticolonial political theory of Frantz Fanon. The link of *Nervous Conditions* to Fanon is apparent from the title itself, which comes from Sartre's preface to Fanon's *Wretched of the Earth*. Though Sartre remains curiously unmentioned, that the phrase derives from *Wretched* is explained in the epigraph to Dangarembga's book: "the condition of native is a nervous condition." When read through the lens of Fanon's works, *Nervous Conditions*' subtle investment in decolonizing nationalism is thrown into relief, and we see that, despite Radhakrishnan's gloomy pronouncement, it is possible to express in literary form a public politics of the nation grounded in feminism.[19]

Sugnet observes of Dangarembga's appropriation of Sartre that she "seized on this particular phrase for her title because her novel redefines Fanon's insights and because she wanted the slight double meaning in 'nervous' in the ordinary sense of anxious, uneasy or worried, but also in the formal medical or psychiatric sense of 'so-and-so suffers from a nervous condition,'" such as Nyasha's anorexia nervosa (35). I agree that Dangarembga redefines Fanon, and would add that she rewrites Sartre's singular "nervous condition" into a plural formulation. Elaborating on Sugnet's point I suggest that Dangarembga is interested precisely in the move from ordinary to formal nervousness, just as she is in the relationship between small and big collectives, "minor" and "major" political questions.

The title's plural form signifies the complexity of Nyasha's anxiety; it also suggests that more than one character in the novel suffers from anxiety. Any reading of "nerves" or "nervousness" should begin with Nyasha but should then extend beyond her, for though she is the narrative's central and most tragic casualty of colonial violence, all of the colonized Africans around her suffer different forms of its consequences—and in a similar mode. For example, Babamukuru, against whom Nyasha is in constant rebellion, also experiences stress, poor eating habits, and "bad nerves." Furthermore, the title proposes an association between anorexia as a quintessentially feminine disorder and the colonized as disempowerment or feminization of the colonized by virtue of their subordinate position. For among those afflicted with anorexia, typically teenaged girls, one reason for its onset is as a response to the victims' lack of agency or power. The afflicted exert control in the limited ways they can, and inhibiting eating, or controlling the body, is a common one. *Nervous Conditions* lends itself to an ironical reading based on this: one might well see Babamukuru's assiduous and patently patriarchal attempts to supervise the sexuality (both in the budding form of his daughter and in the more mature and non-monogamous forms of Lucia and Jeremiah) as a metaphor for the actions of the disempowered. The harmful repercussions of Babamukuru's humiliation of Ma'Shingayi and Jeremiah via the Christian marriage he imposes, his acute repression of Nyasha's choice of dress, her occasional flirtatiousness, and reading materials as well as his compelling her to eat are obvious at the surface level of story. At a secondary level, however, that a colonized adult would seek to control what bodily practices he can through benevolent tyranny serves to underscore his own powerlessness in a system in which he is ostensibly a star product and emblem of power, itself a tragic effect.

A primary sympathetic resonance between the novel and Fanon's work lies in the shared assumption that the native is not born but made, a maxim Fanon pronounces on the second page of

Wretched: "For it is the settler who has brought the native into existence and who perpetuates his existence" (36). Echoes of a shared existentialist tradition can also be heard in Simone De Beauvoir's famous and earlier expressed, "One is not born, but rather becomes, a woman" (267). *Nervous Conditions* depicts both principles equally well. It illustrates the formation of one member of the new nation's bourgeoisie in the person of Tambudzai, the country cousin whose education and upward mobility results in the ability to narrate this tale in reflection, as well as the undoing of elite status and the challenge to that class as posed by Nyasha, the urbanized and Westernized cousin whose criticism and encouragement shape Tambu's self-awareness, but whose insight also makes her vulnerable to incapacitating moral indignation and anxiety.

While it adheres to the main points of Fanon's indictment of colonialism, Dangarembga's forthright feminism combined with her elision from the story of the guerrilla struggle that Fanon so values might be read as riposte to Fanon's own elision of gendered politics from his analysis.[20] On an immediate level, the novel adheres firmly to the anticolonial aspect of Fanon's politics. Nevertheless, it also implicitly indicts Fanon for writing the anxiety of colonialism as a lack of masculine agency, since he occasionally betrays the belief that the colonial subject is a masculine one: "The first thing the native learns is to stay in his place and not to go beyond certain limits. This is why the dreams of the native are always of muscular prowess; his dreams are of action and of aggression" (*Wretched* 52).[21] Fanon's celebration of muscular aggression as a form of rebellion against alienation has been openly engaged in literature by many male African writers. Dangarembga tellingly recasts the Fanonian protagonist's masculine-coded desire for aggression and agency as a teenaged girl's suffering of an eating disorder, and the very opposite of muscularity at the most literal level, thereby exposing the Fanonian protagonist as (universally) male.[22]

I suggested earlier that in *Nervous Conditions*, *Gesellschaft* stands for the unspoken (and unspeakable) nation, a modern, rational, and as female writers have affirmed, remote configuration. However, in that the novel exhibits a strong commitment to decolonization at the level of theme, and at the level of form, there are many parallels between it and the overt nationalism of writers such as Fanon. *Gemeinschaft*, by articulating a meaningful and manageable set of micro-relations of power, offers a way for one to traverse between micro- and macro-relations of power.[23] The interplay between *Gemeinschaft* and *Gesellschaft*, which echoes that of the figural relation between family and nation in women's writing as a whole, offers a way to construct a bridge between the alien and instrumental nature of civic or national politics and the private world of a feminine community which has both social and symbolic meaning for women. Moreover, the connection between the two units of collectivity permits the novel to quietly, if not openly, commit to Fanon's claim that, "[i]ndividual experience, because it is national, and because it is a link in the chain of national existence, ceases to be individual, limited and shrunken and is enabled to open out into the truth of the nation and of the world" (*Wretched* 200).

The genre of the *Bildungsroman* illustrates the making of a normative national subject in Tambu; the political theory of Fanon explains the construction of the native via Nyasha. The ideological connection between the two discourses is that of decolonizing nationalism and feminine subjectivity. Earlier I suggested that, in psychological terms, the *Bildungsroman* charts the development of an interiorized subjectivity, and, in social terms, it depicts the consolidation of the lone, bourgeois, and usually male, subject. Here, via a Fanonian lens, and through the character of Nyasha, one can see a similar exposition of social and symbolic subjectivity in the service of decolonizing nationalism. Fanon's most important contribution to anticolonial theory is his claim that the violence of colonialism is not simply physical but structural as well as psychological and that the threat of violence itself functions as a form of coercion of the colonial disenfranchised. In *Wretched of the Earth* and *Black Skin, White Masks*, his most influential books, Fanon devotes most of his attention to analysis of colonialism's repressive apparatus of psychological and institutional violence. Structural and psychological violence of both the colonial and patriarchal sorts are omnipresent. In a comparable gesture *Nervous Conditions* dispels the notion that colonialism is upheld primarily through brute force in Southern Rhodesia. For with the exception of her grandmother's story of how Tambu's ancestral family is thrown off their land, most of what the novel narrates involves no physical violence. Similarly, with the exception of the fight after the dance, none of the patriarchally configured violence is openly physical. Only on that occasion does Babamukuru strike his daughter. Jeremiah, a far weaker and less admirable man, is never shown to hit his. Both men, however, actively inhibit their respective daughters' ambitions. And the more powerful Babamukuru is also able to frequently coerce Nyasha into eating or not reading forbidden books by threatening to expel her from "his" house.

The buried anger on the part of the female native erupts into violence towards the novel's end. Nyasha's defiance of her father is represented as being of a piece with her defiance of the structures of colonial domination to which she perceives him and herself to be subject. In the following passage, the heretofore largely occluded apparatus of colonial subjugation is tied to the novel's more obvious mechanism of gender discrimination:

> "They've done it to me," she accused, whispering still . . . . "It's not their fault. They did it to them too. You know they did," she whispered. "To both of them, but especially to him. They put him through it all. But it's not his fault, he's good." Her voice took on a Rhodesian accent. "He's a good boy, a good munt. A bloody good kaffir," she informed in sneering sarcastic tones . . . . "They've taken us away. Lucia. Takesure. All of us. They've deprived you of you, him of him, ourselves of each other. We're groveling. Lucia for a job, Jeremiah for money. Daddy grovels to them. We grovel to him . . . ." Nyasha was beside herself with fury.

She rampaged, shredding her history book between her teeth ("Their history. Fucking liars. Their bloody lies,") . . . . "They've trapped us. They've trapped us. But I won't be trapped." Then as suddenly as it came, the rage passed. "I don't hate you, Daddy," she said softly. "They want me to, but I won't . . . . Look what they've done to us," she said softly. "I'm not one of them but I'm not one of you" (200-01).

In the absence of an organized mode of social rebellion, Nyasha's refusal of colonialism and patriarchy first turns inward into anorexia and bulimia. Later she openly objects to consuming colonial history, naming the link between that history and that of the hierarchy of which her father, and she through him, forms a part. Fanon claims that when the native interrupts the narrative of colonization he or she has arrived at a moment of productive crisis: "The immobility to which the native is condemned can only be called in question if the native decides to put an end to the history of colonization—the history of pillage—and to bring into existence the history of the nation—the history of decolonization" (51). Although Nyasha's story produces an ending without a positive role model, her outburst here suggests that she, and through her, the reader, has arrived at such a moment of productive crisis.

The novel ends with Nyasha's mental and physical state unresolved. Nyasha's illness and uncertain condition becomes juxtaposed against Tambu's secure narrative voice and future, calling into question the act of closure typical of the classic realist *Bildungsroman*. *Nervous Conditions* refuses to neatly reintegrate its protagonist(s) into the socius. Earlier, I suggested that instead of a single position of character or reader-identification, this novel manifests a set of hierarchized discourses, one illustrating the coming-into-being of the national subject, the other, a simultaneous unraveling of the self-aware "native" whose discourse gives the novel its vibrancy and moral force. The realist *Bildungsroman* which produces its protagonist--and by extension its readers--as unified human subjects is hereby challenged. Rather than a novel that represents or fails to represent the coming of age of two girls, *Nervous Conditions* lends itself better to a reading of the struggle between the position of a national subject and a native one, and it thereby illustrates how a form normally understood to be flatly mimetic enacts its own limits and incompletions.

Notes

1. "Thus the critical task is not simple; it necessarily implies the superposition of two questions; not in a choice between them, but in the point from which they appear to become differentiated. The complexity of the critical problem will be the articulation between the two questions. To grasp this articulation is to accept a discontinuity, to establish discontinuity: the questions are not spontaneously given in their specificity. Initially, the questions must be asked—asked simultaneously, in a way that amounts to allowing them an equal status" (90).

2. It is critical to remember, however, that the enormous sum of ten pounds that guarantees Tambu's education for at least two school terms, comes directly from a benevolently racist white woman in Umtali. Doris, believing Tambu to be an exploited native child, first excoriates her teacher, Mr. Matimba, then, guiltily upon hearing his explanation of the girl's situation, offers him the money. Dangarembga's choice of narrative strategies here reflects a brutal honesty about neocolonial economies and global markets; she doesn't pretend to depict a level playing field on which developing nations and their citizenry are able to advance without help from external sources of funding.

3. "Thus began the period of my reincarnation. I liked to think of my transfer to the mission as my reincarnation. With the egotistical faith of fourteen short years, during which my life had progressed very much according to plan, I expected this era to be significantly profound and broadening in terms of adding wisdom to my nature, clarity to my vision, glamour to my person. In short, I expected my sojourn to fulfill all my fourteen-year-old fantasies, and on the whole I was not disappointed . . . ." (93).

4. Boumhela, writing about Eliot's *Mill on the Floss*, puts it succinctly:

"Realism, bounded more or less by its project of representing in some typical form the real conditions of social existence, has tended to reduce the options for its female protagonists to either marriage or death. Of course, the virtual interchangeability of the two is itself telling" (326).

5. The prototypical example is Goethe's *Wilhelm Meister*.

6. Carole Vance convincingly argues that the feminine virtues of self-control and watchfulness are signifiers of having been dominated: "Sexual constriction, invisibility, timidity, and uncuriosity are less the signs of an intrinsic and specific female sexual nature and more the signs of thoroughgoing damage" (4).

7. Deepika Bahri perceptively notes that her father's objection to Nyasha's copy of the Lawrence novel marks the first time in the novel that Nyasha rejects food (*Nervous Conditions* 83; Bahri *Postmodern Culture* 5.1).

8. Chido is able to maintain a form of close rapport with the Baker daughter, Nyaradzo, sister of the boy with whom Nyasha dallies after the dance; this friendship, though known to their age-mates and parents alike, does not come in for censure. It does comes in for criticism from Tambu's mother (120 and passim).

9. In feminine form, desire is represented only by the character of Lucia, who through her willful violation of sexual convention serves to illustrate the avenues of power and erotics not normally associated with downtrodden, "traditional" women. In this respect, Lucia's positively-coded sexuality functions as counterweight to the education and earning potential of the "modern" Maiguru.

10. "It was good to be validated in this way. Most of it didn't come from the lessons they taught at school but from Nyasha's various and extensive library. I read everything from Enid Blyton to the Brontë sisters, and responded to them all. Plunging into these books I knew I was being educated and I was filled with gratitude to the authors for introducing me to places where reason and inclination were not at odds. It was a centripetal time, with me at the centre, everything gravitating towards me. It was a time of sublimation with me as the sublimate" (93).

11. I refer to the mother of Tambu and Nhamo as Ma'Shingayi because the text refers to her as such—more than it does to her as Mainini. If the example of Babamukuru's calling of Maiguru Ma'Chido (the mother of Chido) is instructive, Ma'Shingayi refers to the relation she has with a

child we do not know of.

12. "'This business of womanhood is a heavy burden,' she said . . . . 'When it is like that you can't just decided [sic] today I want to do this, tomorrow I want to do that, the next day I want to be educated! . . . . And these days it is worse, with the poverty of blackness on one side and the weight of womanhood on the other'" (16).

13. Note that though she does get pregnant later, her earlier sexual agency is predicated precisely on not being fertile.

14. In an interview of Dangarembga, noted Africanist and Caribbeanist scholar, Kirsten Holst Petersen reveals her disapproval of Dangarembga's depiction of the African Family by asking in the first question: "Do you find that your main character is justified in harboring such an unnatural sentiment?" (345).

15. Tambu's mother does exhibit tremendous grief, but the narrative contains this outpouring; it comes well after the explication of Nhamo's mean-spiritedness towards Tambu and his other sisters.

16. For an insightful discussion of these tropes in the male-authored African literary tradition, see chapter one of *African Literature and the Politics of Gender* by Florence Stratton.

17. See my forthcoming book, *The Nation Writ Small: African Fictions and Feminisms. 1958-1988.*

18. At this point in the text, Tambu cannot articulate her anger and humiliation about the ceremony, though she recognizes it before the ceremony itself and refuses to participate. However, Tambu cannot bring herself to fight openly with Babamukuru. Instead, she becomes physically incapacitated, is unable to get out of bed on the morning of the wedding, and, therefore, is unable to serve as her mother's bridesmaid.

19. I refer here to "Nationalism, Gender and the Narrative of Identity."

20. Only in "Algeria Unveiled" does Fanon make gender a constituent part of his analysis. For an essay that reclaims Fanon for a feminist politics by reading his strategy of contingent polemic as one allied with contemporary feminist strategy, see Madhu Dubey's "The True Lie of the Nation."

21. "The look that the native turns on the settler's town is a look of lust, a

look of envy; it expresses his dreams of possession: to sit at the settler's table, to sleep in the settler's bed, with his wife, if possible. The colonized man is an envious man" (39).

22. Nyasha suffers from bulimia as well as anorexia. The novel seems to indicate that Nyasha chooses to be anorectic, and that she enacts bulimic symptoms only after her father coerces her into eating; see 190 for example of using a toothbrush to induce vomiting.

23. Felski's notion of the relation between *Gemeinschaft* and *Gesellschaft* can be called into play again in order to articulate the relationship of this novel to a public politics, between its expressed investment in a feminine subjectivity and an implied investment in decolonizing nationalism. The smaller collective, *Gemeinschaft*, is the primary and more meaningful association by which women might find or make community. Felski's application of the term does not depend on biological or kin relations and so offers a certain flexibility in constructing community. In contrast, she defines *Gesellschaft* as a far more removed set of associations, characterized by "rational will . . . most clearly exemplified in the division of labor and differentiation of society which develops under capitalism; human relations for the most part no longer possess a meaningful collective base, but are fundamentally alienated and abstract, subordinated to instrumental and quantitative goals" (140).

Chapter 3:
Modernity, Alienation, and Development: *Nervous Conditions* and the Female Paradigm

Ann Elizabeth Willey

*N*ervous Conditions begins with the main character and narrator, Tambudzai Sigauke, declaring bald-facedly, "I was not sorry when my brother died" (1). Most critics take this unusual assertion as something to be explained away—how are we supposed to trust a narrator who does not regret her brother's death? Why should we read the story of such a callous young girl? The most simple answer to this question is provided by the narrator herself when she explains that the events that led to her brother's death "put me in a position to write this account" (1). Tambudzai tells the reader that her ability to write her story is worth losing a brother. I, for one, still find this a callous attitude. But for Tambu, both as the character of age thirteen when her brother dies, and as the older narrative voice, her story is shaped by the imperative of development, both her own and that of her community. In order to tell her story, and she tells us, the story of all the women around her, Tambu must assert a female voice that has the ability to define itself in her rapidly changing environment. The loss of a brother is necessary in order to gain access to the modernity that allows her to write the story that inserts her in a community.

Nervous Conditions is rightly famous in postcolonial circles: it is a compelling text that weaves together many of the concerns that have come to shape the field of postcolonial studies. The novel raises the question of language practice, systems of education, formation of a self in the colonial and postcolonial era, tradition versus modernity, patriarchy, urbanization, nationalism or lack thereof, and a whole host of other concerns central to contemporary discussions. The novel has even been widely incorporated into high school curriculums in the United States as a lyrical coming of age story that may impress upon students the benefits of education (or so teachers hope). I think this novel most significantly brings together three terms that have been central to discussions of African literature: modernity, alienation, and development. For in this novel, Dangarembga challenges our definitions of alienation by linking the question of development as implication in the modern world to the process of a young girl developing into an adult voice. In this, Dangarembga challenges our usually male-defined sense of alienation and modernity to suggest a female paradigm for the understanding of the processes of alienation and development in relation to modernity. For women, the trajectory from "tradition" to "modernity" that describes so much African literature is both more and less unsettling than for their male counterparts. The loss of tradition is not nearly so painful and the gains of modernity are not so nearly liberating as in the typical male paradigm. As with the development of a young girl into an adult female, both advantages and disadvantages accompany change; however, the change is presented as more or less inevitable

When I speak of development here, I mean to understand it in both the grammatical modes that the verb "to develop" can operate. In fact, central to *Nervous Conditions* is a tension between the two meanings of "development" to which the 13-year-old colonial subject that is our protagonist is subject. Through Tambudzai, *Nervous Conditions* argues that the process of development in postcolonial Africa is one that is rife with the tensions between indigenous, internalized forces, that which develops in and of itself, and externalized, exogenous forces, that which is developed *by* someone. Dangarembga separates these two modes of development by transferring the intransitive modality onto the female main character and the transitive modality onto Tambu's uncle and, by extension, the process of education. As Tambu develops into a woman, she is also developed into the educated narrative voice that presents her story. For those of us interested in the articulations of postcolonial and feminist theory, this teasing out of the modalities of development poses some very interesting questions. The character of Tambu, in her two-fold process of development, suggests that both modalities must be in operation for the "story" of the postcolonial female subject to be told. The character of Tambu must negotiate between the internal imperatives of development and the external paradigms of development, specifically the limitations placed on the female gendered subject in a colonial and postcolonial context. It is tempting then to read this as a metaphor for the development of the postcolonial African nation in its struggle to face the internal dynamics of cultural change (or development) while faced with the constraints and opposing forces imposed by the neo-colonial system with its rhetoric of development. [1]

But what gives pause here is the fact that our narrator chooses to portray her development into an educated African woman as precisely this: a clash of internal and necessary forces versus external and incidental forces that are nonetheless irresistible at the same time that they are desirable in their ends if threatening in their means. In the end, the narrative voice that presents her story is one of someone who "feel[s] many things these days, much more than I was able to feel in the days when I was young . . ." (1) and has furthermore "escaped" far enough to be able to tell not only her own story, but also the story of all the women around her. She has developed into an emancipated, fully developed woman who controls the technology of writing and books for her own ends.

The imbrications of these two modes of development, Tambu's intransitive process of maturation and her society's transitive process of being developed by forces outside itself, are made obvious in the first chapter when Tambu describes the twin processes of her and her village's growth. What quickly becomes obvious is Tambu's ambivalence about both types of development. At 13 years old she is happy in her surroundings and enjoys a physical intimacy with her landscape, especially the river Nyamarira. But this intimacy is rudely interrupted by both the advent of a gendered, adult self and the increasing growth of her village. She describes the river as containing flat-topped boulders which provided "exciting equipment for our childhood games . . . the river flowed sparsely in the dry season, but deeply enough in places when the rains were heavy to cover a child's head and engulf me to my nipples" (3). As a child she explored the river at will, all the while noting that "as children we were not restricted. We could play where we pleased. But the women had their own spot for bathing and the men their own too . . ."(3). The women's spot, she notes, is shallow and wide, ideal for doing laundry. Even while asserting that she has crossed over the edge of childhood (the river rises only to her nipples but covers the heads of children) she does not want to claim the wide shallow realms of womanhood.

Just as her relation to the river is destined to change with her development, she traces how the topography of the river changes with the development of the surrounding village. First came the government's decision to build the District Council Houses "less than a mile away from the places where we washed" (3), followed by tuckshops built to take advantage of the people gathered around to conduct business at the council houses, followed by a bus stop which then encouraged the idle youth of the area to linger, leading to the establishment of beer and music halls that cater to the youth. Our narrator remarks wryly that with this increasing concentration of people, "in the interests of decency bathing was relegated to further up the river" (4). Tambu however, does not so easily give up her familiar haunts in the river. Despite the fact that the women of the village have shifted their bathing grounds further up-stream, Tambu continues to swim in her familiar places: "Nevertheless, when I was feeling brave, which was before my breasts grew too large, I would listen from the top of the ravine and, when I was sure I had felt no one coming I would run down to the river . . . and swim blissfully for as long as I dared in the old deep places" (4).

In this relatively short opening chapter, Tambu interweaves the development of her environment and the development of her body. Her relation to the river is heavily encoded by gender and its development: the women bathe in one spot, ideally located for traditionally feminine chores, the men in another, and children can roam freely from one to the other. But Tambu tells us that as the novel begins, she is on the threshold of facing her own growth into the limitations of gender. The river in places would cover a child's head but reaches only to her nipples, surely one of the most obvious indices of a girl's development. Her development into a fully gendered woman furthermore robs her not only of place but also of character. Note that she says that she felt brave enough to return to the old places only before her breasts were too large. She develops as her village develops, not as a function of conscious will, but almost as an accident or fate (the Government decided to build the Council Houses without requesting the input of the village people).

Just as the village in this chapter is the passive recipient of a development that they cannot control, Tambu resists being gendered as her own development takes place. Indeed, Tambu's resistance to being gendered by others is at the root of her callous attitude toward her brother's death, so often remarked on. Before his death but after his transfer to the mission school, Tambu's cherished dream, she asks her brother why she too cannot go to school:

> "But I want to go to school"
>
> "Wanting won't help."
>
> "Why not?"
>
> He hesitated then shrugged. "It's the same everywhere. Because you're a girl." It was out. "That's what Baba said, remember?" I was no longer listening. My concern for my brother died an unobtrusive death. (21)

This interference between her two processes of development, the one she is subject to despite herself (bodily maturation) and the one she actively seeks out (her education), describe the parameters of her struggle for the rest of the novel. The novel, through the development of a female figure that resists external characterization of her development at the same time that she appeals to outside forces to enable her change, frames the question of development that in other terms many Africanists have described. How can postcolonial Africa develop itself? Does Dangarembga end up suggesting something new?

In this context, I think we must answer that Dangarembga at the very least challenges our understandings of the phenomenon of cultural change that has most often been described as alienation as a result of the move from tradition to modernity. This trope of alienation as a result of the shift in African cultural systems toward "modernity" (and this term is never unproblematic) has shaped much of the past and present discussions of African literature. Perhaps one of the most cogent studies of the tensions between interior and exterior pressures on African cultures can be found in Abiola Irele's essay "In Praise of Alienation." In this essay, Irele addresses the trope of alienation which is common in the canon of African literature. One of the most widely recognized examples of this trope at work in African literature is Cheikh Hamidou Kane's *Ambiguous Adventure*, the story of Samba Diallo, an intelligent, sensitive young man from West Africa. Diallo is sent early to western-style schools in order, to quote a famous passage, "to learn the secret of might without right." Diallo's academic career continues prodigiously until he finds himself studying for an advanced degree in Philosophy in Paris. What Kane's novel does so well is question what (in colonial discourse) would be read as a great success by showing the reader what Diallo loses while he gains this western-style education. Samba Diallo ultimately loses his sanity and his life. He is reduced to a metaphysical impasse by the confusion engendered by his very different sources of knowledge and experience.

This story is not exclusive to *Ambiguous Adventure* or West African literature in general. Samba Diallo's experiences are just one example of the phenomena that has come to be called alienation. In this context, alienation is understood to mean a separation from an essential sense of self, a separation from the true self, much as it was used by the pioneers in the field of psychiatry: an alienated individual is one who is not a whole personality. In his essay, Irele describes how this term has come to be used in the study of African literature to refer to the situation of the modern western-educated African. He describes the African educated in European languages as being, "wedged uncomfortably between the values of our traditional culture and those of the West" (212-13). He traces the theme of alienation through several novels claiming: "what runs through all this literature is the feeling that it is within our traditional culture that we are happiest, most at ease with our selves, that there is the truest coincidence between us and the world: in other words, that our true identity is located" (204). Having noted the tendency of cultural nationalism to locate the "true self" within the realm of tradition, and noting the separation to which Africans educated in European languages perforce are subject, Irele recoups the term as a positive one. He posits alienation as the necessary universal force that drives the development of all cultures. He calls on Africans to view their state of alienation as a positive force, one that will enable an increasingly open access to modernity, a choice that he calls a not only "practical necessity" but indeed a calling in of chits as well. Irele says, ". . . we have a claim upon Western civilization as well as considerable stake in it as the instrument for the necessary transformation of our world. It is in our interest to make good that claim, to adopt strategies that will make our investment in that civilization pay handsome dividends" (222). Alienation for Irele is a necessary separation from a realm of tradition that he describes as less and less "apposite" to "the emerging structure of reality" (209) in order to have access to modernity which he posits as necessary for the development of Africa.

Irele ends his essay by asking his readers to re-evaluate alienation as a productive status engendered by an awareness of the "sensitive tension between the immediate closeness of the self and the reflected distance of the other" (224). For Irele, the terms of self and other become defined by tradition, which provides a basis or true self, and modernity, a desired state. In his reading of the novels by Cheikh Hamidou Kane or Camara Laye, Irele stresses how these authors have represented the profound ambivalence that accompanies this quest for modernity. Modernity, in this essay, takes on the meaning of interaction with the western world and all that it usually entails in Africanist discourse: technology, individualism, capitalism, and incorporation into a global economy of goods and culture. What seems to go unchallenged in this essay is the idea that this "idea of tradition" is always a comforting one. By extension, the move away from tradition is always assumed to be one that engenders a type of discomfort, even if that discomfort ends up being positive. The celebration of the idea of tradition, regardless of its applicability to the modern world, is rightly condemned by Irele as often a shallow and cynical move on the part of political leaders to disguise just how much the society has changed to their benefit. However, this very same camouflage by tradition operates in some of the more sincere descriptions of the African cultural universe when we consider the fact that women are often circumscribed by both the realms of tradition and the modernity that Irele so strongly advocates.[2]

In tracing the dynamic of alienation in these terms, Irele sets up a paradigm of alienation that works well to explain the situations of certain characters in African fiction, like Sambo Da lo, but this paradigm does not work as well to describe the experiences of female heroines like Tambudzai of *Nervous Conditions*. Where alienation is described by Irele as the feeling of being removed from the traditional culture where "we are happiest, most at ease with our selves," the female heroine of this novel experiences traditional culture as something that makes her feel ill at ease and profoundly limited. So much so that our protagonist is willing to sacrifice her brother in order to escape the world of tradition. Because this female character starts at a fundamentally different position than that described by Irele for the implicitly male subject, she experiences alienation and access to modernity in different terms. For Tambu the child within the story, the image of the traditional self and the mark against which she gauges her distance from that world is her mother. This is not to say that she experiences this alienation unproblematically—indeed, in separating herself from her mother, she experiences a certain regret. But, in her ability to forge an identity amenable to her desires, Tambudzai accepts the losses as well as gains that come from alienation from a traditional culture that accompanies her education. Tambudzai as the adult narrator, however, creates an equally critical distance between herself and the world of modernity through her ironic statements on the nature of progress, the hypocrisy of the colonial system of education, and other indices of development. Hers does not seem to be a surrender to the "practical necessity" of modernism, but rather an uneasy compromisebetween modernity and tradition based on her ability to forget many things: her love for her brother, her cousin's suffering, and, finally, her own body.

In this, the female subject introduces a new term in the dialectic that Irele traces between tradition and modernity: the body. For the female postcolonial subject, this process of development is played out over the grounds of her body, which is subject to the disciplines of tradition and the technologies of modernity. In order to achieve the development into the adult and educated self that she represents in the beginning of her narrative, Tambu, must negotiate and accept several types of alienation, including finally an alienation from her own body. In the end, I think Tambu no more escapes her double bind than her cousin Nyasha whose self-sacrifice of the body is simply more vocal than Tambu's self-effacement. She develops into the modernized voice capable of recording the stories of the women around her but that is also curiously unable to represent her own developed body.

Tambu tells us in no uncertain terms that these two processes of development are linked in her person. In fact, for her, this is "the point": "I was going to be developed in the way that Babamukuru saw fit, which in the language I understood at that time meant well" (59). While in this passage Tambu frames the external indicators of her development as geography—movement from the homestead to the mission—in the beginning of the same paragraph she also indicates that this development has a bodily implication: "When I stepped out of Babamukuru's car I was a peasant. You could see it in a glance in my tight faded frock that immodestly defined my budding breasts . . ." (58). Very soon however, Tambu comes face to face with the fact that her own process of development into a woman and Babamukuru's project of developing her into "a good African" prepared to advance her portion of the family are at odds with each other. Upon her arrival at his house and enrollment in the Mission school of which he is headmaster, Babamukuru lectures Tambu on her duties as an educated African woman:

> Babamukuru had summoned me to make sure that I knew how lucky I was to have been given this opportunity for mental and eventually, through it, material emancipation. He pointed out that the blessing I had received was not an individual blessing but one that extended to all members of my less fortunate family, who would be able to depend on me in the future . . . Lastly, he explained, at the mission I would not only go to school but learn ways and habits

that would make my parents proud of me. I was an intelligent girl but I also had to develop into a good woman, he said, stressing both qualities equally and not seeing any contradiction in this. (87-88)

Tambu, the older, wiser narrator, indicates that she later realizes that these types of development, mental and eventually material, and gendering into a woman, do indeed contradict each other in the position that the younger Tambu occupies. While she tries to accept Babamukuru's world-view that sees no contradiction, his actions and how they effect Tambu's body eventually force her to confront his contradictions. It is from the vantage point of the interference of these types of development that I would like to think about how Dangarembga presents the trope of alienation and modernity that have come to be so prevalent in our discussion of African literature.

At the beginning of her story, the narrator claims that the young Tambu without hesitation believed that the process of development through education could mitigate the limitations of the process of development into a woman in her familial world. For example, she contrasts her mother, a poor and over-worked woman, with her aunt, a well-educated, well-fed and, in Tambu's eyes, very lucky woman. She regards her mother as someone who is crushed doubly by womanhood and poverty but by her own choice. Tambu believes that she can find a way out of this bind by following the example of her uncle and aunt, who have been educated in the West:

> My mother said being black was a burden because it made you poor, but Babamukuru was not poor. My mother said being a woman wasa burden because you had to bear children and look after them and the husband. But I did not think this was true. Maiguru was well looked after by Babamukuru . . . I decided it was better to be like Maiguru who was not poor and had not been crushed by the weight of womanhood. "I shall go to school again" I announced, .

.. (16)

For Tambu, the process of development in the western sense is a positive step towards a self that seems impossible if she continues to develop into a woman like her mother.

But what she finds upon arriving at her Uncle's house is that the realm of modernity, so hotly anticipated, also limits her development as a female subject. For Maiguru, though equally as developed in the modern world as her husband, is certainly not equal to her husband in any other sense. For Tambu, this comes as something of a surprise: "Is it true Maiguru? . . . Do you really have a Master's degree?" (100-01). What follows is a somewhat bitter conversation wherein Maiguru explains that though the family expected her to focus on taking care of Babamukuru during their stay in London, she struggled to study and gain her degree as well. She ends the conversation saying with a sigh, "What it is . . . to have to choose between self and security" (101). In a heavily foreshadowed passage, Tambu later reflects on this conversation with her aunt: "if it was necessary to efface yourself in order to preserve his [Babamukuru's] sense of identity and value, then, I was sure, Maiguru had taken the correct decisions" (102). As with her brother, Tambu seems to rather unfeelingly accept the sacrifice of one personality for the gains of another. Maiguru's effacement to Babamukuru, like her brother's death, leaves open the path of education and development represented quintessentially by Babamukuru. It is only later in her narrative, when her own corporeal self is implicated in this blind acceptance of modernity that Tambu begins to rethink her relation to modernity.

Thus while the cultural conflict between the Shona world that her mother occupies and the neo-colonial westernized world that her aunt occupies is indeed important, Tambu's story literally embodies the fact that one cannot chose to be developed or not. Tambu must acknowledge the fact of change as her own body develops but also seeks a way to influence that change. On the one hand, the narrative can be read as the story of women, just as Tambu

introduces it and concludes it. On the other hand, it can be read as
the increasing incorporation of her self and her family into the world
system of modernity. A type of development happens to her village, her family, and eventually herself. Indeed, Tambu's stake in
this process of change is first indicated to her by her grandmother.
Tambu's grandmother is mentioned only briefly and only in retrospect, as she is dead during the narrative present. But her influence
on Tambu is obviously significant. Tambu remarks that she is the
patron saint of her efforts to grow crops in order to earn her own
school fees and remembers learning both the techniques of horti-
culture and history from the time she spent in the fields with her
grandmother. The history that Tambu learns is a world apart from
the history that her cousin Nyasha later both consumes and is consumed by. Tambu remarks that this was history "that could not be
found in the textbooks" (17). From her grandmother, Tambu learns
of the Boer Migration northward into Zimbabwe, she learns of the
displacement of indigenous peoples, she learns of the depredations
caused by the system of migrant labor in South African mines, and
she learns of how her grandmother sends her eldest son
(Babamukuru) to the "white wizards" and "begged them to prepare him for life in their world" (19). Thus while Tambu learns the
most traditional, and traditionally feminine, techniques of growing maize, working hard, and remembering history from her grandmother, it is this very same grandmother who first makes a claim
on "modernity" in the name of the family that is first dispossessed
of its lands and then of its men by the colonial structure. Like her
Aunt Lucia who is admirably self-sufficient, yet disreputable,
Tambu's grandmother manages in her own way to make claims on
and incorporate into her own life both tradition and modernity. Development, like growth, in this novel seems inevitable—it is the
shape that this process takes that we must pay attention to. Tambu's
grandmother acknowledges the imperatives of the rapidly developing Zimbabwean world, but Tambu has no models other than
her Uncle for how best to negotiate this development. Tambu, in
short, needs a new discourse to describe the possibilities for women

in a rapidly modernizing Africa.

Having rejected the version of womanhood that was defined by the class status of her village life (underdeveloped), Tambu expects her access to the developed world to allow room for her developing self, just as a new dress will have ample room for her breasts. While in her Uncle's household, Tambu's cousin, Nyasha, serves as a constant point of reference, whether it be through her use of tampons to deal with bodily changes or her distrust of the history that they are taught in school. When Tambu comes to the mission to undergo Babamukuru's development into "an intelligent girl and a good woman," Nyasha is engaged in a constant battle with her parent about the appropriate behavior for a young woman. Tambu tells us that Nyasha's parents are "worried about her development" (97). The narrator purposefully does not elaborate about what aspect of her development her parents are concerned with because in Nyasha's case her burgeoning sexuality is directly related to her early years in the developed world, England. This much is obvious even in her first return to the homestead where Tambu remarks that she is fat and glossy and wears an indecently short dress. But in seeing through her cousin that the developed world is no more modest for the female body than her own immodest poverty, Tambu is forced to face the paradox of development.

The tension that Dangarembga exploits between Tambu's development as a woman and her development by her uncle comes to a head in two parallel scenes, both involving resistance offered by the two young girls to Tambu's uncle. Significantly, for both these girls, the resistance to Babamukuru's project of development must take place within the terms of their internal bodily development; it is against their bodies that he defines their position relative to him, and it is with their bodies that they resist his ideology.

While in her uncle's house, Tambu turns to her cousin Nyasha as a source of encouragement, as well as a warning. Nyasha returned from England literally a stranger to Tambu, who cannot bring herself to accept this scantily clad, non-Shona speaking, timid and pale shadow of the Nyasha she used to know. Once at her Uncle's, however, she relies on Nyasha to show help her acclimate herself to the new surroundings. For all of Tambu's trepidation at embarking on the adventure of schooling, Nyasha has her own battles at home. She is determined to avoid her father's power, especially when it runs counter to her own understanding of how best to develop herself personally and intellectually. One of the first outright battles between father and daughter take place over Nyasha choice to read *Lady Chatterley's Lover.* In Babamukuru's mind, this is not appropriate reading material for a schoolgirl, especially not the daughter of the headmaster. Inevitably, the arguments over Nyasha's behavior take place over the dinner table (the only place the family gathers to interact). Soon, the arguments begin to take place not only over the dinner table, but also literally over dinner. Babamukuru switches his attempts at controlling Nyasha's attitudes to an attempt to control the one thing he is sure he has power over, her body. In forcing Nyasha to eat all her food despite her resistance, Babamukuru exercises what power is still available to him. Nyasha responds in kind by claiming control over her own body through bulimia: what her father Babamukuru forces her to ingest, she literally rejects by throwing it all up once she leaves the table. The text draws a direct parallel between this battle of wills at the table and Nyasha's need to succeed in the nationwide scholastic achievement tests. These tests, based on the British model, become the key to further degrees and respect such as that Babamukuru himself enjoys. And yet Nyasha, as much as she wants to please her father by succeeding in these tests, cannot bring herself to swallow the version of history presented by her textbooks, preferring instead the rather unorthodox histories of colonialism, oppression, and resistance that she finds for herself outside the curriculum. Nyasha becomes so torn between these competing loyalties that she has a nervous breakdown one night and literally chews up and spits out her history textbooks, once again rejecting the narratives that Babamukuru privileges.

The tensions between Nyasha and her father come to a head in a scene that brings together Nyasha's body, her gender, and her implication in the culture of the "developed world." When Nyasha tarries one night outside with a boy, her father accuses her of indecorous behavior, and when she argues with him, he hits her. Nyasha punches him back. Babamukuru reacts to this physical assault by re-gendering Nyasha: "We cannot have two men in this house" (115). Nyasha's resistance ties her corporeal body to her gender in a way that challenges Babamukuru's paradox of an intelligent girl and a good woman. The intelligence that signifies here the world of modernity which allows Nyasha to explore relations with boys (not insignificantly here, a white boy, the son of missionaries) also allows her to point out the inconsistencies of Babamukuru's ideology; "Now why should I worry about what people say when my own father calls me a whore?" (114). It is in response to this question of impeccable logic that Babamukuru slaps Nyasha, once again showing his willingness to discipline the female body when it escapes the boundaries within which he wishes to inscribe it. Nyasha responds in kind by punching him in the eye and the two engage in a knockdown drag-out brawl that leaves Babamukuru speechless for the first time in the narrative.

Most critics note that Nyasha continues this process of corporeal resistance through her eating disorder, but relatively little attention has been paid to Tambu's parallel bodily resistance to the projects of development. After the death of her brother, and a scandal caused by the loose behavior of her mother's sister, Tambu's uncle decides that the family must be purified through a Christian wedding of Tambu's parents—a union that he equates to living in sin. Tambu's "daughter consciousness" forces her at this point to place herself in her mother's position. She describes the wedding as something that ". . . made a mockery of the people I belonged to and placed doubt on my legitimate existence in this world" (163). Tambu's realization, however, is tempered by her continuing admiration for Babamukuru and his language of rightness and sin, the same language that would have her "developed well."

Finally, the contradictions in Babamukuru's world-view become too much for even Tambu to ignore: one cannot be a woman and a girl at the same time, one cannot be educated and emancipated but always subservient. And these contradictions affect not only Tambu, but everyone in the household. Babamukuru is angry and tyrannical when his education comes face to face with his limitations in the colonial system. Maiguru becomes petty and bitter when her education is forced to serve the tyrannical passions of Babamukuru. Nyasha has a nervous breakdown when her own intelligence throws into question her father's position in this world while he insists on controlling her body. And for Tambu, finally, the conflict between being described as well developed and illegitimate, both of which stem from Babamukuru's language, brings her to the point where her mind literally splits in two. The morning of the wedding she refuses to get out of bed. When her uncle chastises her for being stubborn, Tambu thinks to herself, "He did not know how my mind had raced and spun and ended up splitting into two disconnected entities that had long, frightening arguments with each other, very vocally, there in my head . . ." (167). When the conflict between the two seems insurmountable, Tambu feels herself become subject to an even more radical alienation. She becomes alienated from the corporeal body that is being claimed alternately by her mother and her uncle, the symbols in the narrative economy for tradition and modernity respectively. Anticipating the anger of Babamukuru, Nyasha tries to persuade Tambu to rise, but Tambu remains paralyzed: "I was slipping further and further away from her until in the end I appeared to have slipped out of my body and was standing somewhere near the foot of the bed watching her efforts" (166). Tambu surveys the ensuing scene from this vantage point "at the foot of the bed" until her uncle accuses her of being ungrateful in his typically "categorical statements." This categorical quality of her uncle's language gives Tambu something to which she can react. Tambu rejects her uncle's manner of speaking and replies that, while she respects her uncle, she will not go to the wedding. In rejecting her uncle's language through her body, Tambu at least temporarily must acknowledge the connectedness of her process of development as a woman and her integration into "the developed world." Not only are these processes linked, but they are often in conflict, something that Tambu had anticipated but spends most of the novel trying to ignore. While Tambu is ready to sacrifice others, she stops short at sacrificing herself.

The question for the reader thus becomes what compromise can Dangarembga, or Tambu as the adult narrative voice, offer us as a way out of the impasse posed by tracing the two different modes of development that are always necessarily at work and quite often at odds with each other? For Tambu the child, the answer seems to lie in deciding not to forget. She refuses the aphasia that came to characterize her brother's education and instead remains connected to her family and landscape in physical and emotional ways, all the while absorbing all that she can from her western-style education. It is this compromise she asserts, that allowed her to write this story and, in this sense, I think we are meant to see her compromise is a successful one.

In Tambu's mind, the education that she seeks is a way to lessen the burdens on her body and at the same time it is a means of gaining control over her rapidly developing body. When the death of her brother paves the way for her own entrance to the mission school, she envisions a new self, a "clean, well-groomed, genteel self" (59). Indeed, her life at the mission is remarkably easier for Tambu, and she bears few of the burdens that she did at the homestead. Looking back on her first year at the mission, Tambu remarks,

> I could not pretend to be sorry to be leaving the water-drums whose weight compressed your neck into your spine . . . I was not sorry to be leaving the tedious task of coaxing Nyamarira's little tributary in and out of the vegetable beds. Of course, my emancipation from these aspects of my existence was, for the foreseeable future, temporary, but that was not the point. (59)

The physical separation from her mother's world brings a temporary release from pain for Tambu, but her suspicion that it is but a temporary emancipation marks the fact that the material development she seeks can and may well be vitiated by her biological development into a woman. In fact, while she frees her body from physical discomfort associated with tradition, she finds that she has to be literally alienated from her body in order to gain a critical distance on the type of development that her western-educated Uncle Babamukuru offers her.

In fact, modernity seems to demand an effacement of her body. In order to complete the education that she claims made this narrative possible, that allows her to speak for other women, Tambu must for a while also accept alienation from her female body. In her Protestant school, Tambu is significantly enough not only seg-regated by race, but she is also segregated by sex. It is, after all, an all-girls school. Tambu promptly drops any mention of her body and instead reverts to the metaphor of education and reading as eating, reconfiguring the mind as body, and in effect erasing the body as the mind becomes the locus of development. She con-sumes books in the library and loses herself in her studies. In a novel that is so concerned with issues of the body and a narrative in which Tambu so often uses her own body as a point of refer-ence, the last chapter is curiously devoid of any mention of Tambu's corporeal reality. As an embodiment of the process of alienation then, one could argue that Tambu succeeds better than she wants to. Her education does indeed separate her from her own body de-spite her efforts to bring her body back into the discussion during her fight with Babamukuru.

While Dangarembga, through Tambu, seems to agree with Irele that the path of change in Africa implies an ever-deepening immersion into the world of modernity, she resists the celebration of this alienation as the necessary result and action of this develop-ment. The female experience of bodily development that leads to an evermore limited role for women in the traditional world thus becomes a warning about the new burdens and limitations imposed by development into the world of modernity for the African society. What the narrative suggests is that we need to ask what price we are willing to pay in order to have access to the technologies of modernism that Irele labels "practical necessities." Tambu gladly sacrifices her brother and her aunt, more reluctantly sacrifices her cousin,[3] and resists the urge to sacrifice her own body, though in the end, her resistance "may not have been successful." In order to continue her western-style education, the narrative voice must revert to a reifying of the mind which effaces the body as the locus of consumption and development. From the point of view of the female postcolonial subject, the technologies of modernism exercise entirely new disciplines on the body that may end up being as limiting as those of the "traditional" world. For while Tambu develops the voice and technologies to tell the story of the women around her, her own body seems to disappear, covered over by the technology of writing. Perhaps it is her headstrong and unapologetically corporeal Aunt Lucia who represents the most successful example of development as a postcolonial female subject.

Notes

1. It should be noted here that the rhetoric of development was adopted early by African and other postcolonial scholars as a useful term for describing the economic interactions between Africa and the former colonial centers. I am thinking of especially Walter Rodney's 1974 book, *How Europe Underdeveloped Africa*. This monograph is part of a whole series of debates on the relative applicability of words such as "developed," "underdeveloped," "developing," and even "reverse development" that continues to this day in the fields of economics and political science.

2. One is reminded here of Chinua Achebe's statement of the position of English in African literature, a position that he characterized as "the fatalistic logic of the unassailable position of English in our literature." In other words, we might pose other options, but English seems to be here to stay. Achebe has said repeatedly that he has been given this language and

he intends to make it serve his ends. This is similar to Irele's statement that modernity has entered the African sphere, whether we like it or not and now it is up to the African to turn this encounter into a fruitful one.

3. I believe that Nyasha is as much sacrificed for the process of her education as Nhamo. As Susan Andrade has so adroitly pointed out, these two characters are structurally equivalent in this text. And in the end, Tambu is no more willing to be distracted by her gravely ill cousin than she was her brother. When Nyasha writes her a painfully honest account of her mental disintegration, Tambu fails to respond to the letter and admits that though she first feels some guilt about ignoring her cousin's plea for help, "the pang of guilt was no more than a pang which dissolved quickly in the stream of novelty and discovery I had plunged into" (197). The river imagery here is doubly ironic in that Tambu frequently uses the image of the river Nyamarira to express her eternal connection to her homeland and family and "true self."

Chapter 4:
Strategic Fusions: Undermining Cultural Essentialism in *Nervous Conditions*

Jeanette Treiber

> As a result of [the] colonial process, sharply contrastive essentialist pictures of "Western Culture" and of various colonized "national cultures" were reiterated by both colonizers and the colonized, both of whom failed to register the degree to which their very constitution as "Western" or "Non-western" subjects resulted from these putative contrasts between "cultures." (Narayan 90).

> What was needed in that kitchen was a combination of Maiguru's detachment and Lucia's direction. (*Nervous Conditions* 138)

During a question period following a panel presentation on Tsitsi Dangarembga's work *Nervous Condition* at the African Literature Association conference in 1997, one of the discussions surrounded the question of whether or not Dangarembga privileges modernity over tradition in her novel. After all, Tambu, the female protagonist, frees herself from traditional gender oppression by rejecting the ways of her family: "The more I saw of worlds beyond the homestead the more I was convinced that the further we left the old ways behind the closer we came to progress" (147). Other discussion participants objected that this view neglects subtle nuances in the positive depiction of traditional life in the novel and the critique of modernity through the character Nyasha, who suffers from traditional gender oppression, but also from the consequences of exposure to a Western way of life and thinking which the novel openly criticizes. During this same conference Tsitsi Dangarembga herself presented her film *Everyone's Child*, and I could not but read an answer she gave during the question period after the film presentation as a commentary on the earlier discussion. Dangarembga was asked why the female protagonist of the film, who resorts to prostitution to support herself and her orphaned siblings, breaks out of a cycle of abuse through the help of a male friend. This, according to the discussant, weakened the feminist critique of the film. Dangarembga briefly answered that you take help wherever you can find it. What this answer signaled to me was a commitment to strategic maneuver rather than adherence to an ideological correctness that prescribes and forbids various representations. *Nervous Conditions* equally pays tribute to a kind of strategic maneuvering that defies easy ideological identification. The goal of this essay is to show how the novel dismantles gender and cultural essentialism by studying the way in which the text diffuses the geographies of home and "not home," tradition and modernity, essential purity versus contaminated fusions. While Tambu initially naively sees education as a way to elevate her community into a modern, better life, her real educational process lies in learning the shades of gray between the black and white by which she had previously characterized life on the homestead and the life of educated people. Her cousin Nyasha, "whose strange disposition hinted at shades and textures within the same colour," is instrumental in this process of learning, while for her uncle Babamukuru, "black would remain definitely sombre and white permanently clear" (164). As the narrator tells the story of the various women struggling with the harsh realities of their environment, the distinction between what is a better, progressive way to live and what is an undesirable, backward life, becomes blurred at times. Similarly, the symbioses of the traditional and the modern work at times against readers' expectations.

Nyasha's anorexia is one of these symbioses. Identified as a Western phenomenon, anorexia's appearance in a representation of an African female character was seen by many critics as an oxymoron. It has created numerous pages of critical assessment, since the illness has in the past been considered to be a typically Western middle-class phenomenon. It is symptomatic for the strict cultural distinction made between the West and all other cultures that Nyasha's anorexia is predominantly read as a symptom of her Westernization. However, it is very likely that this conclusion stems from the fact that the scientific research on eating disorders in women is predominantly based on Western subjects and that the cultural reasons that have been identified for these disorders are consequently rooted in Western culture. The novel defies gender and cultural essentialism whose "discourses about 'difference' often operate to conceal their role in the production and reproduction of such 'differences,' presenting these differences as something pre-given and prediscursively 'real' that the discourses of difference merely describe rather than help construct and perpetuate" (Narayan 88).

In hardly any other context has the polarization between worlds worked as effectively as in colonialist writing, where indigenous cultures have repeatedly been depicted as "hearts of darkness" in order to uphold Western superiority. Abdul JanMohammed has summarized the cognitive framework of colonialist literature—and I might add colonialist culture—in what he calls the "manichean allegory," which he characterizes as "a field of diverse yet interchangeable oppositions between white and black, good and evil, superiority and inferiority, civilization and savagery, intelligence and emotion, rationality and sensuality, self and Other, subject and object" (82).

Curiously, *Nervous Conditions* plays on the metaphor of purity that underlies the attempts to essentialize and antagonize cultures. Dangarembga uses the cleansing metaphor literally and figuratively. When the narrator reflects back on her childhood, she remembers the surroundings of her childhood homestead and of her uncle and aunt's, Babamukuru and Maiguru's, house where she lives to finally receive her desired education after her brother's death. Babamukuru, the headmaster in a Rhodesian school in the 1960s, has adopted a Western lifestyle and Western standards of hygiene. The description of the respective homes evokes Tambu's early perception of a dualistic world in which Babamukuru's very colonial-looking house is the desired opposite to the backward-ness and dirt the narrator used to associate with her home. In Proustian fashion, the narrator's memory is wrapped in her sense of smell and a heightened awareness of her everyday surround-ings, albeit censored by the reflecting narrator who interprets the sensation as an illusion:

> Babamukuru was God, therefore I had arrived in Heaven. The absence of dirt was proof of the other-worldly nature of my new home. I knew, had known my whole life that living was dirty and I had been disappointed by the fact. . . . I knew, for instance, that rooms where people slept ex-uded peculiarly human smells just as the goat pen smelt goaty and the cattle kraal bovine. It was common knowl-edge among the younger girls at school that the older girls menstruated into sundry old rags which they washed and reused and washed again. I knew, too, that the fact of men-struation was a shameful unclean secret that should not be allowed to contaminate immaculate male ears by indis-creet reference to this type of dirt in their presence. Yet at a glance it was difficult to perceive dirt in Maiguru's house. After a while, as the novelty wore off, you began to see

that the antiseptic sterility that my aunt and uncle strove
for could not be attained beyond an illusory level—enough
of it always remained invisibly to creep up your nose and
give you hay fever, thus restoring your sense of proportion
by reminding you that this was not heaven. Sneezing and
wiping my nose on the back of my hand, I became confident that I would not go the same way as my brother. (70-
71)

Tambu's perception of the colonial or colonial looking space as
desirable and superior reflect an internalization of the colonizer's
manichean aesthetic. In the colonial context clean houses and
hygienic conditions represent desirable whiteness. In *The Wretched
of the Earth*, Frantz Fanon describes the difference between the
native and the settler's towns as spaces that follow the "principle
of reciprocal exclusivity." "The settler's town," he writes, "is a
strongly built town; the streets are covered with asphalt, and the
garbage cans swallow all the leavings, unseen, unknown and hardly
thought about . . . the streets of his house are clean and even." This
is in sharp contrast to the native's village which he describes as "a
town on its knees, a town wallowing in the mire." As a result, the
settler's space becomes a fixation in the natives' mind: "There is
no native who does not dream at least once a day of setting himself
up in the settler's place" (39). Tambudzai's preoccupation with
escaping the predicament of most girls of her background to never
leave the homestead and her desire to make something of herself
through education is inextricably linked with her heightened sense
of sterility and hygiene represented in the clean entourage of more
"civilized" people. She also experiences increasing embarrassment
over her family's living conditions and complains about her
mother's negligence in cleaning the latrines when she visits the
village. In a study of the cultural meanings of cleanliness in post
WWII France, Christine Ross references Edgar Morin's study of
French peasant women, who concluded that the "acquisition of a
'filth complex' is the first step in a process of gaining psychological
autonomy and an expanded personality and horizon that will

eventually propel the peasant woman out of the countryside" (92). Ross' own study, however, reveals that the filth complex, while liberating at first, reveals itself as an illusory means to accomplish the self-determination these women were trying to achieve, once they were confronted with the economic realities of the city environment. I will comment later on a similar realization Tambu has. While in Tambu's own filth complex the modern seems to be equated with the clean and uncontaminated, the polarization between Western/clean/heavenly and homestead/dirty/backwards is complicated by a further distinction between male/ uncontaminated and female/unclean. The latter pair indicates a value system in the narrator's traditional society, which complicates the simple opposite of Western and homestead or modern and traditional. In the value system she grew up with, the clean/unclean distinction has a distinctive gender dimension. In her traditional culture women who are menstruating are perceived to be unclean, their menstruation is a dirty affair to be kept a secret so it will not contaminate men, who by extension are the cleaner, therefore superior, sex. This realization comes at a time when Tambu, who has thus far equated Babamukuru with progress, begins to see him as a tyrannical father and husband.

The duality of spaces whereby the homestead becomes the dirty, rejected (and female) topos while the imitation of colonial entourage becomes the desired (male, godlike) opposite, is super-seded in the text by the ironic voice of the narrator who looks back from a distance in time and reveals the dualities as an illusion. If we examine the passage more closely, we realize that the inside (Babamukuru's clean house) and outside (the dirt of the land) can-not strictly be kept apart. We can read this as a critique of colonial mimicry—colonial strategies and structures that allow the colo-nized to become "the same but not quite" as the colonizer and as a rejection of the "superior" nature of colonial mentality that created the manichean allegory in the first place. Not only had Nhamo, Tambu's brother, been seduced by the luxury of the modern, but he blindly operated under the assumption that rejecting where he came from and entirely adopting the colonizer's ways would liberate him from the old ways, in the process rejecting and betraying his sister. Moreover, her brother was unable to see that the manichean world is a construct, an inability that the narrator equates with irrationality. In an interesting gender reversal, the text reveals rationality as an ability Tambu is proud to possess. "I was very proud of my thinking strategy. It was meant to put me above the irrational levels of my character [and by extension Nhamo's] and enable me to proceed from pure, rational premises" (69-70). Although she admits that this strategy did not seem to work at first when faced with the seductive power of the material shiny goods surrounding her, it ultimately does: "I triumphed. I was not seduced" (70). She is able to see beyond the charade onto the "perversity" of Babamukuru's heaven and to put things "into proportion."

To assert and define herself in opposition to her brother becomes one of Tambu's central preoccupations. Tambu's mother is convinced that colonial education will alienate her child from her family as it had alienated her son. When she leaves for Sacred Heart, her family and friends urge her: "Don't forget, don't forget, don't forget. Nyasha, my mother, my friends. Always the same message . . . Why was everybody so particular to urge me to remember?" (188). The telling of the story itself is ultimately a response to these pleas.

I would like to return for a moment to Kristin Ross' analysis in "Fast Cars, Clean Bodies," where she establishes a relationship between a post-World War II European cult of cleanliness that allows Europeans to distinguish themselves from the colonies they are losing in great numbers. What interests me about her analysis is the connection she establishes between this cult of cleanliness among the middle class and the fact that "clean houses" were the responsibility and domain of women. The accelerated invention and marketing of new household appliances (vacuum cleaners, washing machines, dish washers, etc.) created in turn higher and higher expectations of hygiene and sparkling interiors while at the same time creating a job responsibility that confined women to the home without being paid for their labor. This excursion into the practices of mid-twentieth-century European domestic culture allows us to shed more light onto the critique of colonialism displayed in *Nervous Conditions*. In the quoted passage, the narrator calls the house "Maiguru's house," and she is indeed responsible for the housekeeping. Maiguru is also aware that in spite of her education (she has a Master's degree), and even in spite of the fact that she does work at the school, she is not paid for her labor because she is female. She regrets that she has no independence and remains under the authority of her husband. Rather than looking at her oppression as a stronghold of her traditional culture, we may see it to a large degree as a consequence of a shifting female role in the wake of colonialism. Molara Ogundipe-Leslie confirms this view when she explains:

> The British simply swept aside previous female political structure in society . . . . Modern societies have now inherited . . . the hardened attitudes of male superiority and female exclusion from public affairs which had been introduced by the colonial systems. The colonial systems negatively encouraged or brought to the fore the traditional ideologies of patriarchy or male superiority which originally existed in African societies. (29-30)

Thus, Dangarembga undermines a widely held notion that modernity by necessity holds an emancipatory promise. The strongest female character in the novel is not the educated Maiguru, nor is it Tambu or Nyasha who are on their way to becoming Western-educated women, but it is Lucia, who upsets the gender dynamics on the homestead by asserting herself against and in spite of the limitations placed on her by cultural expectations: she is sexually promiscuous, speaks her mind in front of the male elders, exposes Babamukuru's chauvinism, refuses to be a subservient wife, becomes a single working mother in town going to school part-time. She also embodies commitment to those in her community that are crushed by the weight of cultural pressures: she continues to care about and support her sister Mainini, Tambu's mother, while

Tambu, in her desire to define herself in opposition to her mother, detaches herself emotionally and in a way abandons her.

When Babamukuru takes his family and Tambu back to the homestead for Christmas, Tambu is upset to see it run-down. Its detailed description stands in stark contrast to the earlier image of the mission house:

> The thatched roof of the kitchen was falling down in so many places that it would be difficult to find a dry spot inside when it rained. . . . When I went to the pit latrine that was once a good one and built under Babamukuru's supervision and with his finances downwind from the huts, I gagged. . . . feces and urine contaminated every surface, so that it was impossible to find a place to put your feet and you were tempted not to bother to weave your way to the holes. Glistening pale maggots burrowed fatly into the feces; the walls had turned yellow. Large bottle-blue flies with nauseous orange heads buzzed irritatingly around my anus as I squatted.

At first glance this passage confirms all preconceived associations of African homesteads with infestation, disease, and disgust. Accordingly, Tambu's mother accuses Tambu of falling prey to manichean thinking: "You think your mother is so stupid she won't see Maiguru has turned you against me with her money and her white ways. You think I am dirt now, me, your mother" (140). However, upon examining the dirty toilet episode more closely, the narrator gives us some history. The latrine had been brought to the homestead by Babamukuru in an effort to import a piece of civilization onto the homestead. It had been Tambu's task to clean it, and it was only after her leaving and Mainini's increased work in the fields that the latrine was no longer kept up and became a health hazard. In fact, Tambu and Nyasha decide it is more hygienic to defecate in the bushes "as we had done before the latrine was built" (123). Bringing a piece of modern amenity to the homestead is reminiscent of those foreign aid projects that brought technology

into remote areas of developing countries for the purpose of bringing
fast progress to the village only to be abandoned when grants ran
out and the technology became dysfunctional and useless for lack
of infrastructure and sustainable growth. But the narrator is far from
condemning development altogether. The passage leaves no doubt
that technological progress and capital development are desirable
assets. When reflecting upon cooking on the hearth, the narrator
states, "It alarms me to think of all that carbon monoxide hanging
about in the air to asphyxiate people, and all the inflammatory
products of combustion that we breathed in that had already by
that time made my father permanently asthmatic and bronchitic"
(133). Not only does this characterization of village life defy any
nostalgic or romanticized views of healthy rural life, but the text
goes even further to suggest that this kind of health hazard is
beginning to be eradicated through urban industrialization.
Inadvertently, some villagers escape the health hazard of sleeping
in smoke-infested quarters, because "Tete's husband had started a
small transport business in that year and had come home in his
half-ton truck. The boys slept in the back of it in the clean December
night" (133). What is also striking about this passage is the scientific
language the narrator uses to analyze the hazardous living conditions
of her family, which emphasizes and justifies her insistence upon
receiving an education for the benefit of her community.

Perhaps the most intriguing episode of fusing tradition and
modernity in the novel is the wedding episode because it leads to
Tambu's personal crisis. While she has thus far been able to analyze and cope with the contradictions she has learned about, and
continues to idolize Babamukuru, Tambu has a mental breakdown.
Once again the text operates with a cleansing metaphor. Tambu's
father Jeremiah is to be cured of his continued sexual relations
with Tambu's aunt Lucia, her mother's sister. Jeremiah suggests a
traditional cleansing ritual while Babamukuru insists that his sins
be washed away by a Christian ceremony. Jeremiah is to finally
have an official wedding to his wife Mainini which had never been
performed. The women receive the news in the kitchen with laughter

and ridicule knowing that the real reason for both suggested rituals is the men's desire to manage and control Lucia. The narrator exposes the equally unfit ideologies of traditional belief and imported Christian belief system. Both operate with a similar logic, namely that a ceremony can reinstate a state of purity, a concept that the narrator has repeatedly rejected and undermined. Both are also used as instruments of regulation and control. While thus far Tambu's confrontation with the modern had been on the basis of commodity culture and education, from which she can only see advantages to herself and her community, she now has to come to grips with another colonial import, that of Christian ideology. Since she had fully identified with Babamukuru and never questioned the regular Sunday School teaching, she is all of a sudden confronted with a contradiction that she cannot resolve easily. If it is true that her parents have lived in sin, she must agree to and participate in the ceremony which is supposed to make the sin go away. Tambu has internalized the manichean Christian symbolic structure of sin and salvation, good and bad, life and death. She is therefore horrified to find herself at the wrong side of the manichean divide. Her literal understanding of sin is that "[it] had to be avoided because it was deadly. I could see it. It was definitely black, we were taught. It had well-defined edges, and it was square rather than round so that you knew where it ended. It worked like a predatory vacuum, drawing the incautious into itself and never letting them out. And now Babamukuru was saying that this was where my parents were, which meant myself and my sisters too" (150-51). But once again, the manichean construct has a flip side in this text. The cleansing ritual reveals itself as a dirty, greasy affair when the family goes to the dressmaker to order the wedding dress. The "shop was very small, no more than a booth, so dark and dingy that you wondered how the dressmaker could see to sew. . . . There was dust in every corner, and layers of greasy grime on every surface except the table she used for cutting" (161).

Having already rejected traditional ritual, Tambu now must recognize that the wedding ritual with its supposed cleansing effect is an equally fabricated construct. Tambu's breakdown occurs when the self-proclaimed truth seeker understands that Babamukuru, far from being a god-like figure, is in fact a fraud, a lead actor in a play. The wedding and in retrospect the modern commodity props she was so afraid would have a seductive effect on her reveal themselves as a grandiose spectacle. When she is supposed to play her part in the performance, she is appalled and hurt. During the dress rehearsal for the wedding, "Nyasha was delighted, with the dresses, with the effect I created when I put mine on, with the whole idea of the wedding" (162). Tambu thinks that "the whole performance was ridiculous. The whole business reduced my parents to the level of the stars of a comic show, the entertainers. I did not want them brought down like that and I certainly did not want to be part of it" (163).

Although on the level of the development narrative Tambu's refusal to partake in this spectacle is her first real act of rebellion that has a maturing effect on her, on the reflective level of the adult narrative voice. There is a realization that recognizing societal relations and events as staged performances rather than being informed by ultimate truths is a prerequisite to strategic maneuver. Lucia, who has already come across as the strongest character in this "play," knows how to use her performances to her advantage. When Babamukuru lands her a job in town, she falls to her knees and praises him with ululations, much to the dismay of Nyasha, who believes that it is Babamukuru's duty to use his influence to help his people. Lucia has this to say to Nyasha in response: "Babamukuru wanted to be asked, so I asked. And now we both have what we wanted, isn't it?" (160).

If we take the narrator's statement "What was needed in the kitchen was Maiguru's detachment and Lucia's direction" out of context and use it as a general instruction for the women in the novel, and as a postcolonial strategy in general, we will find that the narrator and perhaps the author have taken the advice to heart. Maiguru attempts to detach herself emotionally and physically from overbearing events and conflicts, but she lacks direction. Her rebellious act of leaving her family is sincere but short-lived. Lucia, however, operates with a strategy, yet her temper often gets the better of her; her compromises are perhaps at times too self-dam-aging. When she moves back in with Takesure whose child she carries and whom she has ridiculed in front of everybody, her ex-planation is that "A woman has to live with something. . . . Even if it is only a cockroach" (153).

One of the novel's distinctive features is its shifting per-spectives on the homestead and modern life. Dangarembga's inno-vation lies in the many ways she fuses the modern and the tradi-tional in a way that disrupts the cultural essentialism so prevalent in colonialist and anti-colonialist writing. As a result, this novel gives African literature a new direction. While this narrative has rightly been characterized as a *Bildungsroman*, a coming-of-age story of a young Rhodesian girl, it is also distinctly different from other African narratives whose purpose for such a development narrative has often been to come to terms with the disruptive ef-fects of colonialism on individuals and communities alike. Often auto-ethnographic in style, novels like Camara Laye's *Dark Child* and Chinua Achebe's *Things Fall Apart* implied Western readers ignorant of the complexities of indigenous societies. These texts therefore contained detailed descriptions of everyday life and com-modities in these societies, allowing for a panoptic view onto a sophisticated world in which colonialism interferes in a most de-structive way. To differing degrees, these texts portrayed the colo-nial event as a conflict between tradition and modernity. *Nervous Conditions* equally depicts ethnographic details, but these depic-tions are not always as flattering as in this African narrative tradi-tion. From the start, the narrative strategy includes detailed every-day-life descriptions of both worlds, the life on the homestead that already shows visible signs of modern invasions as well as the luxury commodities of the Westernized well-to-do Africans. While in the earlier African novels there is a distinctive value attached to the traditional, Dangarembga's novel continuously shifts affinities and at times even confuses readers accustomed to separating the traditional or indigenous from the modern or Western.

In the colonial context, essentializing purification attempts are not limited to the colonizers' strategy of projecting an image of a superior, clean civilization. The birth of negritude, a movement that emphasized the cultural essences and values of African civilizations, is in reaction to colonial attempts to brainwash Africans, who in turn tried to rid themselves of such colonial contamination. Senghor writes in his assessment of the birth of negritude:

> . . . colonizers legitimated our political and economic dependence by the theory of clean sweep. They estimated that we had neither invented, nor reacted, nor written, nor sculptured, nor painted anything. To set our own effective revolution we had first to put off our borrowed dresses, those of assimilation, and affirm our being, that is our NEGRITUDE. (Taiwo 45)

To validate the accomplishments of traditional African culture was a great and necessary undertaking by negritude writers and philosophers, yet to elevate them to a state of uncontaminated holistic purity ultimately had a damaging effect, as it alienated social groups, especially women, whose oppression and struggle remained unrecognized by this construct. When essentialist notions of culture have been used by Western colonizers and anti-colonial nationalist movements to project their respective superiority, the social diversity and historicity of either was largely ignored. When African women writers took to the pen, they attempted to correct the image of an untainted African history by exposing patriarchal practices and structures which in turn brought them the criticism of those who considered this a betrayal of a unified African front against colonialism and neocolonialism. Feminist criticism has largely followed the essentializing trend by distinguishing between Western women and Third World women in order to avoid a seemingly more dangerous essentialism, that of subsuming women under an even larger umbrella that would include all women regardless of their cultural origin (Narayan especially traces this argument).

While the narrator identifies herself as the growing Tambu in this first-person narrative, she also remains removed from the reader—we do not know her physical location or how much time has elapsed between the recorded events and the moment of scripture. We do know that she has taken up a distinctly "modern" activity: that of writing, which necessitates the detachment and distance necessary to reflect upon and interpret the past in written words. The shift from orality and indigenous languages to the activity of writing in European languages has often been considered an act of assimilation. Dangarembga does not seem to agree with this interpretation. When she was asked during the discussion of *Everyone's Child* why she produced it in English instead of Shona, the native language of the people she represented in the film, she answered "so it could reach a wider African audience." This is in line with the commitment she has placed in the book and her film on becoming a spokesperson for and giving a voice to a community, which includes other African people. I would also like to argue that her storytelling is not an activity entirely alien to the people of the homestead. The tradition the narrator follows is more aligned with her grandmother's tradition of bringing the history of her people to successive generations than it is with European or early African narrative tradition. Using the written word, while literally detaching the storyteller from her people, is an appropriate response to the modernization that has already invaded the homestead and to which the grandmother had a strategic response: she sent her son Babamukuru to the white people's school because she anticipated that education was going to help the community to survive. How much intellectualization and detachment from one's indigenous cultural practices threaten the survival of one's culture seems a secondary question to the strategy and direction Dangarembga has chosen. The more burning question she addresses, especially in her film, is how to achieve physical and economic survival in the most humane way possible.

Chapter 5:
Indexing Her Digests: Working Through *Nervous Conditions*

Brendon Nicholls

A decade has elapsed since Tsitsi Dangarembga's *Nervous Conditions* was first published. During this period, a venerable tradition of literary-critical scholarship has developed around this slender, but groundbreaking, novel. The scholars who have contributed to this tradition have all cherished Dangarembga's novel in common, despite their manifestly discrepant theoretical approaches and their avowedly different political agendas. These differences will prove advantageous to my discussion, because I aim to address the difficulty of finding a unified or self-proximate reading position in relation to the nervous conditions elaborated by Tambudzai's narrative. The narrative presents its readers with a series of representational issues, which, in my view, pose a challenge to Dangarembga's critics to embark upon an auto-critique of their own analytico-ideological affinities. Such a challenge is not easily answered, and it will not be my primary aim to offer a corrective or interventionist account of the novel. Rather, I would like to ask what it might mean to *work through* the conditions upon which Tambudzai's narrative is founded—conditions that surely must inspire a degree of nervousness in any reader who attends to the performative aspects of that narrative. My argument will focus primarily upon Nyasha, who seems to me to be the character that most obviously embodies a nervous disorder arising out of the colonial historical moment in which she finds herself—or perhaps it is a colonial historical moment in which Nyasha repeatedly and concertedly fails to find herself. Curiously enough, it is around the anomalous figure of Nyasha that literary critics disposed towards Dangarembga's novel have produced a uniformity of opinion. It is to this comfortable consensus, and indeed to the altogether less comforting orthodoxies it suggests, that I wish to address my discussion of *Nervous Conditions*.

It has been well documented that the "nervous conditions" to which Dangarembga's title refers owe their inspiration to Jean Paul Sartre's preface to Frantz Fanon's *The Wretched of the Earth*.[1] What has been less widely noticed is that there is a divergence between Sartre's preface and its citation in the novel's epigraph:

> The status of "native" is a nervous condition introduced and maintained by the settler among colonized people *with their consent.* (*Wretched* 17)

> *The condition of native is a nervous condition.* (Dangarembga, unpaginated foreleaf; italics in the original)

A problem emerges here, and at its center is the question of one's reading position in relation to the politics of self-representation.

We might wish to ask whether Dangarembga's epigraph comprises a misreading[2] or a re-reading of Sartre's preface. Why does the "status of 'native'" (implying a perspective of external observation) suddenly translate into the "condition of native" (implying an interiorized point of view)?[3] One possible answer to this question is that *Nervous Conditions'* epigraph exposes a crisis of reference in relation to "the native." When one is "native," presumably it is preferable to speak in terms of one's condition rather than in terms of one's status. However, this is not the only possibility. I am also interested in the omission of Sartre's name from the epigraph, which carries the following attribution: "From an introduction to Fanon's *The Wretched of the Earth.*" Is it possible, then, that *Nervous Conditions* speculates somewhat subtly on the impossibility of authoritative citation? In this reading, the authoritative guarantee of credibility that Sartre's preface affords to Fanon's text would be abandoned in Dangarembga's epigraph, by virtue of the re-iterability of "Sartre's" sentiments in contexts or formats that are never entirely his own. Indeed, Dangarembga's skewed citation of "Sartre's" assertion must insist upon his absence.[4]

Two further questions must attend the epigraph to *Nervous Conditions.* Firstly, why does it make no reference to the words *"with their consent,"* which appear so emphatically in the precursor text? Perhaps we might read this omission as a structural concomitant to the shift from the "status of 'native'" to the "condition of native." If "native" is a condition, then consent is not an issue: the "native" is conditioned in such a way as to have no say in the matter of his or her living conditions. In addition, the possibilities for dissent elaborated in *Nervous Conditions* by no means entail the possibility of unbecoming "native." Rather, it is also in unbecoming "native" that nervous conditions consist, as Nyasha's ample experience testifies. Further, Nyasha's nervous conditions are maintained both by the colonial prerogatives of the settler and by the culturally coded masculine prerogatives of the "native." In a sense, my second question encompasses all of the previous questions that I have asked of the epigraph: what are we to make of the conditions in which the epigraph comes to be written of as read? As Charles Sugnet relates, the finalized manuscript of *Nervous Conditions* precedes both its eventual title and, of course, the epigraph from which the title is taken: "Dangarembga says she had not read Fanon until the novel was completed and she was searching for an appropriate title; a friend referred her to *The Wretched of the Earth*" (35). Given that Dangarembga's reading of Fanon and Sartre affords the novel the finitude of a title, are we to read the epigraph as a species of belated foresight or as a species of fortuitous hindsight in relation to the narrative it ostensibly encapsulates? By posing the questions that arise from an attentive reading of the epigraph, I have attempted to demonstrate that it prefigures the act of reading as a double movement that can be neither finalized nor ultimately exhausted. Once one accepts this prefiguration, one's own readership of the novel is itself destined to be overshadowed by a modicum of misprision and hence by a certain degree of nervousness. It is such a reader that Tambudzai's narrative anticipates in its opening sentences: "I was not sorry when my brother died. Nor am I apologising for my callousness, as you may define it, my lack of feeling" (1). The very first sentence of the novel unsettles assumptions and expectations, and the second sentence, with its subjunctive clause, provides the scope for a reader who may (or may not) choose to withhold her[5] sympathy from Tambudzai's unrelenting stance.[6] There is an appeal in this beginning, and it is the appeal to read ethically across asymmetries of reference. In other words, "you" and "I" are asked to imagine a situation in which we are called upon to correspond responsibly with an other. Should we accept this call, and choose to answer it, our readings will comprise a diversity born of situational necessities.

In all but one respect, the tradition of critical work on Dangarembga has reflected a diversity of opinion. *Nervous Conditions* has been read as an African, female version of the *Bildungsroman* (Bardolph, Flockemann), as a novel containing indigenous linguistic embedments (Galle) or a liberational voicing of Zimbabwean women's struggles (Uwakweh), and as an intertext that resonates with Charlotte Brontë's *Shirley* and the Irish potato famine (Plasa). Further, critics have employed a range of theoretical frameworks to the issues raised by *Nervous Conditions*. Their critical approaches include Marxism (Booker), Spivak's elaboration of the subaltern (Woodward), positionality (Bosman), womanism (Pentolfe Aegerter), Fanonian perspectives (Basu, Hill, and Sugnet), psychoanalytic discussions of hysteria (Thomas, Vizzard) and mourning/melancholia (Nair), anticolonial feminism (Bahri, Creamer), Bhabha's notion of mimicry (McWilliams), and a deconstructive reading of ancestral worship and spirit possession (Rooney).

Given the remarkable diversity and complexity of the critical analyses of *Nervous Conditions*, it is all the more surprising that a consensus has emerged on the most problematic and puzzling aspect of the novel: that of Nyasha's ailment. Despite its nascent realization that Nyasha's condition is an anomaly (since eating disorders are virtually unheard of in black African communities)[7] and despite its recognition that she is the product of two unacceptable alternatives (colonial subjugation and indigenous patriarchy), critical scholarship on Dangarembga's novel has agreed almost unanimously that Nyasha suffers from bulimia and/or anorexia.[8] I quote three fairly representative examples:

> Nyasha's anorexia can be understood as a hysterical response to the restraints of the (masculine) colony as partially represented by her father. The representation of anorexia, a condition usually associated with the middle class West, in an African text is one that raises a number of problems, despite the way the text itself invites a selective use of psychoanalysis. (Vizzard 207)

> Dangarembga may perhaps be the first African (woman) writer to explore the theme of anorexia in African fiction. (Uwakweh 81)

> It is interesting that in a larger context of severe malnutri-

> tion, Nyasha suffers from anorexia nervosa and bulimia,
> disorders usually associated with white, middle class
> women. (Nair 137)

In my view, the critical readings of Nyasha contain an interested oversight, and I shall refer to this oversight as the "bulimia diagnosis."[9]   Some scholars have argued convincingly that the (dwindling) figure of Nyasha may be comprehended within Homi Bhabha's elaboration of "mimicry": "a difference that is almost nothing but not quite" (91). If we are to support this argument, then surely we must ask of the bulimia diagnosis what has happened to the "not quite" in its formulation. Nyasha is indeed a category disturbance, regardless of whether we consider her in Western categories or Shona categories, and something of this disturbance is elided in the bulimia diagnosis. In this regard, it is significant that neither anorexia nor bulimia is mentioned anywhere in Dangarembga's novel, even though she was trained in both psychology and medicine. Further, Dangarembga's response to an interview question posed by Kirsten Holst Petersen is instructive here:

> *Nyasha's condition is not just nervous, she has a mental breakdown which takes the form of anorexia. Is it not . . . a provocation to transport, imaginatively, of course, this disease, which is a symptom of the affluent West, to a continent where people still starve to death? Do you think that it could in fact occur in Africa?*
>
> It has happened! Cases of anorexia have been reported in Zimbabwe. The diagnosis of anorexia is something difficult. If a woman in Zimbabwe, rural or urban is depressed, loses weight etc. who is to say whether that is anorexia or not? Of course the extreme form is associated with these images of beauty, which developed in the West during the sixties. That is something else. I find this difficult to answer! When does a depression become so severe that it becomes a disease? And of course, we also have these im-

ages of beauty, we have Hollywood films in Zimbabwe, so women are becoming conscious of their weight. This happens particularly in the middle classes where the women have the leisure to read the magazines and decide that they want to look like these people. I would just like to make a point about the relationship between anorexia, beauty and studying: in the families where anorexia is common, even studying has a positive value, just like beauty, and I sometimes think that one of the reasons why the girls are so prone to this disease is that if you live a very intellectual life you do become more divorced from the physical aspects of yourself, and it may not be easy to determine what is affecting what. This may be the reason why these girls project themselves in that way. (345-46)

In addition to the desire to write Zimbabwean women into the script of Western medicine, Dangarembga's answer reveals a cautious reticence in relation to Nyasha's symptom. The precise rationale behind this reticence remains unclear, but I suspect that the specific socio-cultural co-ordinates of the symptom in a given postcolonial space make anorexia in a Western context "something else"—a different order of debate. In this, I believe, Dangarembga's perspective echoes some of the critical discussion on the different subject-positions occupied by the investigating subject *vis-à-vis* those of the characters in the novel. Brenda Bosman's questions are particularly apposite here: "What is the 'authentic' set of criteria for diagnosing Nyasha's illness? Is this the anorexia of the white Western middle-class family dynamic? To what extent can constructs founded on the class-specific, race-specific, nuclear family model be helpful here?" (95). In attempting to produce provisional answers to unfinalizable questions such as these, I think that it would be useful to bear in mind that Nyasha's symptom does not emerge in any unambiguous way. Quite clearly, her symptom is articulated in more than one place, rendering a certain scholarly nostalgia for "authentic" criteria altogether redundant in this context. In my view, any discussion of Nyasha must proceed by thinking through the mutually interruptive (or contra-dictory) categories that she so stridently embodies: Westernized/native, middle class/colonized, affluent/pathological, and readable/ misreadable.

Were we to look for an alternative explanation of Nyasha's ailment, it would be necessary to trace its formation during the course of Tambudzai's narrative. Why, after all, do food and its consumption become the privileged sites of Nyasha's spectacular rebellion? The first of the confrontations to take place between Nyasha and her father, Babamukuru, is important not only because it signals the beginnings of her overt challenges to his authority, but also because it is the textual juncture that determines the mode of resistance that her future challenges will assume. The passage is prefaced by a conflict between frameworks of cultural reference, since Tambu has arrived at the mission, and she is finding the food served in the Sigauke household unfamiliar, and a little unpalat-able. Maiguru ensures that she receives sadza and a spoon with which to eat it, explaining that when she had first arrived in En-gland, she had found it difficult to become accustomed to the change in diet (Dangarembga 82). Nyasha then interjects, claiming that she could quite easily sleep on an empty stomach, so long as she had a good book to read. At this point, Nyasha becomes aware that her copy of D.H. Lawrence's *Lady Chatterley's Lover* is missing and she begins to suspect that her mother has had some part in its disappearance:

> Nyasha froze half-way out of her chair and then stood up and confronted her mother. "You haven't taken it, have you?" she asked, and then answered herself. "Sorry, Mum. I know you wouldn't do anything like that."
>
> "And what if I have?" Maiguru asked.
>
> "But you wouldn't, would you? Not without telling me, would you?" asked Nyasha in consternation. Maiguru looked so unhappy you could not blame Nyasha for think-

ing her mother had taken her book. "But, Mum! How could you? Without even telling me. That's - that's - I mean, you shouldn't - you've no *right* to -"

"Er, Nyasha," *said Babamukuru to his food,* "I don't want to hear you talk to your mother like that." (83, second emphasis added)

This is the moment at which food *becomes a text* imbued with Babamukuru's authority, and Nyasha (the consummate voracious reader) cannot fail to apprehend the implications. By speaking to his food, Babamukuru unwittingly produces a kind of surveillance in relation to his daughter—he exercises a regulatory power through a technology of visibility. Obviously, the look is bifurcated in this instance: Babamukuru addresses his daughter but speaks to his food. Hence, the discipline that he is attempting to instill in Nyasha must of necessity be ambivalent, or available to the displacements of a strategic misreading that thwarts the internalization of a (repressive) system of constraint. Babamukuru's demand is that Nyasha should not be insolent to Maiguru. He implicitly instructs her to "eat her own words." Rather than occupy the unacceptable position of silence, Nyasha translates/*traduces* Babamukuru's injunction by refusing to eat the food he has provided. Thus, it is not at all surprising that her response to Babamukuru is to leave the table without finishing her dinner. In my view, this passage is crucial to a reading of Nyasha's symptom. During the prefatory conversation with her mother, Nyasha has established the written word as a substitute for a nourishing meal--she thinks it easier to sleep after a good read than after a good meal. The ensuing incident makes use of this substitution to establish an audacious condensation. Not only is the text a substitute for a meal. The meal itself becomes a social text.[10]

The audacity of this condensation is nowhere more apparent than in its implications for Babamukuru's status and standing in the extended family of which he is the titular head. His position of leadership is not merely the upshot of the rank and privilege that

the eldest son in a Shona family enjoys. It is also habitually reaffirmed within an economy of material relations at the family homestead. Further, food is inextricably imbricated in this economy. We
can see this, for example, when Babamukuru travels to the homestead: "On the days that Babamukuru came to visit we killed a
cock. Or rather, we killed a cock if there was one to spare, otherwise just a hen. We also killed a fowl on the occasions that Nhamo
came home, whether he came with Babamukuru or whether he came
alone" (8). The slaughtering of the fowl indicates the position of
respect occupied by Babamukuru. Since Nhamo is the firstborn
male of Jeremiah and Mainini's family, and since their hopes for
the material enhancement of the family rest on his achievements at
the mission school, he is accorded a similar degree of respect.
Babamukuru's rank and privilege, however, extend far beyond the
slaughtering of a fowl that Jeremiah's family unit can ill afford to
expend upon him. As some of the critics of *Nervous Conditions*
have noticed, acclaim for his educational achievements are couched
in metaphors of eating.[11]   Upon Babamukuru's return from England, Jeremiah sings his brother's praises in this way: "Our father
and benefactor has returned appeased, having devoured English
letters with a ferocious appetite. Did you think degrees were indi-
gestible? If so, look at my brother. He has digested them!" (36).
Jeremiah's praises, of course, are calculated to appease his more
affluent brother, who has sent ahead the requisite funds for a goat
to be slaughtered upon his return. After the meat has been cooked
for the extended family that has gathered for the occasion, it is first
served to Tambu's male relations in order of seniority, and then to
the more senior female relatives (40), with the result that there is
not enough meat to devolve down to Tambu and her siblings.
Tambu's response to this incident is one of ironic resignation to
her subordinate status within the Sigauke clan: "We, who rarely
tasted meat, found no reason to complain" (41). Even in
Babamukuru's home at the mission, food is served to family members in the order of their seniority, and Nyasha usurps this pecking
order when she doesn't wait upon ceremony to help herself to a
serving of rice (81).

Throughout the narrative, Babamukuru's power within the family is reinforced by the myth of munificent provision.[12] By refusing to eat, Nyasha effectively abjures her father's material privilege and the magnanimous gestures of generosity that this privilege enables. In my view, her symptom is not merely confined to the recognizable scene of a Westernized, middle-class, and nuclear family unit. It also is informed by, and speaks to, the extended Shona family dynamic of which she is part. In order to demonstrate these assertions, it would be useful to recall some of the cultural expectations and social duties that attach themselves to the female characters of *Nervous Conditions*. Firstly, young women are expected to groom themselves for their future roles as wives and as mothers. It is this expectation that creates discord when Tambu aspires (above her given station) to be educated. Her father's attempt to placate her when she discovers that her family will not have the means to allow her to return to a second year of schooling is cast in revealingly reductive terms: "Can you cook books and feed them to your husband? Stay at home with your mother. Learn to cook and clean. Grow vegetables" (15).

When Tambu earns enough money to send herself to school (significantly enough, by growing and selling vegetables), this provokes a crisis that obtains between two very different economies of material upliftment, both of which construct discrepant outcomes for the value that will accrue to her during her development into womanhood. After she has been helped by Mr. Matimba to sell the maize that she has grown, Tambu relates the difficulty that her father experiences in coming to terms with the advantages of allowing her to receive an education: "It was a difficult time for him because Mr. Matimba had shown him that in terms of cash my education was an investment, but then in terms of cattle so was my conformity" (34). Tambu's initiative has the upshot of bringing the traditional Shona custom of the bride-price (in cattle), with its communitarian[13] notions of property, into conflict with her nascent individualistic sense of an entrepreneurial alternative. Jeremiah is quite understandably concerned that the dowry he expects to receive for Tambu will not ultimately be realized if she continues in her quest for education. After all, a well-bred traditional Shona daughter finds her fulfillment in her unwaged labour in the fields, in her unwaged production of children and in her unwaged home-making activities. His fear is that an educated daughter might choose not to uphold her end of the bargain in quite the same way.

Nyasha's subject-formation is by no means free of the traditional gender-ideological determinants brought to bear on her cousin. Critical discussion of *Nervous Conditions*, however, has not generally remarked upon the social claims that the extended family exerts on Nyasha, nor upon the ways in which these obligations play a part in the emergence of her eating disorder. Rather, the emphasis has been placed on the recognizable affinities between her condition and the characteristics of the Western anorexic or bulimic, despite an almost unanimous recognition that Nyasha is the product of two cultures in conflict. So, for example, one finds the following commentaries on how her rebellion augurs for a Western (and sexist) representational ideal designated as "the feminine":

> [Nyasha's] anorexic body is a parody of a Western ideal of slim, feminine sexual desirability. (Nyasha does not want fat hips.) (Thomas 31)

> The development of eating disorders is strongly connected to the way a young woman feels or is made to feel about sexuality and the sexual development of her body, particularly by her family. When Nyasha and her family return to Southern Rhodesia after a five-year absence, Tambu observes that Maiguru does not look as though she had been to England, but that Nyasha "obviously had. There was no other explanation for the tiny little dress she wore, hardly enough of it to cover her thighs" (37). . . . Having picked up this Western preference, Nyasha transports it back with her to colonial Africa. (Hill 83)

> Symbolically then, Nyasha's nervous condition is symp-
> tomatic of the disease of colonialism. . . . She is punished
> because she resists her father's demands that she stop be-
> having in ways that reflect her hybridity and instead be-
> have as a proper female African child. This script of resis-
> tance and punishment demonstrates the ways in which
> hybridity is symptomatic of the infection of Western influ-
> ence. . . . If her eating disorder is indeed symptomatic of
> the disease of colonialism, then independence must be the
> cure. (Hill 89)

There is nothing particularly objectionable in the first two passages
that I have quoted. They focus on the Western influences on
Nyasha's behavior and self-presentation. The novel clearly points
towards these influences: Nyasha's dieting, her loss of the Shona
mother-tongue, her skimpy attire, her more public adolescent
curiosity in (and exploration of) her sexuality, the breakdown of
suitably respectful demeanour in a gerontocratic regime.
Nevertheless, the latent analytical predicament in such an approach
is that it will always risk constructing a monolithic model of the
West, thereby eliding the Shona cultural components of Nyasha's
characterization. The third quotation exemplifies the difficulties
involved. Nyasha is indeed a hybrid. Hybridity in this instance is
indeed "symptomatic of the infection of Western influence." But it
takes two to make a hybrid. Had *Nervous Conditions* been narrated
differently, in the moment of premature triumphalism
accompanying the advent of national independence, Nyasha would
still have had to contend with other, subtle pathologies. The most
immediate of these pathologies would be indigenous sexism, the
gerontocratic organization of power in her extended family and
the abject poverty of her kinsfolk.

If Nyasha exists in the interstices of two *unevenly distributed* cultures (colonial and indigenous), then one might wish to
ascertain the extent to which her symptom is the result of being
positioned between (and within) two *equally unacceptable* alter-

natives. By framing the question in this way, one would be aiming to avoid constructing the symptom in the simplistic, oppositional logic of strict dichotomies. Indeed, insofar as an analytical model adheres to such explanatory binary categories as unyielding patriarchs/naughty daughters, colonizer/native and domination/victimhood, it also polices their boundaries according to an eminently self-seeking rationale. Quite clearly, Nyasha does rebel against ideological interpellations which insist that she be both the fantasized "good kaffir" (200) of colonial Rhodesia and the good daughter of its patriarchal, Anglicized accomplices. In what sense, though, could we also read Nyasha's symptom as constituting a rebellion against Shona cultural gender-coding? Which aspects of indigenous sexism, if any, do her demonstrative posturings refuse?

To begin with, *Nervous Conditions* does provide us with a description of the "healthy" (or valorized) traditional female body image at the homestead. When Lucia creates such havoc amongst the elders of the extended family, it is because she has been sleeping with both Jeremiah and his equally ineffectual relative, Takesure. The substance of Jeremiah's desire to marry her (despite the fact that she is pregnant with Takesure's child) is particularly significant. Tambudzai explains:

> Lucia had managed somehow to keep herself plump despite her tribulations. . . . And Lucia was strong. She could cultivate a whole acre single-handed without rest. Altogether she was a much more inviting prospect than my mother if you did not scrutinise her past too closely. . . . My father found her desirable and argued besides that the child might be a boy, which would be good since at the moment he only had daughters. (127)

On the homestead, it would seem, slender women are less desirable than their plump sisters. The logic of this preference is evident in the passage quoted above. Plumper women are more likely to have the energy reserves necessary for the back-breaking physical labour required of them. Further, it is this propensity for physical labour that invests Lucia with beauty in the schema of her traditional society. These material considerations far "outweigh" the moral censure that invariably attends the activities of a sexually predacious woman (which Lucia is) in a conservative community. While Nyasha's body ideal rapidly begins to lean towards a very gaunt appearance (she prefers angles to curves [135]), this does not mean that she is free of the traditional female body ideals that Lucia exemplifies. Although she has grown up and has been educated in England, there is evidence as the narrative progresses that she is selectively re-socialized into the symbolic structure of Shona customs, etiquette, and expectations.[14] For example, when Babamukuru, Maiguru, Tambu, and Nyasha arrive at the homestead for the family's Christmas gathering, they go into the room in which an ailing Mainini awaits their arrival. Since there is nowhere to sit, Babamukuru opts for the bed and Maiguru opts for the floor. When Mainini instructs Tambu to bring in a chair, both Babamukuru and Maiguru refuse the convenience in an elaborately self-deprecating fashion. A politics of resentment underlies Mainini's actions. She is ill because she has lost a son, and she lays the blame for this loss squarely on Babamukuru and his "Englishness." The introduction of the chair is an exaggerated gesture of deference to her more affluent in-laws: it is a cultured convenience in the abject scene of impoverishment and incapacitation. Failing to engage with the game of deference and self-deprecation, Nyasha announces in a characteristically forthright way that she will sit in the chair. Mainini seizes on the opportunity to berate Nyasha for making herself comfortable before greeting her aunt, and Babamukuru and Maiguru promptly order her to do so:

> Nyasha jumped out of the chair to embrace my mother, who relished her victory and consolidated it by exclaiming what a big girl Nyasha had grown into.
>
> "The breasts are already quite large," she declared, pinching one and causing Maiguru to wince with embarrassment. "When do we expect our *mukwambo*," my mother teased her niece.

Babamukuru was valiant. Overcoming his inbred aversion to such biological detail, he took my mother's question seriously. "Our Nyasha," he sighed in real distress. "Is she the type to bring us a son-in-law? No, she is not the type. And even if she did, it would be a question of feeding the cattle—the man would soon be wanting to bring them back." (131)

This dialogue goes a long way towards explaining the contradictory situation in which Nyasha finds herself. Inserted into the system of exogamy in a traditional society, she is potentially an object of exchange, and her modestly enlarged breasts are sufficiently ample evidence of her exchange value. Thus it is possible to read her nervous condition as not only a parody of Western-style femininity, but also as a reductive rejoinder to the Shona ideal of the stout and able-bodied mother and cultivator.[15] Babamukuru's response to Mainini indicates the paradoxes involved. Although he appears to vindicate the entire social structure upon which Mainini's remarks are predicated, he will shortly decree that Mainini and Jeremiah must undergo a belated Christian marriage ceremony in order to remedy the "evil" that Lucia has brought to the homestead. Since Babamukuru's own paternal-sororal politics are shot through with contradiction, it is not difficult to understand the reasons underlying his previous outburst upon hearing that Nyasha has stayed out late talking to one of the missionary's sons. While Nyasha manifestly does not approve of Mainini's reference to her in the third person (her foot begins to tap in a typically agitated fashion [131]), she does validate some of the Shona social codes that prescribe respectful conduct:

"*Nyamashewe*, Mainini, *Nyamashewe*, Mainini Lucia," Nyasha intoned awkwardly, her cupped hands, making just the right sound as she clapped.

Babamukuru looked at his daughter, raised his eyebrows and stretched his lips in agreeable surprise, then remembered what he was doing and set his features back into their usual stern contours.

> "Yes," said my mother, flattered by this little attention from her Anglicised niece, "our daughter is really growing up. I tell you, Babamukuru, whatever you say, you will have a fine son-in-law one of these days." (131)

Of course, nothing in Nyasha's previous behavior has prepared Babamukuru for this eventuality. His favourite argument against her is that she lacks a sense of modesty and of the decorum that befits the daughter of a respected member of the community. At this textual juncture though, we can see evidence of Nyasha's reassimilation into Yal codes.

Indeed, Nyasha begins to show a marked interest in aspects of a culture that her five year stint in England has all but effaced. In particular, she directs her attention towards the connubial tribulations of Jeremiah and Mainini, and Babamukuru's peremptory recommendations for an appropriate solution. When Babamukuru first suggests the need for a solution to the problems caused by Lucia's presence at the homestead, Jeremiah enthuses that it will be necessary to get a "good medium to do the ceremony properly with everything—beer, a sacrificial ox, everything" (146). Babamukuru is horrified at the thought of bringing "alcohol" and "witchdoctors" to his home, but Nyasha is more receptive to the prospect of Jeremiah's proposed solutions. Tambu comments:

> She was amused by my father's solutions and the idea of a wedding. She was curious too about the proposed cleansing ceremonies, confessed that her ignorance of these things embarrassed her and asked me about all sorts of fine details, details that I was not very sure of since we did not often perform the rituals any more. (147)

Tambu at first takes Babamukuru's farcical suggestion of a Christian marriage ceremony to be a sign of progress, but Nyasha cautions her against "assuming that Christian ways were progressive ways" (147). It is as if Nyasha's own overexposure to a narrative of progress facilitates the project of re-learning her effaced cultural heritage. In this, her critical approach to both colonial history and Shona tradition stand her in good stead.

Although Nyasha re-engages in part with a Shona traditional lifestyle, she is at a considerable disadvantage. Thus, when she turns to making clay pottery, in what Tambu disdainfully terms Nyasha's "latest craze," Tambudzai hastens to point out that only the very young make pots to imitate their elders (150) or else adults make pots for functional purposes.[16] *Nervous Conditions* refuses the possibility of any unproblematic return to an authentic and prelapsarian nativism. What is important, however, is that Nyasha's crafting of pottery is linked to her symptom, for she plans to use the pots to hold "buttons and jewelery and pens,"[17] and she bakes them in Maiguru's Dover stove (149), which has been brought to the homestead to enable the task of cooking for the extended family.

Understandably, there has been some degree of overlap in the theoretical frameworks employed by scholarly commentary on *Nervous Conditions*. For example, Frantz Fanon, and his latter-day exponent, Homi Bhabha, have come to figure quite importantly in the fairly extensive critical work on the novel. Fanon's importance to this critical work is relatively straightforward: he is one of the first—indeed one of the few—theorists of colonialism and neocolonialism to view racism or liberation struggles as having the capacity to institute a psychic force. Fanon's insights in "Colonial War and Mental Disorders" are absolutely crucial in this context (*Wretched* 200-50). It is possible to claim that the mental disorders that Fanon treated during the Algerian War of Independence were by no means confined to the constitutionally delicate or to those predisposed towards deviance (perversion): the symptom is actively produced within a culture in conflict. If the symptom is culturally produced, it has a socio-economic history and, more importantly, a subject-specific politics. It cannot be reduced to normative criteria; its uniqueness admits of the ideological particularities that work in and through differently classed, racialized, and gendered human subjects. However, Fanon also presents us with two cautionary notes on the dangers of an excessively hasty recourse to a universalizing psychoanalytic discourse, or to Western medicine for that matter. Directing a polemic against Mannoni's "Malagasy complex"—which legitimizes the Madagascan colonial project by arguing that the colonized suffered from a "dependency complex" which pre-dated the French incursion—*Black Skin, White Masks* offers a re-reading of the colonized subjects' dreams that Mannoni recorded as evidence for his suspect conclusions: "The enraged black bull is not the phallus. The two black men are not the father figures—the one standing for the real father, the other for the primal ancestor. . . . The rifle of the Senegalese soldier is not a penis but a genuine rifle, model Lebel 1916" (106). Elsewhere, Fanon has this to say about the colonized's reactions to Western medicine in an Algerian colonial context: "Introduced into Algeria at the same time as racialism and humiliation, Western medical science, being part of the oppressive system, has always provoked in the native an ambivalent relation. This ambivalence is in fact to be found in connection with all of the occupier's modes of presence" ("Medicine and Colonialism" 121). Given that so much of the literary critical work on *Nervous Conditions* hazards medical diagnoses of Nyasha's eating disorder, it is all the more surprising that this work has not heeded the pertinent caveats that Fanon supplies. If Nyasha is something of a curiosity in an African context, in what sense is it possible to speak meaningfully of her "anorexia" or "bulimia"? Surely this ill-considered diagnosis works counter to the most astute insights that Dangarembga's critics advance. It is an entirely specious maneuver to evade this complication by noting that Fanon speaks of anorexia in relation to Algerian psychiatric patients during the war of independence. In places, Fanon's vocabulary is symptomatic of his assimilation into precisely those discourses[18] that he seeks to critique and, in any event, Algeria during the mid- to late Fifties was clearly not remotely equivalent to Rhodesia during the late Sixties, despite any broader historical rubrics under which they might be subsumed for purely descriptive purposes.

I would now like to comment on the most disempowering aspects of what I have previously referred to as the "bulimia diagnosis." While Dangarembga's critics have been quite happy to note the anomaly of a black Zimbabwean having "bulimia" (a "Western" illness), they have not interrogated the ease with which they have arrived at their diagnosis. In seeking to admit Nyasha to a Western discourse of psychopathology as an interesting anomaly, these critics have also foreclosed on her resistance to the Shona patriarchy represented in the novel. Thus, in my view, the "bulimia diagnosis" covertly reinstates the West as the sovereign context of Nyasha's symptom, in an act of naming that is profoundly catachrestical.[19] I have attempted to delineate some of the traditional Shona expectations that exert pressure on Nyasha's sexuality and upon her gendered positionality. I am inclined to argue that Nyasha's eating disorder is proleptically indexed during an early confrontation with these expectations. Tambu comments on one of Nyasha's first visits to the homestead in this way:

> One day she behaved very badly indeed. They arrived at eleven o'clock in the morning, in a season when there was very little in the garden in the way of vegetables. However, there was a cow in milk, so my mother was relieved when Nyasha, having been asked whether she would have milk or vegetables, said she would have milk. Unfortunately, when lunchtime came, Nyasha tucked into vegetables with the rest of us. When my mother offered her the sour milk she had asked for, she became very morose. She refused to eat anything, although by this time everybody was very concerned and sympathetic and saying she could have whatever she wanted. (52)

Why should Nyasha become morose upon receiving the milk she has asked for? Is it because she was not expecting to receive *sour* milk, but fresh milk instead? Perhaps these questions make a meal of slender pickings, but I think that the passage does tentatively broach the question of Nyasha's misreading of a culture and a cuisine that are no longer her own. Further, this is the first instance in which Nyasha refuses food. If this narrative juncture anticipates the later development of Nyasha's eating disorder, then it seems to me that we need to account for cultures in conflict when we deliver our diagnoses, and this is what the "bulimia diagnosis" so spectacularly fails to accomplish.

This problem raises a second, more serious, one, that is, the problem of finding a reading position with which to articulate the novel. While the majority of Dangarembga scholars have cautioned against the dangers of universalizing a Western-style feminism, the overriding concern of a number of articles has been to reclaim *Nervous Conditions* for "feminism,"[20] thereby reinstating at a subterranean level precisely those outmoded and politically fraught modes of intelligibility that these articles have explicitly renounced. Although I am broadly sympathetic to the explanatory potentials and the social agendas of feminism, I feel compelled to question the legitimizing motives behind such wayward interpretations. For some time now, the proper name, "feminism," has justifiably been viewed with great suspicion in the black intellectual climate of Southern Africa, since even the name "feminism" has historically entailed the sorts of privilege to which black women have not generally had access. Dangarembga herself has made this point in interviews with Kirsten Holst Petersen and Flora Veit-Wild:

> I used to adhere to a Western model of feminism, but even this problem between men and women in my part of the world, and in America as well, seems to me more and more to be a policy of divide and rule. . . . [W]omen in Zimbabwe are very wary of being called feminists. It is really a dirty word. (Holst Petersen 347)

> The white Western feminism does not meet my experiences at a certain point, the issues of me as a black woman. The black American female writers touch more of me than

the white ones. (Veit-Wild 106)

This final statement suggests Alice Walker's *The Color Purple* as a possible literary precursor to *Nervous Conditions*[21] and Walker's elaboration of "womanism" as an active influence on Dangarembga's political persuasions.[22] "Womanism" is currently, and with good reason, extolled as Southern African women's answer to "feminism," since it provides a means of fighting both colonial and indigenous gender-oppression while uniting black communities against institutionalized racism. On a regional level, feminism could conceivably be touted as a panacea to the injustices of sex-discrimination, but it has done little to eradicate the widespread "madams and maids" syndrome. I am tempted, then, to suggest the possibility of an ideological blindness in the critical work on *Nervous Conditions*. Since Nyasha has been ubiquitously read in terms of anorexia/bulimia, and since Tambu's narrative has been widely reclaimed for feminism, then surely one must suspect that the misguided diagnoses of Nyasha's condition owe their inception to the impulse to constitute Nyasha as the subject of a Western-style feminism. Expressed otherwise, the "bulimia diagnosis" amounts to a monolithic explanatory strategy that enables an auto-sympathetic structure of recognition.

Given that Nyasha's symptom introduces a politics on at least two fronts, and given that this politics exceeds anything the Western bulimic has to offer, we need to find another name for her symptom in order to arrive at non-appropriative conclusions. This act of naming would have to account for Nyasha's insertion into two conflicting cultural matrices, and it would have to be highly provisional, an interim category conceived of in the current absence of other, more available designations. Hopefully, such designations will eventually emerge as part of the discourses of postcolonial medicine and psychoanalysis. My suggestion is that we should risk a strategic misreading of *Nervous Conditions* and attempt to think through "bulimia," understood in its etymological sense: from the Greek *bous* (ox) and *limos* (hunger), the hunger of an ox. In my view, "boulimia" can account for the recognizable aetiology of Nyasha's condition and for the anomalies that she produces. This reading would not deploy the etymology in order to reinstate an overarching Hellenic heritage, which has, since Plato, held a privileged philosophical place in classical Western myths of origin.[23] To deploy the etymology in this way would be tantamount to making the same mistake as those critics who have opted for the "bulimia diagnosis." Rather, my strategy here is to use the etymology's referent ("the hunger of an ox") as an expedient *metaphor* with which to displace the fantasy of the origin as it operates in critical accounts of *Nervous Conditions*. The "hunger of an ox" is quite easily linked to Nyasha's self-starvation, which stretches hunger beyond physiological dictates in order to adumbrate the gendered zones of a broader cultural discomfiture. However, we could also read Nyasha's symptom as an instance of translation/ *traduction*. In much the same fashion as Dangarembga's skewed citation of Sartre, the symptom revises the authenticity and the authority of its context. In other words, reading in translation entails a necessary misrepresentation (*traduction*). In this reading, Nyasha has a "hunger for an ox": she can be read as the daughter who refuses to participate in the economy of exogamy. This final move requires a little explanation. If women are unwaged labour in the Shona patriarchy, and if they are granted a diminished status within the Shona patriarchy's material relations (evidenced by the gendered division of food—men eat first and have the pick of the choicest morsels), then we can see this violence being exposed in Nyasha's "boulimia." She also destroys her own value as a potential object of exchange (in exogamy).[24] It should be remembered here that cattle are imbricated both within the outer signs of masculine privilege (men eat first, animals are slaughtered in their honour) and that they function as units of wealth within exogamy (women are exchanged for cattle). However, there is a further sense in which Nyasha's protest "castrates"[25] Babamukuru's familial power, which is based on the myth of munificent provision. She refuses the food he provides, and, with it, the filial obligations this provision demands in return. If Nyasha's gendered body is viewed as a politico-legal text (at least partially implicated in customary law—which is, in turn, thoroughly implicated in colonial legislation),[26] then her willfull self-mastery amounts to an attempt to re-author colonial history, Settler law, and Shona tradition. It is no coincidence that Nyasha finally breaks down and rants semi-coherently at Tambudzai and Babamukuru, while taking bites out of a history book and plunging the shards of mirrors and of her clay pots into her own flesh:

> Nyasha was beside herself with fury. She rampaged, shredding her history book between her teeth ("Their history. Fucking liars. Their bloody lies."), breaking mirrors, her clay pots, anything she could get her hands on and jabbing the fragments viciously into her flesh, stripping the bedclothes, tearing her clothes from the wardrobe and trampling them underfoot. . . . Then as suddenly as it came, the rage passed. . . . "I'm very tired," she said in a voice that was recognizably hers. (201)

In my view, the objects that form part of the chaotic action during Nyasha's breakdown contain significant overtones for the way in which we might read her symptom. Her aversion to colonial history books is unsurprising, given that she has persistently questioned their content throughout the narrative. One might also make a case for the mirrors' importance to her body image, and the clothes that Nyasha tears from the wardrobe have formed one of the bases of contention between her and Babamukuru. However, it is also interesting that the clay pots should re-emerge at this juncture. In my view, the pots are a metonym of the Shona mother culture that Nyasha must also finally refuse.[27] It is significant that the passage quoted above follows the logic of the symptom by interrupting the mind-body dichotomy. Nyasha's flesh is no less textual for being sentient. Equally, the history book is no less material for being written, since it provides an alibi to Settler exploitation of Rhodesia.

No doubt, the case for employing "boulimia" as an analytical classification will appear slightly fanciful, or perhaps even unwarranted. I would argue that when dealing with a category disturbance in a postcolonial context, an ethical reading consists in keeping the question open by emphasizing the disturbance, rather than the available explanatory categories. In "Medicine and Colonialism," Fanon adopts a broadly similar disposition, claiming that "[it] is necessary to analyze, patiently and lucidly, each one of the reactions of the colonized, and every time we do not understand, we must tell ourselves that we are at the heart of the matter—that of the impossibility of finding a meeting ground in any colonial situation" (125). What is important for the purposes of my discussion is that "boulimia" allows for Nyasha to be read as embodying a syndrome broadcast within incommensurate culture/s, even if the limits of our present knowledge prevent us from naming this syndrome in its entirety. "Boulimia," as I wish to define it, is a provisional term that enables the Western feminist-aligned critic to read cultural difference in *Nervous Conditions* ethically, by resisting the impulse to recuperate African women's lived conditions for Western-based or auto-sympathetic diagnoses. The notion of a culturally broadcast syndrome accomplishes two things here. Firstly, it resists a certain nostalgia for origins that consists in locating pathologies within a bounded culture ("anorexia and bulimia are Western afflictions"). Secondly, the culturally broadcast syndrome acknowledges cultural differences, and their impact upon subjects positioned between these differences in a colonial encounter.

By way of conclusion, I would like to point out some of the practical ramifications of my argument thus far. While the anecdote that follows does not provide empirical support for my claims in relation to "boulimia," I hope that its import will at least prove to be illustrative of my concerns. In 1996, I taught *Nervous Conditions* on a literature Bridging Year course under the auspices of the English for Academic Purposes program in a South African university. The students were second-language speakers of English and those that passed the course were permitted to proceed to a first year in literary studies. The class attendance of one student, a young woman named A.K., decreased abruptly as the semester progressed. When a fellow graduate teacher asked the class members why A.K. had not been attending tutorials, they laughed and told him that A.K. had *amafufunyane.*

Amafufunyane is an affliction that is specific to the Xhosa- and Zulu-speaking South African communities (Swartz 66). It is a "culture-bound syndrome." This means that it is a locality-specific syndrome (a symptom-complex; or the sum of signs of any morbid state) iterated within a folk diagnostic category.[28] Its dictionary entry describes it as a "rapidly spreading disease with insanity; mania; hysteria" (Doke, Malcolm and Sikakana II: 65). *Amafufunyane* primarily affects "women over the age of 13 years" (Mkize 329). Frequently, the onset of the illness may be marked by abdominal rumblings, abdominal pains, or abdominal swelling.[29] Ngubane describes the typical behaviour associated with the *amafufunyane* sufferer:

> She becomes hysterical and weeps aloud uncontrollably, throws herself on the ground, tears off her clothes, runs in a frenzy, and usually attempts to commit suicide. She reacts violently and aggressively to those who try to calm her. She is said to be possessed by a horde of spirits of different racial groups. Usually there may be thousands of Indians or Whites, some hundreds of Sotho or Zulu spirits. (144)[30]

Ngubane's assertions regarding the typicality of these symptoms has been challenged recently by research findings in which a number of informants have applied the term "*amafufunyane*" unevenly to psychological and physiological conditions that a Western medical practitioner would recognize as discrete nosological phenomena (hysteria, schizophrenia, epilepsy).[31] Therefore, the general understanding of *amafufunyane* has moved towards the view that it exists: "less as a discrete diagnostic entity with attached symptoms than as a construction or explanatory model, which patients use to make sense of their experience. It is a ready-made, socially sanctioned model, by which experiences of inner conflict can be incorporated" (Swartz 163). Perhaps the most interesting aspect of *amafufunyane* is its correlation with socio-cultural upheaval. In other words, it can be linked to the historical injustices in South Africa. Mkize notes that the term *amafufunyane* became common currency during the 1920s and 1930s (330). He goes on to describe the social conditions affecting the Zulu community at this time:

> [*Amafufunyane*] is a response to perceived threats by the influx of people from overseas, more particularly during the period of the great depression in Europe after World War I. Zulus in South Africa perceived this to be an intrusion, threatening their lives. With increasing mobility and intensified migratory labour, contacts between peoples of various racial groups grew daily. . . . The feeling of "insecurity" grew, and both Indians and whites combined were seen as a formidable force bent on disrupting the equilibrium of Zulu society. (330)

This historical dimension of *amafufunyane* explains why the "culture-bound syndrome" may include hallucinations involving white or Indian spirits. It is almost as if the syndrome preserves a species of cultural memory in the historical absence of other legitimate forms of political dissent. In this context, *amafufunyane* emerges as a symptom of inter-cultural conflicts. It is not enunciated from only one place, or in a bounded Xhosa or Zulu culture. I am therefore sceptical of the term culture-bound syndrome, since it enables a slippage between thinking about *amafufunyane* as a condition specific to two South African communities and assuming that it is produced only within these communities. It is possible, on the contrary, to show that the *amafufunyane* is not an oddity or idiosyncratic propensity amongst the Xhosa or Zulu that enables a bit of medical-anthropological tourism and little else. The syndrome points towards a dramatic history of cultural conflict, an eminently colonial history in which pathologies are culturally broadcast. And this shift in emphasis is precisely the reason for entertaining the "boulimia" reading of *Nervous Conditions*.

Amafufunyane is considered to be psychosomatic and untreatable by Western medicine. Understandably, A.K. missed the majority of my literature tutorials because she was shuttling back and forth between Cape Town and the rural Transkei—a journey of approximately 600 miles—in order to receive treatment by a traditional healer. A.K. submitted a draft essay on *Nervous Conditions* on time, but handed in the two full drafts required of her beyond the final deadline. The draft essay failed with a mark of 46%. Since A.K. had not produced a doctor's note excusing her absence, and since the university did not recognize illnesses treated by traditional healers as a valid excuse for a lax academic performance, only the draft essay counted towards her final mark for the course. The outcome of this particular student's attempts to complete the literature component of the course, despite the adversities she experienced, continues to bother me. To begin with, it is clear that the university's failure to grant formal recognition to traditional ailments and to their traditional treatment speaks to a history of institutionalized ethnocentrism that is all too familiar within a South African context. In addition, I think that the essay merits a rereading. I cite it in full:

> In this essay I am going to show the expectations of Tambudzai about the new world in which she is in and how she compares in the old world in the homestead. I will then deal with her background which is not exactly shown in this passage and I will trace Tambudzai's choices that are affect and develop her life according to author's language in this passage.
>
> Tambudzai is from a very poor family in rural area. She even saw herself as a peasant (par 2, p.g. 58). She was untidy from hair to toe. A peasant is a person w(h)o is working to death and has got little or no chance for education. Tambudzai was learn(v)ing behi(n)d. That is where she got different expectations in the new world.

In the new world Babamukure was the saviour. So in this passage we found her entering his new ~~wout~~ world which seemed very different from her old world. To support my argument she said "It was relief (par, 1 p.g. 58). It was relief from hard work of the homestead. She made it clear when she said "This new me would not be ~~over~~ a enevertate by smoky kitchens that leave eyes smarting and chest bronchit (par: 2, p.g. 59). That is what she really showed her relief in this passage

In Babamukuru's house she expectet cleaness, to be well-groomed and herself who could not have been bred, and be encouraged to consider questions that had to do with the survival of the spirit (par 2 pg 59). Whereas in homestead it was survival of the body because women were the ones who almost do everything. At Babamukuru's everything was just easy and Tambudzai could focus on a life of the mind.

To conclude this passage is showing us important different world that Tambudzai is dealing with and the new life she was going to develop for her future [strikethrough denotes the student's deletions; parentheses denote the student's insertions]

I shall not be commenting on the merit of the essay in relation to "objective" academic/literary critical criteria. Rather, I shall attempt to ask to what extent the essay might be symptomatic of the nervous conditions governing its emergence. Since *amafufunyane* is an under-explored field, and since I am inexorably part of the institutional violence to which this essay was submitted, I must remain suspicious of any analytical maneuvers that might articulate the essay in terms that finalize it as an object of knowledge. Accordingly, my investigation will proceed by way of questioning. Given that we are dealing with a student afflicted by a "culture-bound" syndrome, how far can a psychoanalytic framework account for the essay? Are the parapraxes (slips of the pen—for example:

"wout", "over" and "learn(v)ing behi(n)d") that we encounter significant, or are they merely the result of an English-as-a- second-language-speaker's less confident approach to her written expression? What is the extent of the student's identification with the novel, given that her own entry into the educational system may arise from humble beginnings equivalent to those of Tambu, and given that she inhabits a nervous condition comparable to that of Nyasha? Has the student's reading of *Nervous Conditions* (as a sympathetic cultural encounter) contributed to the formation of *amafufunyane*? Has the classroom dynamic (as an antagonistic cultural encounter) contributed to the formation of *amafufunyane*? Does *amafufunyane* have a cultural logic that may be detected in the essay? Leading on from the previous question, does the phrase "The new me would not be over" have any correlation with the suicidal impulses attributed to *amafufunyane* sufferers? Further, given that "wout" is an Afrikaans word (meaning "wood," as in "copse"), does its inclusion into the essay amount to the student "writing in tongues," or does it merely indicate that the student is trilingual? Does the clause "Tambudzai was learn(v)ing behi(n)d" reflect on the student's own situation as she shuttles between learning in Cape Town and leaving for the Transkei? Does the same clause not resonate with some of the central preoccupations of Dangarembga's novel; leaving in order to learn versus learning as an activity that forces one to leave one's loved ones and cultural co-ordinates behind (or "behid")? Are the student's classmates correct in their diagnosis, given that *amafufunyane* is a way of negotiating illness, rather than a strict diagnostic classification? Is the student's illness perhaps not *amafufunyane* but *isimnyama esikolweni* (school anxiety or "brain fag"[32])? Whatever our answers to the questions listed above, is it not probable that the student has inhabited *Nervous Conditions* better than a cursory glance at the essay suggests she has? If this were indeed true, how might one begin to make a case for the recognition of this situation in the regulations governing marking procedures in a South African university?

I believe that an investigative exercise of this kind sounds a cautionary note for those literary critics who have been too ready to find answers to the questions posed by *Nervous Conditions*. When a Western psychiatric discourse is applied to colonial contexts, it cannot in every example account for the pathologies that it finds. Furthermore, Western psychiatry provides only one understanding of psychopathology among many, and we need to question its unilateral instatement in texts such as *Nervous Conditions* and *amafufunyane*. Even though the name of the symptom may be on the tip of one's tongue, one must refrain from indexing it too exactly.

Notes

1. See Bahri (par. 1), Thomas (26), Woodward (85), Bosman (93), McWilliams (108), Vizzard (204-05), Booker (190-91), Nair (133), Creamer (350-51), Plasa (35), Hill (79), Sugnet (35, 38), and Rooney (130). Sugnet and Rooney extend their discussions to the differences between the citation and its source.

2. I should make it clear that I am not referring here to the contemporary strategy of "creative misreading," although Dangarembga's epigraph could be apprehended in precisely these terms.

3. Although "condition" in French translates into English as both "condition" and as "status," it is curious that Sartre's sentence in *Les Damnés de la Terre* does not contain the word "condition." Sartre writes: "L'indigénat est une névrose introduite et maintenue par le colon chez les colonisés *avec leur consentement*" (19, emphasis in original). According to the *Collins Robert Comprehensive French English Dictionary*, "l'indigénat" was an "administrative system applying to indigenous populations of French colonies before 1945" (Duval and Marr 487). This historical specificity is lost in the translations "the status of 'native'" and "*the condition of native*." Further, "une névrose" is, strictly speaking, "a neurosis" rather than a "nervous condition." Hence, Dangarembga's epigraph is the product of a double misreading.

4. It is possible to read this insistence as a gender-political gesture. Spivak notes that "[quotation] in Derrida is a mark of non-self-identity: the defining predication of a woman, whose very name is changeable" (171).

5. This gesture on my part is not intended to imply any facile affiliation or alignment with a corrective feminist account of the universal "reader." Rather, the gesture is informed by Lisa Jardine's claim that seventy-five percent of the book-buying public in the United Kingdom is female. It would be interesting to know how this figure would compare with the demographics of the book-buying public in Zimbabwe, where one would suspect that the gendering of poverty and the gendering of illiteracy might considerably complicate the scenario. In any event, since this piece of work considers two specific African women readers, I have chosen to designate the abstract reader as female.

6. Supriya Nair makes an astute observation on this stance when she writes: "[t]he categorical tone of the first-person narrator signals a critical self-examination, quite conscious about rejecting the guilt associated with 'unnatural' sisterhood, inhuman lack of feeling" (133). I would simply add here that any unexamined critical approach to *Nervous Conditions* that seeks to establish commonality with Tambudzai/Nyasha in the name of a universal feminism risks the reconstruction of another "unnatural sisterhood."

7. See Bahri (3), Thomas (31), Vizzard (207), Uwakweh (81), Booker (194), Creamer (357), Nair (137), Plasa (36), Pentolfe Aegerter (238).

8. The critics who have read Nyasha's symptom as anorexia include Flockemann (45-46), Thomas (30), Vizzard (206), Uwakweh (81), Holst Petersen (345), Woodward (88), Rooney (135), Bosman (95), Booker (194 and 196) and Plasa (37 and 44). The critics who have understood the symptom as bulimia include McWilliams (110), Sugnet (35), Nair (137), Hill (82), Bahri (5, para. 9) and Pentolfe Aegerter (237-38). Only Bosman and Bahri extend their discussion so as to question such unilateral diagnoses. Creamer actively refuses to name the symptom (359-60, note 8).

9. My terminology here should not be understood as a flippant dismissal, but as expedient shorthand. I should add that I am not altogether convinced that anorexia is an issue in *Nervous Conditions*, since it is not typically associated with the purging of food.

10. It would be a mistake, I think, to claim that Nyasha occupies a posi-

tion outside of discourse, a position that is antithetical to "power." After all, the progression of her illness indicates that she inhabits a macabre disciplinary structure. She reads, she questions, she eats, she disgorges. She is the self-regulating subject *par excellence.* Discussing the panopticon, Foucault writes: "He who is subjected to a field of visibility, and who knows it, assumes responsibility for the constraints of power; he makes them play spontaneously upon himself . . . he becomes the principle of his own subjection" (202-03). It would be interesting to think about Nyasha's self-enclosure in the bathroom for the purposes of disgorging as a species of cellular confinement that approximates the spatial distributions of the panoptical machine. Of course, the gagging is not visible to her parents, but its effects upon her body most certainly are.

11. See, for example, Bahri (6, para. 12) and Hill (81), Plasa (40).

12. This myth is later deflated when the reader discovers that Babamukuru's provision for his poor relations is sustained only by redirecting Maiguru's earnings to this end.

13. "Communitarian" is something of a euphemistic misnomer here, since exogamy in Shona customary law is an exchange conducted between patriarchs, with whom possession of the properties exchanged ultimately rests.

14. Biman Basu views Nyasha in similar terms (15).

15. It is worth noting here that "the feminine" is a sign produced in exogamy. Further, it is produced in such a way as to consolidate numerous social interests. Firstly, exogamy forges alliances of affiliation between otherwise unrelated men, and these alliances are based upon the bride-price (or *roora*) in cattle. Since wealth in the Shona community is measured in head of cattle, an entire economy hinges on the bride-price. The family is the locus of this economy, just as it is the locus of normative gender criteria. Secondly, cattle are a foodstuff associated with affluent families and an increased social status (Dangarembga 91 and 141). Thirdly, when we do encounter meat being served in *Nervous Conditions,* it usually forms part of a sacrifice for an honoured male family member, and the male characters are always served first, with the occasional result that some of the more junior (or disempowered) female characters do not receive their portion of edible meat (41 and 135-36). Thus, in theory at least, exogamy is by no means free of the institution of gender hierarchies in everyday ceremonies of nutrition.

16. Even here, Tambu notes that she has never seen anyone "make a proper *hari* [pot]" because people use "two- and five-gallon drums these days" (150). Nyasha's insertion into a narrative of the colonized's progress under internal colonization is understandably rendered as an instance of her regression.

17. Nyasha's refusal of food is also intimately linked to the pressures brought to bear on her to succeed in her education: "[W]hen breakfast was ready she had been studying in a concentrated state for an hour or more. At night it was the same: by eight o'clock she was curled up in bed with her books, but the light rarely went out before one. Everybody agreed that she was overdoing it. She was looking drawn and had lost so much of her appetite that it showed all over her body in the way the bones crept to the surface, but she did not seem to notice." (107) In my reading, the pens are metonyms for Nyasha's education at this textual juncture.

18. It would be worth adding here that I remain slightly sceptical of orthodox psychoanalytic readings of *Nervous Conditions*, since they leave a number of questions unanswered. If Nyasha can be read in terms of mourning and/or melancholia, what is the lost object being mourned? Maiguru's body? Her father's esteem? *Lady Chatterley's Lover*? A precolonial Shona society? Her English upbringing? Her Shona infancy? Further, psychoanalytic readings of the novel do not generally discuss the implication of Freud's project in broader Imperialist narratives, nor do they speculate on the dynamics that miscegenation or mixed-race relationships bring to bear on an Oedipalized female subject (Nyasha's only represented paramour is a white missionary's son). Finally, they do not attempt to explain the implications that Nyasha's hybrid subject-formation might hold for a psychoanalytic framework, nor do they question whether the unconscious can be addressed in the same way across differently interpellated subjectivities, obtaining in different historical moments and settings.

19. Catachresis is defined by J. Hillis Miller as "the violent, forced, or abusive use of a term from another realm to name something which has no 'proper' name" (72). As we shall see, the proper name instituted by the "bulimia diagnosis" is "feminism."

20. See Bahri (par. 2), Thomas (33), Bardolph (43-44), McWilliams (103-04), Vizzard (202-03), Uwakweh (77), Sugnet (33), Plasa (35) and Sugnet (33). To be fair to these scholars, much of the discussion has centred on

"anticolonial feminism" and "black feminism," and these designations obviously do acknowledge the fact that there are substantial differences between Western feminist concerns and the gender politics of the margins. My point is simply that even the name "feminism" may be viewed with suspicion by some constituencies.

21. Jacqueline Bardolph also makes this connection (38).

22. Pentolfe Aegerter reads *Nervous Conditions* within the rubric of womanism (231). Bosman, on the other hand, raises objections to the terms "feminist" and "womanist" in relation to Dangarembga's novel (99).

23. Caroline Rooney makes an interesting comment on this point: "A certain Western fascination with Hellenism may also be allied with a fascination with primitivism" (143, note 42).

24. For a similar argument, see Bahri (par. 16).

25. The ox is a castrated bull. Nyasha would thus hunger for a breakdown in the reproductive economy of bridewealth in patriarchy.

26. Wendy Woodward's article outlines the legal and historical background to the novel.

27. Pentolfe Aegerter also views the significance of the pots in this way (238).

28. I have followed Mkize's definition of the "culture-bound syndrome" (329).

29. I am grateful to Dr. Chris Welman for providing this information, and for first bringing *amafufunyane* to my attention.

30. The interested reader should compare these features with Nyasha's final outburst (Dangarembga 200-01). Further, Nyasha's voice takes on a Rhodesian accent and is not recognizably hers until the outburst is at an end. Significantly, *amafufunyane* attacks may only last for several minutes, and one of the associated symptoms is the patient's "speaking in tongues." So, for example, Swartz states that "a Zulu-speaking woman may speak in a male voice, and in Xhosa or English" (163). Given that traditional healers provide the explanation of "spirit possession" for *amafufunyane*, it would be tempting to relate this explanation to a point that Caroline Rooney makes in relation to Nyasha's outburst. Rooney argues that the "they" Nyasha refers to might apply to the ancestors equally

as well as it applies to the colonizers (138). Nyasha says that she does not hate her father and that "They want me to, but I won't" (Dangarembga 201). Rooney asks why the whites would want Nyasha to hate Babamukuru. Indeed, since "they" is a shifter that may map onto any signified, the ancestors would surely be a better candidate than the whites in the logic of the narrative. Although it is tempting to suggest that *amafufunyane* (as "spirit possession") exists as a possibility in *Nervous Conditions*, my emphasis on the socio-cultural determinants of Nyasha's illness must prevent my reading from developing in that direction. Rather, the analogy in this instance is anamorphic.

31. See Mkize 329.

32. Once again, there are interesting correspondences between the notion of school anxiety and Nyasha's hyperactive approach to her schoolwork. I have not found any evidence thus far of the prevalence of school anxiety in Zimbabwe.

II

MATERIAL CULTURE

Chapter 6:
Moving Forward From Death: Cultural Autopsy as a Guide to the Living

Jeffrey L. Geller

*N*ervous Conditions begins and ends with meditations on death. On the opening page, Dangarembga expressly introduces the themes of death and dying only to deny their centrality to the novel. *Nervous Conditions* is about survival, she protests, about successful struggle against untimely death. Her denial appears plausible: the novel's narrator and focal character, Tambudzai manages by means of her wit, determination, and wisdom, to overcome the forces arrayed against young African women and to enter a promising future.

There are three considerations, however, that show the limits of Dangarembga's denial. Beginning with the most obvious, her counterclaim that the novel's theme is survival reintroduces death as the complementary opposite: the threat of premature death is precisely what makes survival problematic. Second, *Nervous Conditions* chronicles the generation of a novelist, providing a portrait of the artist as a young woman. The artist, as portrayed by Tambu, is drawn toward the prospect of death as though she were forthrightly confronting a stalker. Inasmuch as the novel is about someone eminently concerned with death, it is also about death. Third, the concept of death has broad application in *Nervous Conditions*, covering the cessation of biological life functions, as exemplified by Nhamo's premature death and by Nyasha's moribund deterioration, as well as loss of identity and disintegration of community. In common parlance, we speak of a person's being dead *to* someone else. Falling under the influence of the English, Tambu's mother Mainini suggests, is another form of death (202). Mainini's contention can be paraphrased as follows: the loss of one's identity as a member of the community is as serious as biological expiration because it tends to destroy the family and the community. The most persuasive proof of Tambu's survival is the story she narrates of her own character development. Though the novel is a proclamation of survival, its power comes from the fact that Tambu's continued survival, like Nyasha's, remains an open question. *Nervous Conditions* is, after all, written in English. Bearing these considerations in mind, we can read *Nervous Conditions* as a case study of a survivor *and* as a series of strategic examinations of the obstacles that must be overcome.

The Cultural Autopsies: Achebe and Dangarembga

Given the broad application of the concept of death in *Nervous Conditions*, the novel fits into a genre that might be called "cultural autopsy." This genre brings together history and fiction, biography and fantasy, psychological inquiry and the tropes of suspense and mystery. As coroners are charged to determine whether suspicious deaths are the result of natural causes or foul play, novels within this genre address the question of whether a particular culture reached a dead end because of internal disintegration, external assault, or a combination of both. Unlike a coroner's inquest, which, in the majority of cases, is an either/or proposition, the issue in a cultural autopsy is a matter of degree.

The post-colonial period offers the opportunity for a critical survey of the events that led to colonial domination and of the devices that sustained the domination for several centuries. These events and devices have been a major theme, if not the major theme, of African literature. If any single work epitomizes this young tradition, it is Chinua Achebe's *Things Fall Apart*, which explores the conditions that contributed to the end of a way of life in Africa. Whereas most contemporary understandings of the novel emphasize the role of the individual and focus therefore on Okonkwo's problems within Igbo society, the interpretation that follows will examine the novel for the light it sheds on fatal flaws of Igbo society itself. Though Achebe might have written the novel with a view to recuperating vestiges of a bygone way of life, as though the colonial period were a prolonged interruption, his primary interest is in understanding current circumstances by tracing them to ancestral events. To understand the post-colonial period requires an understanding of the colonial period, which requires in turn an understanding of its antecedent, the precolonial period.

Achebe constructs a heroic narrative that traces the collapse of precolonial Africa to a set of tragic flaws, to specific excesses and deficiencies inherent in precolonial African societies. The general thesis of Achebe's novel, as indicated by its decidedly un-ironic title, is that societies wear out and fall apart. Like a swath of fabric that has outlived its usefulness, it becomes frayed and begins to disintegrate, a process that is part of the natural course of events. The success of European territorial expansion would not have been possible without the internal weakness of African societies, Achebe suggests, the tendency of African culture to disintegrate of its own accord. Moreover, the tendency toward disintegration from within, the impulse to unravel, is as inevitable as the passage of time. *Things Fall Apart* follows the rise and fall, the life and death, of one of the greatest men in Umuofia, Okonkwo. The conjunction of Okonkwo's suicide, an abomination and "offense against the earth" (190), and the shift in the final chapter to the perspective of the District Commissioner, whose book will be entitled *The Pacification of the Primitive Tribes of the Lower Niger,* leads to a sense of finality and resignation. By contrast, Dangarembga's *Nervous Conditions* joins the coroner's thought process in a gesture of hope that focuses on the future instead of the past. Dangarembga's Tambu is neither paralyzed nor disabled by the specter of death. She is determined to learn from the consequences of past events and to get on with life as modified by the insights.

While *Things Fall Apart* documents a failure to adapt, *Nervous Conditions* explores a quest for adaptation and inquires into the costs of adaptation. Though Tambu personifies the drive to adapt, she is no psychic contortionist, bending or modifying her attitudes and ideas in a manner that would compromise either her personal identity or her identity as a member of her family and people. From Nyasha, Tambu learns that resistance to character deformation is possible. In Nyasha's words, "[y]ou can't go on all the time being whatever's necessary. You've got to have some conviction, and I'm convinced I don't want to be anyone's underdog. It's not right for anyone to be that. But once you get used to it, well, it just seems natural and you just carry on. And that's the end of you" (117). In Nyasha's case, however, we find that resistance may displace, and not solve, the problem of character deformation. *Nervous Conditions* raises the following question: Does the kind and degree of adaptation necessary to succeed in the context of post-colonial Africa entail the sacrifice of individual, group, or cultural identity?

Some theorists have responded pessimistically to this question. For example, Cilas Kemedjio, in his analysis of Maryse

Conde's *Segou*, argues that at least one kind of cultural domination, "the conversion from orality to the written word" (126), undermines identity by destroying the unique qualities of African life. Kemedjio characterizes this change as an "identity mutation" (127). According to him:

> The collapse of the world order where existence and structuration determine the manifestation of the traditional word, of the universe which in its organization and functioning gave pertinence and validity to the griot and to his word, brings with it the reformulation of the conditions of survival for the word. The first movement in the invasion of imperial writing begins with the negative definition of peoples and cultures whose majority does not practice the written word: the polarization between simplifications and confusions that create essentialist and hierarchical categories attributing an overvalued primacy to the written word to the detriment of orality. (139)

Without the knowledge embodied in orality, Kemedjio concludes, African societies cannot maintain autonomous institutions (139).

Buoyed by her own experience, Dangarembga is decidedly more optimistic. In disagreement with both Achebe and Kemedjio, Dangarembga maintains that cultural death is not the inevitable consequence of either the passage of time or absorption into a new world order. She presents a picture of mutual accommodation that interweaves African and European ways of life. Though this essay will argue that she discovers and formulates an accommodation between traditional practices and the unique pressures of contemporary life, the success of her endeavor is no more important than the fact that she desires such an accommodation. By actively seeking viable options she takes the first step toward overcoming a pervasive sense of helplessness and victimization, toward defeating the mental habits born of colonialism. Active searching sheds the colonial mentality and shifts from the tragedy of passive submission to a story of active accommodation. It is no trivial matter that Dangarembga is writing her own story. The quest motif that is integral to the genre of autopsy literature, to in-quest, displays a harmony of form and content: activity on the part of the author, as reflected in the main protagonist, demonstrates that passive submission to externally imposed conditions is a thing of the past.

The respective story-telling devices employed by Achebe and Dangarembga are also worth comparing. Whereas Achebe tells his story in the third person from the perspective of a sympathetic but impersonal narrator, Dangarembga tells her story in the first person, from the perspective of one of the parties affected by the events in the narrative. Though much of *Nervous Conditions* can be understood as a coroner's inquest, as we will see below, Dangarembga shifts to the perspective of a medical doctor or psychotherapist who distinguishes morbid conditions from healthy conditions with the intention of benefiting future generations.

The Bewitchment of English Education

The question around which *Nervous Conditions* pivots, even while this question appears to recede into the background, is: "What caused Nhamo's death?" The autopsy is relevant to several related questions, which differ from the first in terms of the affected person and, more importantly, tense. What is killing Nyasha? What is threatening to kill Tambu?

Reinforcing the link between death and the loss of cultural identity, Dangarembga stresses that Nhamo had already begun to die to his family before his physical death. Before departing with Babamukuru, Nhamo had become "puffed up with his own importance" (47), belittling Tambu as though she were the African equivalent of chopped liver. Nhamo's identity had begun to erode during his first year at school, as marked by "the terrible change [that he] had forgotten how to speak Shona" the native language of his family (52). While Dangarembga describes this change as a sort of aphasia (53), she also sympathetically reports Mainini's more global view that Nhamo was "bewitched" (53-54). Having anticipated the tragic loss of her son, Mainini intuitively senses the terrible news of Nhamo's death before Babamukuru can make the announcement. While her anticipation appears at first to be a case of "feminine intuition," something a child's mother senses by extraordinary means, it has another more ordinary aspect. Given Mainini's reactions to her son's departure and to the ever increasing psychic distance between him and his family, we can understand Mainini as having *hypothesized* her son's death. Though tragic and shattering, Nhamo's death does not take her by surprise. Before Babamukuru announces the tragic news, Mainini spits at his feet, intoning "[y]ou and your education have killed my son" (54). By contrast, Nhamo's death takes everyone else, with the exception of Tambu, by complete surprise. Though perplexed, Babamukuru takes the loss stoically. He attributes the death to "the plans of the heavens," which are unknown to us (55). Consoling Nhamo's father, he suggests that "the One who knows . . . will keep you and comfort you even when evil strikes against you" (55). At this point in the narrative, Nhamo's mother has the upper hand, for unlike the others, she has not only a "theory," but also a confirming instance.

Tambu's response to her mother's explanation is cautiously agnostic. While hardly indifferent, she remains non-committal in the midst of the emotional turbulence. Her ambivalence in the face of what would otherwise be an unmitigated tragedy comes partly from the fact that Nhamo had already been lost to his family. Tambu was sad for her parents' loss more than for any loss of her own, because her brother had become a stranger to her (55). Of course, her ambivalence also arises from the fact that she is allowed to pursue her studies only after and because her brother is dead. Tambu is "vindicated" when she is offered the opportunity to take her brother's place at school (57). Having been the only person to take her mother's perspective seriously, Tambu must distance herself at this point from Mainini's position on English education. This distancing gestures at the possibility that Tambu will become every bit as estranged from her family as Nhamo had. The collision between the daughter's aspirations and the mother's fears take an enormous toll on Mainini. The prospect of losing her daughter to the same process of bewitchment causes her to fall ill. Once the decision is final, Mainini's position on the effect of English education has taken such firm hold in her mind that Tambu's impending departure causes her mother to become "so haggard and gaunt she can barely walk to the fields" (57).

Following Tambu's departure, the suspense builds because Nhamo's death, notwithstanding Mainini's initial explanatory success, remains a mystery. For anyone trained in the tradition of enlightenment metaphysics and scientific methodology, Mainini's hunch appears to be a "lucky" guess. Tambu is enough of a border dweller to appreciate her mother's thesis while at the same time treating it with skepticism. Tambu's agnostic response invites the reader, who in all likelihood is steeped in the Western tradition, if not in English education, to engage the question with an open mind. To her credit, Tambu is able to maintain an open mind despite the urgency of her situation: she must get to the bottom of the mystery, for her own life depends on it. While she does not dismiss her mother's position, she obviously cannot accept it, for that would entail that she abandon her aspirations and resign herself to village life.

Despite Tambu's confidence that she can withstand the pressures that proved fatal to her brother, the parallel between Tambu and Nhamo is unmistakable. Indeed *Nervous Conditions* serves as a demonstration and reminder that, all else being equal, a female may be more capable than a male. To make this point, the *ceteris paribus* clause must be established. This is no trivial matter, as Mary Wollstonecraft emphasized: until social conditions approach gender equality, "objective" empirical observation is useless as a means of assessing relative gender capabilities. In *Nervous Conditions*, a fictionalized account, the conditions can be equalized by poetic stipulation. Fusing the interests of social critic and novelist, Dangarembga's establishment of the *ceteris paribus* clause strengthens the analogy between Tambu and Nhamo, thus adding to the novel's suspense. Not only do Tambu and Nhamo draw from the same genetic material, the same bloodline, they have similar familial and cultural backgrounds. The parallel goes even further, far enough to build suspense concerning Tambu's endangerment. Tambu describes her state of mind when she is informed of the decision to accept her at Babamukuru's school as "triumphant" (57), which is reminiscent of Nhamo's being "puffed up." The potentially enriching process of cultural assimilation and the potentially lethal process of cultural dis-assimilation begin anew, to the horror and regret of Tambu's mother.

The sustained inquiry into the conditions of Nhamo's death is both aided and complicated by the novel's other primary sub-plot, Nyasha's life-threatening "rebellion." Whereas in the former case, the action takes place at a distance, thus heightening the mystery surrounding the death, the latter case takes place under conditions of the most intimate proximity. Sharing the perspective of the narrator, readers become co-participants, implicated as though they were Nyasha's bedfellows. Despite the greatly diminished distance and the fact that many of the pressures on Nyasha are the same as those that had been on Nhamo, her case remains every bit as perplexing as his. Clearly, the factor of gender constitutes a significant difference between the two, a difference that would favor Nhamo and place even greater pressure on Nyasha. However, the threat to identity posed by "English" education is present in both cases, and even more dramatic in the case of Nyasha, given her additional exposure to British culture.

The suspense associated with Nyasha's rebellion is never resolved, nor is there any promise along the way that it will be resolved. On the opening page of the novel, the narrator adumbrates the inconclusiveness of Nyasha's story when she states that the rebellion "*may* not in the end have been successful" (1, emphasis added). Yet Tambu has a keen interest in Nyasha's rebellion, and not only out of love. As students identify with the heroic characters in the novels they read and adopt the perspectives of the authors of their textbooks, if only to pass their classes, they absorb, as though by osmosis, the values implicit in English education. This would be one way of parsing Mainini's term "bewitchment." A rebellion of some form is necessary to preserve identity in the face of these transformative forces.

In addition to the pressures of race and gender, Tambu's identity is threatened by a third factor, her relatively modest socio-economic background, which further jeopardizes her survival as an *educated* member of her familial and social group. Confronting threats from every angle, Tambu is grateful to the "far-minded" Nyasha for attempting to negotiate the dangers of self-loathing, self-effacement, and shame concerning origins. Unfortunately, Nyasha's prognosis is not promising. By leaving Nyasha's case unsettled, Dangarembga guides the reader from the past, from a preoccupation with causal antecedents, to the future, placing greater emphasis on the vastly more promising days that await Tambu.

From Fanon to Dangarembga

Consistent with her proactive approach, Dangarembga focuses not on an internal impetus, not on a spontaneous tendency for things to fall apart, but on external threats to viability, specifically, on the threats of economic predation and social domination. Her narrative of survival draws attention to the necessity for defense on the part of those threatened with subordination. Specific defensive maneuvers can ward off psychological deformations that follow from and lead to relations of dominance and submission.

The title of Dangarembga's novel comes from Jean-Paul Sartre's preface to Frantz Fanon's research on the psychological impact of colonialism, *The Wretched of the Earth*. In that preface, Sartre observes that: "The status of 'native' is a *nervous condition* [emphasis added] introduced and maintained by the settler among colonized people *with their consent*" (20, emphasis in original).

The fact that Dangarembga takes her title from a treatise that concentrates primarily on the effects of colonialism should not blur the distinction between colonialism and its post-colonial aftermath, each of which presents a unique set of problems. By adopting this title despite the twenty-seven intervening years between the respective publications of *The Wretched of the Earth* (*Les damnes de la terre*, 1961) and *Nervous Conditions* (1988), Dangarembga asserts that post-colonial living conditions continue to jeopardize mental health. Like Fanon, Dangarembga traces the appearance of nervous disorders to power relations. Also like Fanon, she is concerned with power relations as they filter down from the macro-politics of regional domination to the micro-politics of family life.

The colonial period in Africa was characterized by colonial powers' haughty dismissal of indigenous practices. Fanon argues that "[t]he colonial world is a Manichean world . . . [the] settler paints the native as a sort of quintessence of evil" (41). With the curiosity predators have for their prey, colonial powers collected information and then denounced local cultural practices as primitive, going so far as to consider the obliteration of such practices their paternalistic responsibility. According to Fanon, "[t]he customs of the colonized people . . . are the very sign of . . . poverty of spirit and of their constitutional depravity" (42). Colonized populations were persuaded to renounce their cultural affiliations and to embrace the superior culture of the European conqueror. For example, French colonial subjects were induced to adopt French ways, to aspire to join the French in their ongoing celebration of national superiority. Colonial subjects who changed their allegiance, however, found themselves outside of their original culture and also outside of the culture they aspired to join. Regardless of their efforts, they would never be accepted as French. The ambivalence that resulted from these frustrated aspirations was a factor in the etiology of colonial *Nervous Conditions*. The effort by colonial powers to subvert indigenous culture can be seen as a more or less successful attempt at ethnocide. The extent of the destructiveness was lost on the colonizer, however, whose Manicheanism, according to Fanon, "goes to its logical conclusion and dehumanizes the native, or to speak plainly, it turns him into an animal. In fact, the terms the settler uses when he mentions the native are zoological terms" (42). Armed with Manicheanism, colonizers could administer large-scale cultural death without the burden of awareness.

Dangarembga suggests in *Nervous Conditions* that the ethnocidal tendencies Fanon had diagnosed in colonialism are also evident in post-colonialism. Having recognized the association between English education and death, Dangarembga's Mainini must confront not only the corrosive effects of such education on rural cultural patterns but also the fact that the persons for whom she cares most deeply *desire* to undergo the process. Aspirations to become educated play a central role in the drama of estrangement. When she accuses Babamukuru of having killed her son, her anguish is multiplied by the fact that Nhamo had been delighted to go away to school. Though Nhamo may have been too young to know better, he clearly welcomed the opportunity to be educated. The complicity of the victim, the *desire* to receive an English education, decreases the plausibility of explanations in terms of pure victimization. Dangarembga expressly connects education to suicide in the following passage:

> The debate and the tensions surrounding Babamukuru's departure [for England] centred not so much on the question of his going as on what to do with the children. Babamukuru was appreciative of the opportunity that had been offered; and further, to decline would have been a form of suicide. (14)

From Mainini's perspective, however, it is the acceptance of an English education, not its rejection, that constitutes a form of suicide.

The theme of suicide recalls the concluding chapters of Achebe's *Things Fall Apart*. With the help of Obierika, Okonkwo recognizes with perfect clarity that his time, and the time of his people, is up. In Obierika's words:

How do you think we can fight when our own brothers have turned against us? The white man is very clever. He came quietly and peaceably with his religion. We were amused at his foolishness and allowed him to stay. Now he has won our brothers, and our clan can no longer act like one. He has put a knife on the things that held us together and we have fallen apart. (162)

Okonkwo's ostensible suicide is the logical outcome of a series of events that spell the end of his way of life. Taking the broad sense of death that runs through *Nervous Conditions* and that is common to the genre of cultural autopsy, Okonkwo is already dead at the time of his suicide.

The issue of suicide, which resurfaces in the self-inflicted deterioration of Nyasha, helps distinguish the relative brutality of colonial ethnocide from post-colonial *seduction*. Notwithstanding Sartre's claim that colonial rule was maintained with the consent of the colonized people, a claim to which he was bound by his philosophy of absolute freedom, there is a qualitative difference between the consent of the people under colonialism and post-colonialism. Dangarembga's novel reveals the virtually irresistible allure of *wealth*, both educational and material. Whereas colonial subjects endured a campaign that asserted the inferiority of their culture, post-colonial subjects experience a barrage of images that suggest, often with great subtlety, the superiority of exogenous culture. From Mainini's point of view, death is death, regardless of whether it is colonial murder or post-colonial seduction and suicide. For her, the mere aspiration to leave the village to attend Babamukuru's boarding school gestures unwittingly toward suicide. Tambu's position is more subtle: being forewarned that English education produces character deformations that threaten individual and community identity, she is confident that she can receive the education offered to her without contributing to the death of her family and community. Potential victims may avert this disaster by withholding complicity. Tambu believes it is possible to receive an education *and* withhold complicity. To reach the point at which she can deal effectively with the threat, Tambu must take her mother's warnings seriously. Instead of seeing English education *per se* as lethal, however, she maintains that the attitudes normally induced by this education constitute the threat. For her, the key is to retain both pride of origin and a critical stance on the process of education she is undergoing.

As sympathetic as Dangarembga's treatment of Tambu's mother is, Mainini does not represent a viable option. She is an anachronism, immune to the seductive power of European culture. Generalizing from Tambu's solution, we might view her emphases on pride of origin and criticism of exogenous authority as imperatives for post-colonial identity retention. More significantly for the purposes of this essay, Tambu's imperatives provide a key to understanding the psychopathologies that confront post-colonial Africa. The primary obstacles to meeting the first imperative are shame over one's origins, in the event that English education demeans indigenous culture (explicitly or implicitly), and indifference to the plight of one's original culture, as though history had rendered it irrelevant. The primary obstacle to meeting the second imperative is the tendency to indulge the exogenous.

The Concealed Deficit of Wealth

According to the foregoing analysis, the change from colonial to post-colonial *Nervous Conditions* can be approached in terms of the shift of metaphors from murder to seduction and suicide. Whereas complicity plays a minimal role in the former, it is essential to the latter. The rhetoric of post-colonialism displays a marked shift away from domination toward cooperation. A tract entitled *Africa: World's Last Frontier*, published by the U.S. Foreign Policy Association in 1959, appeals for a "partnership in progress" (54). The tract claims that Africa's inhabitants "would like to become both producers and consumers" (55). The word "partnership," the author explains, "embodies the concept of brotherhood so deeply rooted in the Christian ethic. It embodies the concept of economic cooperation and the idea of racial harmony, both so necessary in dealing with Africa today" (55).

The rhetoric of Africa's "leap ahead . . . to create markets for commodities as well as for processes and techniques" (55) shifts to an even more patronizing tone when it discusses "interesting and challenging job opportunities for scores of thousands of Western technicians" (55). The seduction that leads to the abandonment and eventual death of indigenous culture is accomplished by a relentless transmission of images and information that represent the intellectual and material wealth of exogenous life. Departing from colonialism, post-colonial powers resist the impulse to derogate, to pass judgment on the inferiority of prospective "partners." Blatant hostility has given way to a highly refined iconography of luxury and privilege. By means of magazines, films, television broadcasts, and music videos, post-colonial powers evoke with their message of inclusiveness the simple and seemingly harmless desire to join up. Unlike the colonial period, in which loyalty to indigenous cultures was (and was correctly seen as) a source of resistance, the post-colonial period is marked by indifference on the part of powerful nations and multinational corporations to local practices. The seductive effect is enhanced by explicit statements of universal equality, even concerning the relative merit of different cultures, for such statements create a relaxed atmosphere in which admiration seems mutual and defense seems misguided.

Dangarembga's "fictional" treatment of post-colonial nervous conditions draws attention to the problem of wealth, thus to the role of economic factors in the formation of nervous disorders. Following her lead, I want to examine the relation between economics and psychopathology. The incidence of social and cultural degradation can be expected to rise as Africa is absorbed into the post-colonial international economic system. The process of degradation begins on the macro level. To progress economically, a developing nation must secure a significant influx of capital. "Capital infusion" or "capital penetration" as economic analysts refer to the necessary financial backing, comes from multinational corporations, "donor" countries, and the World Bank, among other sources. As a source of reserve capital, the International Monetary Fund offers assistance to nations facing problems concerning balance of payments, that is, to net importers of capital. Attracting an investment from a multinational corporation or procuring a loan from an international lending agency is contingent upon the supplicant-nation's ability and willingness to comply with guidelines laid down to govern domestic political and economic arrangements. These guidelines are referred to as "political conditionality" and "structural adjustment" respectively. Demands for structural adjustment include dissolving linkages between private corporations and the government, enacting labor law reform, minimum wage law reform, changes in tariffs, changes in import restrictions, changes in currency supply, changes in foreign currency relations, and measures to control inflation. Designed to increase stability and efficiency, these demands are sometimes resisted because they impose hardships on the population. Financial experts point out, however, that temporary hardship is the cost of long term prosperity. While this is true, it overlooks another cost exacted by such prescriptions, namely, that overhauling the political and economic patterns of a population causes changes in the group's identity. Though the imposition of democracy and free market economy seems from one perspective to bring unqualified advantages, these advantages alter the social fabric.

If Dangarembga were a social theorist writing an economic treatise, she would need to establish the linkage between the macro-level and the micro-level, demonstrating precisely how large-scale political and economic phenomena affect social and personal relations. As a novelist, she can be content to offer a compelling picture of a small group of people affected by the changes. *Nervous Conditions* personifies the necessary linkage in the character of Babamukuru, who, though not a purveyor of material goods, is very wealthy by African standards and is a purveyor of what Pierre Bourdieu calls "cultural capital." If the thesis linking political and economic transformation to social and psychological transformation is correct, multinational corporations, international lending institutions, and donor countries create the world in their own image.

Members of the community who administer the influx of capital, both material and cultural, while first to realize economic gains, are also more susceptible than other members of the community to the nervous conditions associated with post-colonial development. The debt owed by the local elite, the indigenous administrators who represent the population, is exacted partly as allegiance. In *Nervous Conditions*, Nhamo's uncle, aunt, and cousins acquire "English" habits, practices, and values. The cultural capital they acquire distinguishes them from their relations. Though this appears to be a boon, adding to their freedom by enabling them to be equally comfortable in London and in the Shona villages of Zimbabwe, it serves instead to distance them from both possible "peer groups." Babamukuru's family cannot readily readjust to village life. As Tambu observes upon their return, "[i]f they could not enjoy themselves with us, there was no reason for them to have come home" (43). Burdened by their hard-won distinction, they lose the spirit of unity that once connected them to their extended family. To his credit, Babamukuru retains his sense of loyalty to and responsibility for his extended family despite the increasing cultural estrangement. What remains, a shadow of the robust network of common interests and concerns that had united the family, is a paternalistic relationship between rich benefactor and poor supplicant.

The burden of distinction imposes the obligation of keeping up appearances, of justifying privilege by appearing superior. In large measure this is accomplished through the mystique of education. The only person to see through the facade, to question the value of European education is Mainini, who is suspicious that the new tastes and mannerisms, if not superficial affectations, serve only to alienate relatives, friends, and associates. The rich uncle's beneficence, though estimable, does not compensate Mainini for her sense of loss. Dangarembga does not lay blame for this estrangement on Babamukuru, preferring instead a structuralist approach that traces his behavior to his position. When one becomes a prime mover of society, one turns the spheres of the social universe by eliciting imitation. To serve in this capacity, a person must accept the obligation to behave impeccably, as though he or she were divine, which gives rise to a condition that might be called Distinction Maintenance Disorder. The primary symptom of this disorder is the compulsion to be perfect, at least in appearance, which may lead to such secondary pathologies as anxiety over being "seen through" or narcissistic absorption in one's public image. Though these pathologies are evident to some extent in Babamukuru, Dangarembga concentrates on the consequences of his unrealistic expectations for those nearest to him, particularly Nyasha.

As a person of distinction, Babamukuru imposes severe constraints on his immediate family, constraints that do not allow Nyasha the normal range of human frailty. Trapped by conflicting needs, she must try to reconcile the drive for perfection, a drive imposed on her by her father, with the desire to be human. Consistent with the latter, she has a deep desire to demonstrate her fallibility *to her father*, as revealed by her tendency toward deliberate carelessness in her social dealings. After one of her deliberate curfew violations (111-12), her father perceives her as having behaved "like a whore" (114). One of her tactics, of course, is simply to quit eating (118). Opposed to this desire, and bolstered by affection for her father, she also wants to honor his excessive demands. Her frustration comes to a head, so to speak, when she punches her father, a transgression that is so far outside the (cultural and transcultural) bounds of acceptability that it cries out for attention:

> "I told you not to hit me," said Nyasha, punching him in
> the eye . . . Babamukuru bellowed and snorted that if
> Nyasha was going to behave like a man, then by his mother
> who was at rest in her grave he would fight her like one.
> They went down on to the floor, Babamukuru alternately
> punching Nyasha's head and banging it against the floor,

> screaming or trying to scream but only squeaking, because
> his throat had seized up with fury, that he would kill her
> with his bare hands; Nyasha screaming and wriggling and
> doing what damage she could. Maiguru and Chido could
> not stay out of it any longer. They had to hold him. (115)

The impossible situation in which Nyasha finds herself may shed
light, incidentally, on the mystery of Nhamo's unlikely death.
Though there is little explicit textual evidence to this effect,
circumstantial evidence suggests that his general weakness of
character made him particularly susceptible to his uncle's demands.
Nhamo's experience at Babamukuru's house, for example, was
simply overwhelming:

> Nhamo had had a refrain with which he had punctuated
> his enthusiastic and reverent descriptions of the luxury and
> comfort of Babamukuru's house. "Not even the Whites,"
> he had used to carol in an impressionable descant, "not
> even the Whites themselves could afford it!" (61)

Of the competing explanations, including undiagnosed mumps (the
medical opinion, 55), jealous spirits (Nhamo's father's explanation,
55), bewitchment (his mother's hypothesis), and the unbearable
burden of excessive expectation (by analogy with Nyasha), the latter
has at least some claim to etiological significance.

On a parallel course with the overt conflict between Nyasha
and her father, another conflict rages inside her. The nervous condition Dangarembga addresses most explicitly in the novel is
Nyasha's eating disorder, which ties together in a single pathology
problems of identity under assault by conflicting expectations. In
addition to her struggle to be both human and perfect, Nyasha has
two other mutually antagonistic desires, namely, to avail herself of
the plenitude that signals and rewards her family's rise in status
and to retain her identity. These desires correlate with the desire to
eat, to consume in proportion with one's ability to procure, and the
desire to remain thin, to prevent the physical "deformation" that
normally attends eating.

As is often the case in psychopathology, Nyasha's condition illustrates a convergence between the literal and the figurative, the concrete and the symbolic. *Nervous Conditions* establishes an analogy between physical and intellectual wealth and an analogy between ingesting food and taking in information. Greeting his brother Babamukuru upon his return from England, Tambu's father, Jeremiah, makes the following speech:

> Our returning prince. Do you see him? Observe him well. He has returned. Our father and benefactor has returned appeased, having *devoured* English letters with a *ferocious appetite*! Did you think degrees were *indigestible*? If so look at my brother. He has *digested them!* (36, emphasis added)

Other speakers echo these sentiments, noting that the prince has returned "Full of knowledge" (36). Given these analogies, Nyasha's eating disorder represents symbolically the simultaneous desires to absorb and expel English education. The desire to expel, in this context, is an expression of Tambu's second imperative, namely, to remain critical of exogenous authority.

On the problems of maintaining criticism in the face of pressure to adopt Western values, Dangarembga is more insightful than Fanon. During decolonization, Fanon argues, there is a shift from a strategy of direct assault on the conditions of native culture to an appeal to the virtues of Western culture:

> As soon as the native begins to pull on his moorings, and to cause anxiety to the settler, he is handed over to well-meaning souls who in cultural congresses point out to him the specificity and wealth of Western values. (43)

The appeals to the superiority of Western culture, according to Fanon, fall on deaf ears:

> But every time Western values are mentioned they produce in the native a sort of stiffening or muscular lockjaw. During the period of decolonization, the native's reason is

appealed to. He is offered definite values, he is told frequently that decolonization need not mean regression, and that he must put his trust in qualities which are well tried, solid and highly esteemed. But it so happens that when the native hears a speech about Western culture he pulls out his knife, or at least he makes sure it is within reach . . . [In] revenge, the native laughs in mockery when Western values are mentioned in front of him. (43)

Using images that tie his analysis to Dangarembga's emphasis on eating disorders, Fanon argues that:

In the colonial context the settler only ends his work of breaking in the native when the latter admits loudly and intelligibly the supremacy of the white man's values. In the period of decolonization, the colonized masses mock at these very values, insult them, and vomit them up. (43)

Contrary to Fanon's confident assertions, Dangarembga suggests that a new generation of *Nervous Conditions* makes the "vomiting up" of Western values highly problematic.

To see the precise connection between Tambu's second imperative and Nyasha's symptoms, we need to recognize that moral criticism that depends for its existence on economic prosperity all but forecloses challenges to the system that generates prosperity. The style of living required for intensive, sustained moral reflection, as conceptualized by Stanley Cavell in his *Pursuits of Happiness*, requires more than a fleeting satisfaction of needs. Cavell contends that such moral reflection requires freedom from the pursuit of necessities, leisure time to contemplate what really counts in life (Geller and Vela). Though he does not expressly generalize this thesis beyond the American context, its implications are worth considering, if only to reveal its limits. Objecting to the conditions necessary for critique appears to be performatively self-contradictory, susceptible to the adage, "Don't bite the hand that feeds you." Given this folk logic, a cloak of immunity protects economic success from criticism. Moreover, high economic productivity is widely accepted as a criterion for assessing not only "standard of living" but also "quality of life." Despite the wisdom embedded in folk logic and the comfort of consensus, Africans must examine critically the material foundation of post-colonial culture. For them, the key question is not whether needs are met, but how they are met. Reflecting sentiments that are widespread, though only ambivalently endorsed, *Nervous Conditions* challenges the legitimacy of using productivity as an essential criterion for assessing quality of life.

From the point of view of the post-colonial subject being assimilated into an international order, surplus production creates not only the ability to exercise moral insight but also a distinct range of moral blindness. English education, together with its con-comitant economic privileges, instills a prejudice in its own favor, a prejudice that masquerades as common sense. This disorder, which might be called Selective Criticism Occlusion, is often part of a syndrome that also includes Fetish of Economic Success. The para-dox of prosperity-dependent criticism is that economic success becomes an article of worship that transcends criticism.

From Tambu's point of view, English education is a port of entry into a new range of experience and possibility. But if this education and the conditions that make it possible are virtually exempt from criticism, other cultural backgrounds, including tra-ditional forms of culture, will inevitably appear inferior. Thus, the innocent and all too human desire to enter a new world slides im-perceptibly toward the desire to escape the old world. The better the students, the lower their resistance to "reform," even to the point of wishing to hasten the process. The imperatives to main-tain pride of original affiliation and remain critical of the new are thus linked: failure to achieve the second predisposes one to fail at the first.

Returning from abstract imperatives to concrete courses of action, we find that Tambu manages with surprising ease to cel-ebrate her education while resisting complete assimilation. One might say that the balancing act comes naturally to her. Recall that balancing opposed attitudes toward English education is an ongoing requirement for Tambu, her uncle representing extreme sympathy and her mother representing extreme antipathy. Ambivalence, which would normally be regarded as symptomatic of a nervous condition, is instrumental in maintaining the necessary balance, hence instrumental in combating post-colonial nervous conditions. Given the pervasiveness of such ambivalence in post-colonial Africa, Tambu's balancing act is merely one instance of a widely distributed survival skill.

Another of Tambu's personal strengths that aids her in reaching the necessary balance is also widely distributed in post-colonial Africa. Her identity as an African is a significant asset, serving as a source of ironic distance: the ineliminable sense of her own otherness *vis-à-vis* her education impedes complete absorption, prevents her from becoming a mere product of that education. The unbridgeable gap of alterity that, according to Fanon, was a cause of identity deformation under colonialism, is a source of resistance, a measure of identity protection, in the post-colonial period. The ironic distance provides an incentive to turn criticism acquired by means of an English education back on English education thereby effectively disarming the implicit judgements of the inferiority of African culture.

Conclusion

Reviewing the findings of three examples of cultural autopsy, this essay has explored Chinua Achebe's *Things Fall Apart*, which addresses the transition from precolonialism to the colonial period, Frantz Fanon's *The Wretched of the Earth*, which addresses the transition from colonialism to the period of "decolonization" and Tsitsi Dangarembga's *Nervous Conditions*, which addresses the transition to the post-colonial period. Unlike the first two, Dangarembga's future-oriented narrative demonstrates the advantage of putting autopsy to work, of harnessing death as a resource for the living. By noting the condition that led to severe identity deformations and to the extinction of many indigenous cultural practices, Africans can guard against the recurrence of the tendencies that define colonialism. Dangarembga's novel is rich in such practical wisdom. Of greatest significance are Tambu's two imperatives, namely, to avoid undervaluing indigenous culture and to avoid overvaluing exogenous culture. There are various obstacles, however, to meeting these imperatives. Material and educational wealth can bring a dangerous combination of arrogance and hidden intellectual poverty. But they can also create conditions for intensive cultural critique, for the even-handed analysis of both indigenous and exogenous influences. One advantage of the post-colonial period, as indicated in this essay, is that it allows for this manner of critique. But if potential critics are dazzled by the new system, educational and economic, or seduced by the prospect of personal gain, the post-colonial dividend will disappear. The promising new period will be marred by psychological deformations as troubling as those under colonialism.

Chapter 7:
Dangarembga's Dirty Work: Acting Up and Speaking Out, "Good Medicine" for Africa

Giuliana Lund

Illness has long been a central trope in European discourse on Africa. This colonial obsession with pathology has, moreover, left its mark upon African writers and theorists of the postcolonial. While colonial writers emphasized the need for European medical intervention in Africa, anticolonial writers commonly viewed illness as a mark of transgression, of excessive intimacy with the African environment and peoples. This anticolonial literature of ecological, cultural, and sexual "miscegenation" paved the way for a postcolonial vision of hybridity as pathology. The highly influential work of Frantz Fanon, in particular, has encouraged the appropriation of Western medical discourses to articulate the pain and suffering of colonized peoples. Tsitsi Dangarembga distinguishes herself from the majority of writers who apply Western medical discourse to postcolonial criticism in that her critique has a double edge—one cutting to the heart of colonial ideology, the other taking a stab at the patriarchal tendencies within postcolonial theory itself. Dangarembga not only undermines the Western stereotype of the African woman as a source of contagion, she also challenges the propensity of male writers to critique the corruption of the colonial or postcolonial state through an abstract language of pathology that constructs woman as a symbol, rather than a participant, in nationalist struggles.

To properly measure the radical transformation wrought in traditional medical discourse by Tsitsi Dangarembga, it is essential to place her works within the larger context of colonial and postcolonial discourses on pathology. This essay will thus begin with a brief foray into colonial and postcolonial constructions of Africa as the "hot zone" before engaging in a close reading of medical discourse in *Nervous Conditions* and "Everyone's Child."

European colonists, lacking previous exposure to tropical environments, were highly susceptible to the wide range of unfamiliar diseases that met them when they attempted to penetrate into the interior of the African continent.[1] However, while the conception of Africa as "the white man's grave" was based to a degree on historical experience, it also reflected European fantasies about the "dark continent." The image of Africa as a hotbed of disease and African women as the agents of disease took center stage in a racist colonial discourse that viewed the African environment, and thus the African people, as inherently inferior. Jean Comaroff has shown that from the early nineteenth century "'Africans' personified suffering and degeneracy, their environment a hothouse of fever and affliction," and that as the century progressed, "the black body became ever more specifically associated with degradation, disease, and contagion" (305-06).

In contrast, Europeans considered medical prowess as evidence of their superior civilization and therefore used it to justify imperialist expansion.[2] To this day, Western medicine and hygiene are widely considered the greatest gifts of colonization; public health is one of the few arenas in which foreign intervention in Africa is usually accorded unquestioned legitimacy. However, in the colonization of Africa, "public health was to serve in the discipline of black populations," and what health facilities were available for natives were operated by the colonial state—often the police or military.[3] Comaroff has revealed that from the earliest evangelical expeditions to Africa, imperialism was justified as a "healing mission" that would save Africans from the "plagues" of barbarism, slavery, and disease. The exploration of Africa was imagined in terms of the medical discourse of the period, which emphasized an invasive gaze that could explain a patient's symptoms and penetrate the inner secrets of the human body. According to Comaroff, this medical gaze "became increasingly tangible in discourses about exploration in Africa, where the quest for knowledge of the interior likened the continent to the human body." Indeed, explorers like Mungo Park "reduced Africa to the body of a black female yielding herself to the white male explorer," and "it was science that articulated and authorized such imagery" (Comaroff 308).[4] The pathological qualities of the African environment were thus embodied for Europeans in the African woman. Because of her presumed sexual availability to male adventurers, her porous flesh formed the key interface with the jungle; she was represented as the covert agent of darkness, a creature whose very intimacy threatened to infect the explorer and by extension his race.[5] One of the greatest preoccupations of missionaries in southern Africa therefore was controlling the sexuality of the African woman by confining her body in European clothes and restricting her relations to men through Christian marriage.

Significantly, metaphors of disease appealed as much to

anticolonial writers as to colonial writers because such metaphors could be construed to imply that colonization was as dangerous and corrupting for the European as it was for the African. Thus Conrad's anti-imperialist novel, *Heart of Darkness*, confirms the pathological vision of Africa and the African woman present in imperialist novels such as Rider Haggard's *She*. Despite the implicit critique of Western culture at the obscure heart of anti-imperialist literature by writers like Conrad and the influential French author, Louis-Ferdinand Céline, these works consolidate a vision of Africa in which bodies decompose, individuals are corrupted, and civilization disintegrates. The Africa of Conrad, Céline, and their cohorts is perceived as a site of excess that, as Christopher Miller has pointed out in *Blank Darkness*, baffles Western teleologies and subverts representation. Conrad's wildly dancing and strikingly inarticulate cannibals find an echo in Céline's savages, who are described as frenzied, hysterical pieces of the night. For European protagonists encountering the African environment with its medley of incomprehensible cries, language itself becomes deranged and madness ensues.

The "horror" engendered by this supposedly diseased continent, so evident in *Heart of Darkness*, is figured by Céline as visceral, gut-wrenching disgust—that is, as nausea. Indeed, the concept of nausea so crucial to existentialism was first developed in Céline's pseudo-autobiographical novel, *Journey to the End of the Night* (1932), in which Africa is depicted as a phantasmatic terrain of disease and death. In addition to interminable bouts with parasites, the narrator repeatedly succumbs to delirium, hysteria, and a nausea that seeks to expunge from the body all environmental contaminants. The concept of nausea was further developed by Sartre in his pre-war novel of the same name, and became standard currency in existentialist circles. Frantz Fanon took up this existentialist preoccupation with nausea in *Black Skin, White Masks*, adapting it to the colonized man's [sic] experience of social alienation, self-loathing, and disgust. Like the tradition it draws on, Fanon's colonial nausea is male-centered, taking as its (anti-

)hero the lone male intellectual who stands against the hypocritical constraints of a society that wants to dictate, amongst other things, whom he is allowed to bed.

Fanon was certainly not alone in challenging European discourses of pathology. Many early writers from Africa and the Caribbean engaged with this aspect of the European tradition, most notably, Aimé Césaire, whose *Notebook of a Return to the Native Land* seems to revel in images of corruption and obscure biomedical terminology. Césaire, however, traces the mental and physical corruption of his people not to any innate debility, but to the traumas of colonization. Like Césaire, Fanon shifts the ground of colonialist discourse on illness from the racial flaws of the native to the social pathology of domination and the crisis of the hybrid subject. In both *Black Skin, White Masks* and *The Wretched of the Earth*, he articulates a vision of the colonial as pathological that turns his Western medical and philosophical training back upon Europe. In addition, he extends the psychoanalytic notion of the talking cure to the socio-historical world of colonialism, using writing to diagnose the ills of the colonized.

Yet, while writing is an important analytic tool for Fanon, he argues that only violent revolutionary action can ultimately end the colonial crisis and cure African ills. Despite the fact that Fanon recognized that extreme violence was the cause of the Algerians' symptoms, he believed in the power of violence as therapy, viewing war as a cure for the Algerians' ills, and maintaining a connection between health and soldiery that makes the back-to-the-front attitude of World War I psychiatrists like Rivers seem tame. Of course Fanon's overall objectives differed from that of Rivers, since part of Rivers' task in treating shell-shocked soldiers was to make them fit enough to fight once more for queen and country, whereas Fanon did not wish to send his patients back to the colonial system that had scarred them but into battle against it. Fanon appropriates from psychoanalytic theory the conception of hysteria as a physical manifestation of mental anguish. His understanding of hysteria, however, is closer to that of Rivers and other post-World War I psychiatrists than it is to Freud's, particularly in terms of gender. For while Freud primarily treated women for hysterical symptoms caused by repressed sexual urges, Rivers treated soldiers for the traumatic stress inflicted by trench warfare, in which men could not adequately defend themselves or act out their aggressive impulses.[6] In consequence, Fanon reads hysteria in the Algerian context as a "reactionary psychosis" resulting from emasculating fear and domination. Almost all of the case studies he records center around male experience. The rare case that deals in any depth with an Arab woman does so peripherally. One case, for instance, involves the treatment for impotence of a soldier whose wife has been raped.[7]   For Fanon, hysteria is not caused by the repression of female sexuality, but by the Algerian man's inability to adequately control access to the body of "his" woman. The rape of the woman functions as a symbol for the rape of the land, and nation-building relies upon a construction of the native woman as a violated symbol whose purity—and chastity—will be restored through the violent self-assertion of the Algerian man.

Ironically, Tsitsi Dangarembga's novel *Nervous Conditions* opens with an epigraph from *The Wretched of the Earth* attributed to Fanon, although actually taken from Sartre's introduction, that draws immediate attention to the pathology of colonialism. Dangarembga's elision of Sartre's role, and by extension European philosophy's role, in the elaboration of pathological discourses on colonization is revealing. It points to her refusal to become entrapped in the Western paradigm of pathology, a refusal that is played out within the novel by Tambudzai, the narrator. Of course, such attempts at escape are never totally successful, and this is as true for Dangarembga as it is for Tambu. Considering her training in Western modes of psychiatry and medicine, it is difficult to imagine Dangarembga leaving all of that intellectual baggage behind in her diagnosis of gender relations in Zimbabwe. However, while Dangarembga does employ a rhetoric of pathology that has its origin in Eurocentric views of Africa, she clearly undermines the hegemony of Western scientific discourse.

As a young girl, Tambudzai, the narrator of *Nervous Conditions*, is keen to escape from her village because she has already begun to internalize the colonial perspective of rural Africa as dirty: not only unpleasant, but unhygienic. At the time she believes that joining white society (in the form of a convent school) means "to take another step upwards in the direction of [her] freedom. Another step away from the flies, the smells, the fields and the rags; from stomachs which were seldom full, from dirt and disease, from . . . mother's chronic lethargy" (183). Yet even in this state of relative naiveté, Tambu recognizes that embracing this Western conception of progress necessitates leaving something behind, namely the river Nyamarira that she loves (183). This river has great symbolic importance for Tambu's community because it represents purity, cleanliness, and feminine vitality. In abandoning Nyamarira, Tambu forsakes more than local geography: in fact, she relinquishes native conceptions of freedom, femininity, and health.

When Tambu arrives at the mission where she is to be educated, her first lesson is that cleanliness is next to godliness, or at least whiteness:

> The absence of dirt was proof of the other-worldly nature of my new home. I knew, had known all my life, that living was dirty and I had been disappointed by the fact. I had often helped my mother to resurface the kitchen floor with dung. I knew, for instance, that rooms where people slept exuded peculiarly human smells just as the goat pen smelt goaty and the cattle kraal bovine. It was common knowledge among the younger girls at school that the older girls menstruated into sundry old rags which they washed and reused and washed again. I knew, too, that the fact of menstruation was a shamefully unclean secret that should not be allowed to contaminate immaculate male ears by indiscreet reference to this type of dirt in their presence. Yet at a glance it was difficult to perceive dirt in Maiguru's

house. After a while, as the novelty wore off, you began to see that the antiseptic sterility that my aunt and uncle strove to achieve could not be attained beyond an illusory level. (70-71)

In this passage, the mature Tambu reveals her childhood disappointment that "living was dirty." At the same moment, however, she hints that the very concept of "dirt" is problematic. Indeed, Dangarembga seems to support the idea, summed up by Mary Douglas, that "dirt" is merely matter out of place.[8] In her village, Tambu observes, smells, animals, and even dung have their proper place; they are only qualified as dirt according to the Western perspective propagated in the missions. Moreover, the "antiseptic sterility" of the mission is ultimately proven to be an illusion: every time a bus passes through it raises a pall of dust that blankets every surface. Every lifestyle inevitably produces its own form of dirt, the Westernized Christian lifestyle of the mission being no exception.

With regard to women, the Western biases inherent in the mission conception of dirt are compounded by the patriarchal biases of traditional Shona society. Menstruation, for instance, is considered dirty, as is speech about menstruation: as Tambu explains, "the fact of menstruation was a shameful unclean secret that should not be allowed to contaminate male ears by indiscrete reference" (70-71). Babamukuru, a devoted Christian as well as the patriarch of his clan, beats his daughter Nyasha and treats her like "a whore with dirty habits" as much for her vocal protestations as for her flirtations (117). This link between dirt and the imposition of silence upon women is crucial to understanding the double thrust of Nervous Conditions in its attack against Western constructions of hygiene and indigenous repression of women's sexuality and self-expression. Indeed, by even discussing female sexuality and bodily functions in her novel, Dangarembga has broken social taboos and opened herself to the accusation of writing a "dirty" book. Dangarembga's novel could never find a place in the immaculate library at the nun's school with its abundance of approved "books whose glossy covers never seemed to get dirty or torn" (195).

   Nervous Conditions opens with Tambu's bold statement that "I was not sorry when my brother died. . . . I shall not apologize but begin by recalling the facts as I remember them that led up to my brother's death, the events that put me in a position to write this account . . ." (1). In recounting Nhamo's death, Tambu dwells on the fact that her brother "did not like travelling by bus because, he said, it was too slow. Moreover, the women smelt of unhealthy reproductive odours . . ." (1). The interjection of "he said" marks off Nhamo's point of view from that of the narrator, who clearly does not share his perspective about the objectionable nature of public transportation or of the functions of the human body, most particularly the female body. Fittingly, Nhamo's end comes not through the dangers of public transportation but in a sanitary Western hospital that nonetheless fails to save him or even allow him to die surrounded by his family. Like Western hygiene, Western medicine falls painfully short.

   Tambu opposes Nhamo's attitudes about dirt, relating them metonymically to his death. She cannot comprehend Nhamo's distaste for walking home from the bus terminal along the river Nyamarira, for "[t]he road wound down by the fields where there were always some people with whom to pass minutes of the day— enquiring about their health and the health of their family, admiring the broadleafed abundance of the maize crop when it was good, predicting how many bags the field would yield" (2). Where Nhamo only sees squalor and dirt, Tambu sees a thriving, productive community. The fact that Tambu pauses to enquire about the health of other families is not incidental here. Rather, it indicates her awareness that health flourishes in the same environments where communication and community flourish. Speech and the expression of mutual concern is no mere formality; such fellowship provides vital support that saves individuals from alienation and the conse-

quent mental and physical decline experienced by Nhamo and later
Nyasha.

Tambu eventually realizes that the healthful appearance
of the mission is merely a facade hiding painful, festering sores,
though primarily of a psychological rather than a biological nature. While Tambu's mother has an exaggerated distrust of European ways, her claim that her son's and niece's illnesses derive
from their leaving the traditions of their homeland is not unfounded.
Her concerns about Tambu going to the mission are justifiable, if
extreme: "You, Jeremiah, are you mad? Have you eaten some
wild shrub that has gone to your head? I think so, otherwise how
could you stand there and tell me to send my child to a place of
death, the place where my first living child died! Today you are
raving. She will not go. Unless you want me to die too. The anxiety will kill me" (56). The mission, and by implication colonialism, is thus characterized as the cause of death and madness, both
for those who embrace it and for those who suffer the consequences
of being left behind. Dangarembga deftly reverses the Western
stereotype of Africa: no longer is Africa "the white man's grave";
instead, colonization is the African's grave. In her anxiety for her
daughter, Tambu's mother becomes severely depressed: she "hardly
ate anything . . . when she was able to swallow something it lay
heavily in her stomach" (57). This inability to eat foreshadows
Nyasha's nervous condition.

Even Tambu is "unnerved" by her encounters with colonial culture (110). Upon arrival at the mission, with its surfaces
scrubbed to the point of dullness, Tambu assimilates its sanitary
regime, taking a long bath after which she admires herself in the
mirror—thus hygiene writes Western civilization upon the home,
the psyche, and the female body. Nyasha, too, spends a great deal
of time grooming and studying herself in front of a mirror to see
whether she measures up to the idealized Western image of the
"svelte" woman. The conflicting forces of Western and Shona feminine ideals eventually result in Nyasha's mental breakdown. On
the one hand, Nyasha attempts to embody the Western standard of

the healthy, attractive body; on the other hand, she aspires to the silent acceptance expected of Shona women with regard to their sexuality. Paradoxically, Nyasha's bulimia and vocal outbursts represent her rebellion against and her simultaneous entrapment within these gender constructs. The Western food Nyasha is force-fed by her parents becomes a symbol for the Western culture that is habitually stuffed down the throats of the colonized. Nyasha's silent consumption of this food is soon broken by the sounds of her "retching and gagging" (198-99). Shortly thereafter, the surface quiet of her docile and dutiful studying of Western textbooks is torn asunder by a screaming fit in which "[s]he rampaged, shredding her history book between her teeth ('Their history. Fucking liars. Their bloody lies.')" (201).

Through the multiple symptoms of her protagonists, Dangarembga not only underlines the pathological nature of colonization, but highlights the postcolonial "pathology" of split subjectivity. Indeed, for Dangarembga, hybridity is a nervous condition—and a nervous condition that affects women doubly because their position within the traditional African patriarchy duplicates their inferior status as colonized subjects. Nyasha's nausea signifies her inability to incorporate and assimilate Western and Shona expectations of female behavior, which she expels both literally and symbolically through her mouth. Her nausea is a sign of her hybridity, the recognition that "I'm not one of them but I'm not one of you" (201). Indeed, the entire Shona elite suffers from a cultural indigestion of the first order (40): after all, argues Tambu's mother, "you couldn't expect the ancestors to stomach so much Englishness" (203). Being unable to stomach "Englishness" implies a male point of view; bulimia, on the other hand, is an explicitly female gendered version of nausea. Dangarembga also transforms the trope of nausea by insisting that it is actively self-inflicted (bulimia, is not, after all, the same as anorexia): even in her greatest moments of crisis, Nyasha maintains her agency, her rebellious spirit, and her ability to articulate her trauma.

Ironically, the modern appliances of Western hygiene—
toothbrush and toilet—become the very instruments of Nyasha's
purges. Tambu, too, falls awry of Western and Shona notions of
cleanliness. From a traditionalist point of view, she is not unlike
the dirt she attempts to scrub away from her mother's toilet, for
like Nyasha's, hers is a body that refuses to conform to colonial
and patriarchal norms, a body out of place, a nauseous body doing
"dirty work" (140). By virtue of their hybridity, Tambu and Nyasha
fall into the cracks between the reified roles dictated to them by
European and Shona customs. In some respects their situation parallels that of the hysterics discussed by Hélène Cixous and
Catherine Clément in their essay "The Sorceress and the Hysteric,"
though the woman of color finds no place in their discussion. Indeed, *Nervous Conditions* pushes the limits of Western feminism
just as it pushes the limits of postcolonial theory and medical discourse.

Nervous Conditions contains numerous scenes of hysteria, manifested in the classic symptoms of psychosomatic illness,
paralysis, muteness, deranged language, and frantic outbursts. The
symptomology of Nyasha's nervous condition indicates that the
crux of her problem lies in the double imposition of silence on the
colonized woman: the cost of submission and self-effacement is
depression, psychological paralysis, and spiritual starvation. In this
respect, the depictions of Nyasha's outbursts recall the Freudian
observation that excessive repression is the primary culprit in neurosis. However, whereas Freud would have been inclined to return
these women to their homes resigned to their lot, Dangarembga
follows Fanonian social psychology in illustrating the impossibility of "digesting" colonial oppression. Clearly, women's acting
out of rebellion in pathological symptoms cannot be treated through
discipline or the performance of a strict sanitary regime, since treatment enforcing social conformity is sure to provoke further problems.[10]

Nyasha's initial contacts with Western psychologists are
thwarted by racist presumptions about the African personality. It

is doubtful whether even a sympathetic doctor will be able to halt Nyasha's downward spiral of self-destruction. Yet, in contrast to the painful failures of Western medicine in the cases of Nyasha and Nhamo, Lucia, a rural woman without significant formal education, is able to save her sister, Tambu's mother, from emotional paralysis and starvation through an insightful approach that Dangarembga dubs "very good medicine." Lucia's "good medicine" involves breaking the taboo of silence to acknowledge publicly her sister's depression, despite the fact that usually "an illness of this nature is kept quiet and secret" (185). "Good medicine" involves bringing Tambu's mother back out into the community and reviving her desire to nurture others. In saving her sister, Lucia ignores Western medical practices that generally focus on curing individuals of specific illnesses without reference to their environment or community. In order to be successful, however, Lucia must also challenge the sexist reign of silence that would deny the real suffering of her sister. "Good medicine," then, is based in acting up and speaking out.

Lucia carries on the African woman's tradition of nurturing and healing. Like Tambu, who stops along the road to inquire about the health of her neighbors, Lucia's vocal nature, though rebellious, ultimately sustains her local community. Like women before her who have nourished life, whether through motherhood or the cultivation of the land, she plants a seed for women's liberation as well as national independence and vitality in Zimbabwe. Despite the fact that Tambu has much more formal education than her aunt, she takes a page from Lucia's book when she writes at the end of her tale that "seeds do grow. . . . Quietly, unobtrusively, and extremely fitfully, something in my mind began to assert itself, to question things and refuse to be brainwashed, bringing me to this time when I can set down this story" (203-04). Though this "process of expansion" is "long and painful," it is ultimately successful to the extent that it allows Tambu to speak out and tell her own story as well as the story of the women she loves, to reap the seed that was sown in her childhood by the example of women like Lucia (204).

Instead of relying on the radical, interventionist model that characterizes European medical treatments, Dangarembga employs a writing cure: by vocalizing her complaints, Tambu is able to overcome her anguish and gain a new perspective on her suffering. Unlike the Freudian talking cure, however, this writing cure does not necessitate a doctor-patient relationship built upon the authority of the former and the submission of the latter. On the contrary, this autobiographical writing is a "composing" of the self strong enough to counter the social forces of de-composition that threaten the health and sanity of the protagonists. Moreover, this composition of self takes place in the public sphere and involves a community of readers. Thus, for Dangarembga as well as her characters, healing emerges from solidarity and mutual support. Writing, like speaking out, is "good medicine" for Africa: it neither spits in the face of tradition, nor submits to a pained silence; it neither vomits up all European nourishment nor forgets the taste of the sustaining, local sadza. Indeed, Dangarembga has truly digested the Western tradition, incorporating it into her own African corpus, transforming it utterly.

Dangarembga is not only skeptical of Western biomedical and psychoanalytic models of cure; she is also wary of the more radical Fanonian resolution dependent on a violent social transformation born of psychological angst. The violence exhibited in Nyasha's wild outbursts is largely self-destructive and does little to reshape society. As Charles Sugnet has argued, *Nervous Conditions* rejects "the usual terms of heroic, masculine, national narrative" (42). Rather than forming an extension of the Fanonian call to arms, it departs from the arguably Eurocentric and patriarchal notion that subjectivity must be affirmed through aggressive objectification of an "other." Perhaps it is for this reason that Dangarembga makes no explicit references to the *Chimurenga* struggle for independence contemporaneous with the time-frame of the novel.

Françoise Verges has demonstrated that for Fanon colonialism "acted as a 'screen' obscuring the complexity of social organisation" (59). By returning to the sexual roots of hysteria, Dangarembga offers an important corrective to Fanon's construction of the "reactionary psychosis," which ignores the impact of extra-colonial factors—such as culture, religion, family structure, and gender—in determining the victims and forms of colonial pathologies. Moreover, she identifies sexual repression as parallel and contributive to colonial oppression, thus rebuking the "virile masculinity" of the Fanonian revolution and revealing the faulty logic of a liberation movement taking the pure woman as the symbol of the nation. Though she does not wholly reject the biomedical vision of illness as a result of the body's invasion by some external agent of infection, Dangarembga does overturn the equation of such biomedical infection with sexual penetration. She thereby undoes the analogy of health and chastity, reconceiving colonial pathology as sexual as well as cultural repression. In place of Fanon's symbolic rape, avenged by the soldiers of the revolution, *Nervous Conditions* focuses on the struggles of actual women to overcome the double domination of colonization and patriarchy. Instead of advocating sexual repression, Dangarembga suggests nationalists should be lifting all forms of political and cultural censorship and fighting for sexual liberation as a vital part of national liberation. Otherwise, this cautionary tale warns, the society for which the revolutionaries are presumably fighting will fall apart at the roots and will be plagued by social instability, psychological crises, and ill health.

Whereas narrative clearly performs a curative role in *Nervous Conditions*, its efficacy is limited by the fact that it is only available to a small elite that has the knowledge and means to read and write. Writing is, moreover, a comparatively solitary endeavor which belies in some ways the communitarian values supported in Dangarembga's novel. In light of this, it is not surprising that Dangarembga has subsequently turned to film to get her message out to a wider audience. In contrast to literature, film is both cooperative in its production and generally communal in its reception. As an oral and visual medium disseminated widely across the public sphere, cinema is ideally situated in Africa to function as a healing art. The propaganda value of film was realized early on, both in Europe (for instance by the Nazis) and in the colonies, where it was used to promote Western values and lifestyles. Indeed, documentaries on hygiene and medicine were amongst the earliest films produced in Africa for a local audience. This legacy certainly represents a mixed blessing for African filmmakers. Even today, in independent African nations, the vast majority of productions rely upon foreign capital and sometimes foreign technology and expertise.[11] With foreign investment involved, artistic control is a crucial issue, and *Everyone's Child*, directed by Dangarembga, has been accused by some detractors of supporting the agenda of development agencies rather than a truly African perspective on the current health crisis on the continent. Quite to the contrary, *Everyone's Child* marks a radical departure from the historically dominant genres and styles of development cinema. It also makes a break from Western approaches to dealing with AIDS, whether medical or sociological.

There is no question of denying the tragic spread of AIDS on the African continent over the last twenty years. However, as with other diseases that originated or took root in tropical Africa, the representation of this history in the Western press has been colored by notions of Africa as the "dark continent" and the "white man's grave." Under the guise of scientific theory, ahistorical, racist stereotypes have been bandied about: the argument was even put forth that HIV entered the human population through African bestiality. This late-twentieth-century specter of savages copulating with their monkey "next of kin" echoes strikingly the visions of bestiality presented in late-nineteenth-century novels like *Heart of Darkness*. Seemingly more innocuous statements about the prevalence of anal sex in Africa are highly inflamatory when placed in the context of the predominant view of AIDS in the West as a divine punishment for sodomy (in addition to promiscuity and addiction). Yet, in the case of Africa as in America, a realistic assessment of the prevalence of the disease in certain communities does not preclude challenging interpretations of the pandemic as a plague visited upon a particular people due to their evil behavior or inherently threatening environment.[12] In *Everyone's Child*, Dangarembga takes on the difficult task of making a film that can intervene in a significant way in the health crisis in her native Zimbabwe without reinforcing negative stereotypes of Africans or of people living with AIDS.

Everyone's Child opens just before the crisis comes to a head for the Maputsa family through the death of the children's mother (the father precedes her). Yet, rather than beginning with the funeral of the mother, the film sets the stage by introducing Tamari, the eldest daughter, via her innocent love affair with Tabiso and her devoted care of her dying mother. Indeed, the opening of the film offers a model of how a family and community should function. The innocuous, monogamous devotion of the two youngsters suggests that they would not normally be at risk for HIV infection. Similarly, Tamari's selfless care of her mother is a model that the whole community might profitably follow in caring for "everyone's child." As the situation of the orphaned children deteriorates, they are not only forced into painful choices, suffering, and alienation, but they are also, significantly, placed at great risk for catching AIDS and perpetuating the vicious cycle of the virus. The townsfolk marginalize those they know or suspect are infected: they avoid contact, neglect the customary mutual aid vital during the planting season, and resent having to share communal wells. By ostracizing the children, and thus condemning them to emotional turmoil and destitution, the townsfolk place them at high risk. Tamari is forced to have intercourse with a much older man whose behavior suggests habitual promiscuity; she further exposes herself to possible infection when her hand is cut sifting through garbage for crafts materials. Itai, the eldest son, is similarly put at risk by living on the streets in Harare: his resistance is lowered due to hunger and unsanitary living conditions; he narrowly es-

capes prostitution; ultimately, he is raped by a street-hardened gang-
ster while in a juvenile reformatory (the rape is not actually shown
but clearly suggested). Only Nhamo, the youngest child, has no
need to fear AIDS: he dies more quickly from simple neglect.

Agency is extremely important in *Everyone's Child.* Although the community as a whole is crucial to the long-term survival of the children, every character in the film must first choose
not to be saved, as in a Christian ethic, but rather to save themselves. While Tabiso defends Tamari from the abusive store owner
who has been exploiting her sexually, he steps forward only after
she herself has taken the decision to reject the shopkeeper and end
her relationship with him. Likewise, her brother must make up his
own mind to return from a life of delinquency in Harare. Thus, not
only is self-help crucial to this African community, which is not
encouraged to rely on Western medicine or other forms of external
aid, but self-help is also the rule for individuals. While the general
ethic of work and self-improvement might be interpreted in a facile manner as echoing Western notions of morality and the Protestant work ethic, in fact it rejects these in favor of a vision which is
much more communitarian in orientation, that, while emphasizing individual agency, also recognizes that individuals need support from the community. The film also emphasizes that failure
does not necessarily signify the fault of the individual or a measure of divine wrath: lyrics from the prominent soundtrack remind
the audience not to rush to judgement against those in an unfamiliar situation.

The centrality of agency in this film sets it apart from the
vast majority of films made by international organizations on health
crises, in which the norm is to emphasize the helplessness (and
innocence) of the African—usually in the form of a poor, starving
child with big eyes and flies buzzing round its head. Though
Everyone's Child was funded by an international development organization, it does not pander to the agenda of such organizations
without regard to local African values. In spite of its own dependence on external funding, the film promotes self-reliance rather

than dependence on national or international relief. It is neither a slave to the economic and political interests of foreign states nor to the preponderant aesthetic of the development documentary or charity advertisement genre. The overall view of official aid institutions in the film is quite critical. At the Church, Tamari receives only sympathy and prayer; a traveling crisis group asks the townsfolk for information but offers no material support; the school seems unwilling to make an exception for the girls to allow them to stay in class—the teacher will only offer Tamari a place in exchange for sexual favors; the government detention center exposes Itai to physical and psychological abuse; the reformatory psychiatrist ignores Itai's actual plight and instead accuses his parents of abusing him, an entirely unfounded accusation that smacks of the Western desire to find a scapegoat for illness in the failures of Africans.

Even the hospital offers no help. When the children take their mother there, the nurse tells them that she is better off at home. On a literal level, this comment seems to indicate that there is no hope of recovery in the hospital so she may as well die at home. This comment sets the mood for the failure of all institutions to offer material aid to people who are suffering. But the idea that the mother is better off at home is not merely a negative commentary on the state of the hospital and other public institutions; it also suggests that the home is the best place for care, even when the patient is terminally ill. For Dangarembga, health begins in the home with the family and the community. When the hearth is broken, the children are flung out of it as far as the big city slums. The film makes the point repeatedly and emphatically that the solution is not money but resources everyone can offer: compassion, acceptance, cooperation, time, shelter, and food. No doubt this is a conscious part of the ideology of the film, especially as it is directed mainly at people who live on a subsistence level and who have very little monetary assistance to give. The film works hard to convince the audience that everyone, no matter how poor, can lend a hand and make a difference. And, since what comes around goes around, helping others in their need is a good insurance policy against future tragedies. For, while self-reliance on an individual basis is brave, it is insufficient; only communities can be effectively self-reliant.

Dangarembga relates the crisis in the community to the over-burdening of women as mothers and caregivers. Tamari's very first utterance is a request that her boyfriend take her away, yet even as she speaks these words her tone of voice indicates that she knows this is an impossible dream. Later, when he returns in the hopes of whisking her off to Harare, she explains that she cannot go because she must care for her younger siblings. Not burdened with the care of children, men find it easier to shirk their responsibility to the family and escape to the city, where for a time they can sustain a pretence of independence, however illusory it ultimately turns out to be. The family patriarch fails to live up to his family duties by making off with the cattle and plow, the children's sole livelihood, and then abandons them to their own devices. Another male role model, Uncle Jimmy, brags irresponsibly about the economic opportunities of Harare only to disappear to South Africa without leaving a forwarding address. Amongst the younger generation, both Itai and Tamari's boyfriend are lured by the economic promise of Harare. Though their intentions are to earn money to help Tamari, they are also shown to be motivated in part by ambition and escapism. Both young men eventually return, but arguably too late, since Nhamo, the little boy who wishes to fly away like his male role models, has already perished in a blaze caused by the untended hearthfire that burns down the family home. The flight of all these male figures has tragic consequences for the women who are left behind to bear the brunt of the immediate burden of keeping the family, and by extension the community, together. It is the loss of the mother that initiates the drama, while the removal from the home of Tamari, the substitute mother, brings the film to its tragic climax. Not incidentally, these crucial events, both followed by funeral processions and scenes of communal mourning, form the frame of the narrative. In this manner,

Dangarembga links the survival of the community to a vision of gender politics that recognizes the crucial role played by African women and their need for greater material and emotional support from their male partners.

In *Everyone's Child*, Dangarembga does for physical illness what she had done for mental illness in *Nervous Conditions*: she demonstrates that the health crisis in Africa is based not on some congenital or cultural failure; it is situational, historical, and, thus, however long the odds and difficult the struggle, reversible. Like Fanon, Dangarembga reveals that the true enemy of the African is not genetic inferiority, a tainted environment, or even an invisible microbe, but instead the concrete effects of poverty, ignorance, fear, and fatalism that form part of the complex legacy of colonialism. While she does not paint a rosy picture of the situation in Africa, she certainly shows that famine and plague need not be its inexorable fate. Significantly, the statistics with which *Everyone's Child* closes, though frightening enough, are not of the number of Africans infected with AIDS, nor the number of the projected dead, but the number of children who will be orphaned by the disease.[13] This is no mere diversion tactic, shifting the public's concern from disease carriers to innocent children. Even in the film's most patently scientific moment (statistics being a favored tool of scientific method as well as development agencies), Dangarembga keeps the focus firmly on future generations, leaving open the possibility that Africans may save their children and thereby themselves.

Breaking from the tradition of the development documentary, *Everyone's Child* is not, after all, a film about AIDS, but a film about the struggle for life. Whereas the film does not deny the biomedical aspects of the disease, it departs from most American prevention programs (at least the early, mainstream efforts) which placed blame on individuals for engaging in dangerous behavior, targeted only habitually marginalized communities rather than the heterosexual white majority, and emphasized a repressive, and arguably unrealistic, "just say no" attitude to sex, which assumed that amongst women only prostitutes would be at risk. In stark contrast, *Everyone's Child*, as indicated in the title, focuses on the entire community: it makes the biomedical facts of AIDS secondary to the breakdown in native customs that enables its spread; it blames desperate circumstances rather than individual caprice for infection; it makes health as well as illness everyone's business. The message of the film is deceptively simple: the community should not and cannot afford to allow death to enter where there is the capacity to support life. Thus, despite horrifying statistical projections on the fallout from the AIDS pandemic, Dangarembga insists that the acknowledgment of tragedy and loss be complemented by the equally crucial recognition of the power of Africans to draw on their communal strength, traditional values, and local knowledge to sustain life. The task of Africans is to cultivate the African roots of health buried so deep under the debris of colonization, warfare, and underdevelopment, and thus bring them to fruition once more.

Indeed, throughout her works Dangarembga supports a culture of care rather than a culture of cure. *Nervous Conditions* and *Everyone's Child* share a vision of health as a social product, as much spiritual as physical, that emerges from the well-guided home and community.[14] Whereas in both novel and film Western-style hospitals typically fail—whether in colonial Rhodesia or independent Zimbabwe—native methods of healing hold out some hope. This is particularly so when a distinction is drawn between healing and curing, healing being a communal practice aimed at improving well-being in all its multifaceted aspects, while curing is a narrowly focused biomedical endgame. Although healing is central to Dangarembga's work, the healing process is not synonymous with psychological or biomedical cures, which are totally goal-oriented, their narrow focus blinding them to the social and psychological factors that are crucial to determining not only the ultimate outcome of illness, but the patient's quality of life and dignity in death. Both of Dangarembga's works are characterized by a telling lack of closure indicative of this avoidance of the radically cure-oriented medical practice of the West: *Nervous Conditions* ends without resolving the question of whether Nyasha will live or die, and *Everyone's Child* comes to a close without any indication of whether Tambu and Itai are already HIV positive.

The impetus for change, according to Dangarembga, must come from individuals joining together and overcoming their anxieties and inhibitions through dialogue. In short, communication of ideas—rather than diseases—fosters a healthy community. This principle is illustrated in the opening scene of *Everyone's Child* when Tabiso proclaims "I got a voice, Tamari," ostensibly referring to his singing voice and making an argument for the success that awaits him in Harare as a musician. There is another, more subtle meaning to this affirmation, particularly as it contrasts with Tamari's relative silence and resignation about her situation. Both youngsters must come together before they can truly save themselves and each other. Tamari must find the voice to say "no" to the shopkeeper who is exploiting her, while Tabiso must return to the village with his voice in order to reach his true audience and inspire Tamari to resist. This lesson has broad implications: the healing of Africa necessitates both the empowerment of Africans, including African women, to find their own voices and the rededication of those voices to the community. It is precisely this formula for healthy discourse that Dangarembga cooks up in her "dirty works."

Dangarembga's oeuvre is at once highly engaged with the longstanding discourse of colonial pathology and innovative in its interpretation of social crises. It undercuts popular Western conceptions of plague as the wages of sin. Moreover, it challenges imperialist representations of the African landscape and people as sources of contagion by revealing the ways in which illness is produced by oppressive, hierarchical, social structures. Unlike male writers of the colonial-as-pathological, Dangarembga avoids the allegorization of disease and the usurpation of the female body as a symbol of the continent or nation. Dangarembga's women are unique individuals who resist easy typing and who insist on taking part on the most immediate, material level in the fight for political, cultural, and sexual freedom.

Dangarembga's fluid transformation of colonial pathology into postcolonial pathology does raise a nagging question: is medical discourse the most constructive way to understand a socio-historical phenomenon? The equation of postcoloniality and hybridity with mental instability may serve to confirm damaging stereotypes about people of mixed race or mixed cultural heritage. There is also considerable danger in reinforcing the longstanding association of Africa and Africans with illness. Such issues are especially troubling in an age of increased anxiety over Africa as a "hot zone" incubating diseases such as AIDS and Ebola.[15] Although they seem to be growing ever more prevalent, pathological discourses may already have outlived their usefulness for theorists of the postcolonial.[16] Even so, in drawing attention to the self-inflicted and self-destructive aspects of postcolonial malaise, Dangarembga illustrates the insufficiency of a symptomatic acting out and points the way towards a more healing nationalist-feminist discourse. In that sense, *Nervous Conditions* may prove the last word in (post-)colonial pathologies and *Everyone's Child*, in its turn away from biomedical discourses to community resources, the first word in "good medicine" for Africa.

Notes

1. On the facts and fictions of disease in Africa during the colonial period, see Philip Curtin's informative works *Death by Migration* and *The Image of Africa*. On the origins of the image of the "dark continent," see Patrick Brantlinger's "Victorians and Africans: The Genealogy of the Myth of the Dark Continent."

2. For a range of discussions on the role of medical discourse throughout

the empire, see Sheldon Watts' *Epidemics and History: Disease, Power and Imperialism*, as well as the following edited volumes: David Arnold, *Imperial Medicine and Indigenous Societies*; John MacKenzie, *Imperialism and the Natural World*; Roy Macleod and Milton Lewis, *Disease, Medicine and Empire*.

3. Comaroff, 321. Medicine was frequently used as a tool of discipline in Southern Africa and Maynard Swanson has argued convincingly that European fears about the contagiousness of the African population and the concurrent desire for its separation and containment led to a regime of "sanitary" segregation that eventually contributed to the ideology and infrastructure of apartheid ("The Sanitation Syndrome"). For further discussion of the South African context, see Shula Marks and Neal Andersson's "Epidemics and Social Control in Twentieth-Century South Africa"; on North Africa, see Frantz Fanon's "Medicine and Colonialism"; on East Africa, Megan Vaughan's *Curing Their Ills*; on India, David Arnold's *Colonizing the Body*.

4. Comaroff draws on Foucault's concept of the medical gaze as elaborated in *Birth of the Clinic*.

5. Comaroff 311. On the pathological, hyper-sexualized representation of the black woman in European literature and art, see Sander Gilman's "Black Bodies, White Bodies." On imagery of science as masculine reason unveiling female nature and penetrating the secrets of the female body, see Ludmilla Jordanova, "Nature Unveiling Before Science," and Evelyn Fox Keller, *Reflections on Gender and Science*.

6. On gender and the psychology of Rivers, see Elaine Showalter, *The Female Malady*. For a discussion of Fanon's relationship to other schools of psychology, see Francoise Verges, "Chains of Madness, Chains of Colonialism."

7. Fanon, "Case No. 1: Impotence in an Algerian following the rape of his wife," *The Wretched of the Earth*, 254-59.

8. Douglas, *Purity and Danger*, passim. Ann McClintock shows how imperialist ideology formulates the opposition between dirt and civilization in the context of southern Africa in the chapter "Soft-Soaping Empire: Commodity Racism and Imperial Advertising" from *Imperial Leather*, 207-31. The uncanny promise of hygiene for Africans is that if

they clean themselves with the appropriate brand of British soap, their darkness (read dirt) will be scrubbed right off, revealing a glowing, healthy, white skin beneath (213-14).

9. See Robert Young, "Hybridity and Diaspora," *Colonial Desire* (1-19). Homi Bhabha, *The Location of Culture.*

10. Freud's perception of the sexual roots of hysteria are evident in *Dora: An Analysis of a Case of Hysteria,* as is his therapeutic goal of helping hysterics to cope with the status quo (rather than attempting to change it). A number of important feminist critiques of this case are collected in Charles Bernheimer and Claire Kahane's *In Dora's Case: Freud - Hysteria - Feminism.*

11. For a discussion of the development and current situation of African filmmaking see Manthia Diawara's *African Cinema.*

12. Two of the more influential treatments of this topic are Susan Sontag's *Illness as Metaphor* and *AIDS and Its Metaphors,* and Sander Gilman's "AIDS and Syphilis: The Iconography of a Disease."

13. For a scientific discussion of the AIDS pandemic in southern Africa, see Douglas Webb's *HIV and AIDS in Africa,* which contains a section entitled "Community Responses to AIDS Orphans: Whose Responsibility?" (181-90).

14. Historical and anthropological evidence supports the view that traditional African cultures have approached healing from a communitarian point of view. See, for instance, S. Feierman and J. Janzen's collection *The Social Basis of Health and Healing in Africa.*

15. One example of the popular new genre of alarmist epidemiology is Laurie Garett's bestseller, *The Coming Plague.*

16. The use of medical discourse in postcolonial theory has, until quite recently, remained largely unselfconscious. This tendency reflects a general cultural trend related to the authority of science and medicine in the developed world, the obsession with youth and health, and growing concerns about globalization and the increased risk of pandemics. The presence of medical discourse in postcolonial studies also reflects the central contribution of psychoanalysis to contemporary theory (even as it has been reinvented by Lacan, Fanon, Deleuze and Guattari, and others).

Since the early 1990s, however, a more critical discussion of the role of medical discourse in postcolonial literature and theory has begun to develop, particularly within the Francophone sphere, and so far has produced two valuable publications from Harmattan: Bernard Mouralis's *L'Europe, l'Afrique et la folie* and the conference proceedings of the Association pour l'Etude des Litteratures Africaines, *Litterature et maladie en Afrique*. Much work still remains to be done in this area.

Chapter 8:
Some Very *Nervous Conditions*: Commodity, Culture, and Identity in Dangarembga's Novel

Sally Ann Murray

Tsitsi Dangarembga's *Nervous Conditions*, first published in 1988, is a retrospective narrative of female coming-to-consciousness in colonial Rhodesia during the mid-1960s to early 1970s. Critics agree that Dangarembga feminizes "Fanon's findings on colonial cultural alienation" and neurosis in order to represent "different forms of black women's estrangement and self-possession" (Boehmer 228). The story is conveyed through the insightful presence of the mature narrator, and guides readers to conclude that patriarchy is Tambu's "primary incentive" in learning to shape her own life: "everywhere around her she perceives the injustice intrinsic to the position of woman" (Veit-Wild 332). Yet patriarchy is only one of the powerful cultural claims made upon the characters.

My purpose is not to ignore either an authorial or critical interest in exploring patriarchal oppression as an influential experiential logic in the novel. I want to probe beyond the obvious in an attempt to understand the cultural dynamics of Dangarembga's story. Let me begin by pointing out a few instances where critics suggest that Dangarembga's subject matter and style, far from being unitary or stable, break beyond the bounds of "patriarchy" and even the conventions of the *Bildungsroman*. Some critics acknowledge this volatility rather paradoxically, by granting Dangarembga complete authorial control over the nervous energy of her characters. Veit-Wild maintains, for instance, that since one "of the aims of the story is to explore the contradictions inherent in . . . the psychological development of a young African," it is inevitable that "Tambudzai's path to self-discovery is not straightforward but full of trials, crises and troubles" (332). More interesting, though, is Chapman's response, which implies that whatever Dangarembga's manifest focus in *Nervous Conditions*, there are latent authorial "nervousnesses" in the story she publishes. As he explains, "Tambudzai's own 'theme' cannot be confined to what she herself insists upon: the gendered character of complicity and consent." Instead, "*Nervous Conditions* remains jittery about its own attempts to transfer African issues, contexts and values to Western-style dialogues, and vice versa" (308). Chennells' essay is also a useful reference point. It highlights the cultural tensions in the novel between Shona belief systems and the "hybrid" cultural identities of Dangarembga's characters. I cannot give an exhaustive list of articles in which critics hint that patriarchy alone is not the interpretive key to *Nervous Conditions*. I can simply indicate that despite patriarchy having been emphasized in the academic reception of Dangarembga's novel, some respondents suspect that the novel's cultural domain is more accurately to be understood as shaped by complex, even contradictory cultural vectors. Furthermore, in writing the novel Dangarembga has drawn on uneasy, shifting cultural resources rather than producing a coherent critique of patriarchal oppression in modern African women's experience.

In all of this, we also need to consider what kinds of distinctions we are willing to allow between fictional convention and social fact. In one sense, any attitudes to consumption that we glean from the novel are most immediately those of the mature narrating consciousness, who is not synonymous with Dangarembga herself. In another sense, though, while we try to avoid facile conflation of author and character-narrator, we might also recognize this fictional consciousness as a product of the author's own interests and blindspots. (Many have even pointed out loose parallels between Dangarembga's own life experiences and those of her imaginary characters.) The focuses and evasions of the narrator, then, might well be considered suggestive traces of the author's preferred "worldview." Critics' momentary nods towards cultural volatility in *Nervous Conditions* provide the impetus for my own investigations: the representation (or not) of commodity relations as they bear upon the identities evolved by Dangarembga's characters. Near the beginning of the novel, we see a brief evocation, within a text whose primary concern is the critique of patriarchy, of the wider interrelation of cultures that mark colonial modernity and its paradoxical opportunities and limitations for black people. In representing the adult Tambu's recollections of her girlhood, Dangarembga has Tambu explain, for example, that while the building of the Government's District Council Houses "to enable the administration of our area" (3) fundamentally altered the domestic-social routines of the surrounding homesteads, not all of these changes caused abjection and alienation. A subsistence economy where people grew their own food stuffs co-existed with new forms of commercial exchange: The "entrepreneurial among us . . . built their little tuckshops which sold the groceries we needed—bread, tea, sugar, jam, salt, cooking oil, matches, candles, paraffin and soap" (3). Some even began to extend such commerce into forms of popular cultural expression that were simultaneously pleasurable and political. They set up a gramophone "where the youth could entertain themselves with music and dancing. They played the new rumba that, as popular music will, pointed unsystematic fingers at the conditions of the times" (4). Here, the narrator acknowledges the capacity of people to wrest meaningful kinds of identity and collectivity from compromised commercial exchange. Tambu refers to a "solidarity," a "stamping of feet to the pulse of these social facts." The narrating voice is clearly critical when it recounts that the authorities, alarmed by such bonding, curtailed it through duplicitous measures: by erecting a beer-hall, where people could buy cheap mass-manufactured beer and be lulled into cultural acquiescence, away from any independent entrepreneurial—or political—action. Such pointed observations about the mutable forms of popular and official culture, however, are scarce in the novel. Official culture in the novel tends to be present as the masculinist morality of the modern mission household, but as the design and decor of "Babamukuru's" home indicate, this authority is also inflected through fashionable codes of consumption and beliefs about what it means to be well-educated. (In color-coded rooms, encyclopedia are displayed alongside fine china.) Thus as my paper argues, in *Nervous Conditions* consumption and learning also become "official" cultures and they are treated ambivalently in the text. They are represented as being compromised since they work to adjust individuality to systems of social control, yet they are discourses which are also subject to creative reworkings by individuals.

If *Nervous Conditions* does not immediately strike the reader as a deliberate response to the kinds of consumer cultural relations which were characteristic of Rhodesia in the 1960s and 1970s, the very context of the novel's action means that we cannot simply dismiss as irrelevant Burke's observations. In *Lifebuoy Men, Lux Women* (1997), Burke argues that Rhodesia after World War II saw the proliferation of "capitalist functionaries and state officials whose interest in penetrating what they called the "African market" necessarily demanded that they try to change the nature of African selfhood" (11). While this emergent 'African market' is not coherently evident in the novel, the economic symbolic pressures and possibilities which it entailed do contribute to the characters' nervous conditions. Moreover, Dangarembga does make a significant assumption: her reader will understand that the novel's action occurs within the context of commodity capitalism associated with modernity. This incipient "globalism," if you will, even though it takes a back seat in a novel which is set particularly within a colonized Rhodesia, must surely bear upon the way in which we read the experiences and identities of Dangarembga's characters. This is a curious reworking of the "universalist" principles upon which good literature was once thought to be based. As Chapman has remarked, for instance, the "African specificity" of the novel "is sufficiently muted" to allow the culturally particular to encompass also a more generalized cultural domain. The educated, mission-inflected version of Shona patriarchy on which the novel focuses also reaches beyond the immediate socio-historical context in order "to operate as an analogue of the general topic of patriarchy" (307). This uneasy shifting gives us characters who are trying to locate meaningful identities at the interface of cultural particularities such as "Shonaness" and "Africanness"; modernity, capitalism, and individualism. Although she does not find these cultural intersections untroubled, Dangarembga herself has commented on the likelihood that the cultures which make up Zimbabwean life will increasingly be obliged to accommodate the styles, designs and beliefs of the influential West (Chapman 307).

Nervous Conditions sometimes suggests that modernity (in its complicated guise of education, development, and commodities) betrays the black Rhodesian through hyperbolic promises of freedom, enlightenment, and fulfillment. Modernity fails to deliver the serious social good, or delivers Africans into the hands of false gods who require from them the uncritical worship of goods and the good life. Within this scenario (one drawn by many African writers and theorists), consumer culture appears as a form of con-

tinuing colonialism through which otherwise independent indigenous people are unequally reconciled to western capitalism. Pertinent here is Zimbabwean Dambudzo Marechera's scathing ridicule, in *The House of Hunger*, of the way in which "the Modern
African Family" was produced through the consumption of both
western commodities like "Fanta Orange Tastes So Good" and of
Christian religion (151). Several sections of *Nervous Conditions*
corroborate this view.

At other points in the narrative, though, the position is
slightly different. For the movement of the various characters from
the homestead to the mission and beyond is not a simple journey
deeper into the clutches of racist capitalism. Rather, the characters
are faced with the need to negotiate various cultural codes and
practices. Many of the characters have a contradictory relation to
consumer capital, given their status as members of an emergent
black elite. Yes, we find them being culturally assimilated, forfeiting what some would see as their "authentic" Shona culture. But
we also see their moving and awkwardly innovative attempts to
devise new kinds of socio-cultural repertoire. It is to the ensuing
contradictions—which are variously enabling and disabling—rather
than simply to neuroses provoked by colonialism, that their "nervous conditions" may be attributed. Modernity has the negative
capacity to induce mysterious illnesses, bodily and psychic dys-
functions, but in addition it enlarges horizons, presenting different
dreams and possibilities.

It is worth reminding ourselves that while Dangarembga
writes as a Zimbabwean from a postcolonial perspective, she does
so about characters who are located within the timeframe of colonial Rhodesia. They have not achieved political independence, nor
have they experienced the Machiavellian will of western nations
to retain cultural-economic control over former colonies while re-
linquishing overt political power. It is perhaps because
Dangarembga writes of an earlier historical stage, of pre-Zimba-
bwean life, that she does not make the issue of commodification
central to the novel's "message." A number of colleagues who

read this paper in its draft versions, for instance, described having lived in Rhodesia during the 1960s and 1970s. Many a commercial center of what was thought a major city consisted of only a single main shopping street which quickly petered out into small-time suburbia. And this thoroughfare was not a comfortable shopping space for black people: they could wait a long time before the shopkeeper deigned to serve them at the separate entrance reserved for "non-Europeans." However attractive commodities may have been to black Rhodesians, colonial economics preferred to restrict black buying and selling to township stores, truck outlets, and local trade stores. These are not spurious points. Firstly, they remind us that the historical-geographical context of Dangarembga's novel is one in which commercial exchange was not thoroughly mediated by the symbolic and discursive glamour of "the commodity," and that black people's needs and desires were in any case both materially and ideologically structured by the needs and desires of colonial racism. Secondly, though, the points hint that in the 1960s and early 1970s context in which Dangarembga locates her story, commodification was emerging as an important social dynamic, an excitingly "new" presence through which self could be shaped, announced, and symbolized through consumption. (We should bear in mind that "new" here does not mean entirely without history or socio-cultural precedent. As Burke indicates, long before the commodification of fashion and style, there always were in place the Shona and Ndebele equivalent of sumptuary codes which reserved the wearing of certain fabrics and garments for the elite.) Given this, readers would be misguided to expect Dangarembga's novel to show characters living in the commodity-rich/culturally-impoverished network society which many of us now take for granted. And if we allow the social excitement generated by modern commodities in 1960s and 1970s Rhodesia, we might find it in ourselves to judge humanely, rather than harshly, the inflated role played by goods in the subjectivities of several of Dangarembga's characters.

Dangarembga's own preferred subject matter deserves

comment. She does not choose, unlike so many male Zimbabwean authors, to write a novel about obvious cultural resistance with *chimurenga* as its subject. Instead, she displaces "resistance" into a field of experience where cultures are more relative, shifting, uncertain, where cultural authority derives from curious co-ordinates of masculinity and femininity, tradition and modernity, rejection and incorporation. If she clearly values the forms of inventiveness which mark the popular resistance of gramophone playing and politically charged rhumbas, she does not pursue this political populism. Instead, the novel rather haphazardly refracts the "popular" into forms of commercialized culture of the 1960s—whether youth culture, mass culture, or middle-class culture, and this hybrid cultural space becomes the informing context of her narrative of female empowerment. Commercial "popular" culture, Dangarembga implies, can disable young women like Nyasha and Tambu, offering them insubstantial role models; but aspects of her story also imply that commercial cultures are inevitable constituents in the formation of her characters' identities and futures. (Throughout this paper, readers will see that I am intrigued by the extent to which Dangarembga controls—or not—the values which she associates with the official and the unofficial, the popular and the commodified. The novel blurs the boundaries to such a degree that, when it comes to consumer culture, I am left uncertain about what it is that Dangarembga sanctions. Appropriately enough: "to sanction" may mean "to approve" or "to forbid"!)

Let me proceed by discussing some examples from *Nervous Conditions* which illustrate the unstable life of modern commodity culture and the ambivalent place of the commodity in the lives of Dangarembga's characters. Obliquely, Dangarembga shows in her novel that new forms of market production are associated with the increased consumption of a range of generic product types like soap, toothpaste, and Vaseline petroleum jelly. Partly, Dangarembga is critical of the fact that the use of these commodities (and the bodily display of difference which such use entails) confers an elite status on several characters, separating them from traditional cultural conventions and destabilizing customary hierarchies. Yet she occasionally implies, through sympathetic observations from a generally hard-nosed narrator, that this is not a simple process of consumption as self-aggrandizement. (Think of the mature Tambu's brief extension of understanding to her brother: as a boy, he was not merely being pig-headed and arrogant towards his sisters; instead, as society expected of him, he was being male.)

A sympathetic view of the status use of apparently ordinary commodities such as soap admits that consumption is oddly connected to the uneven imagining of new selves. The characters' perceptions of self intersect with the symbolic value of otherwise banal goods. The basic "groceries" that could be purchased from the "little tuckshops" (3) beside the Council Houses and the bus terminus, items which the local people have come to "need," become symbolically invested with desire, associated with the exchange of an old self for something thought to be better, improved, more modern. From at least the early 1940s in Rhodesia, commercial agents such as advertisers and market researchers had been laboring to produce the black person as "market" and "consumer": products as diverse as "pens, clothing, beer, education, automobile supplies, and especially toiletries of all kinds . . . were . . . pitched to African consumers as the definitional essence of glamour and 'smart' living—commercial code-words for the African elite" (Burke 155-56). We are also by now familiar with the (social) fact that in colonial race relations, toiletries were associated with complex ideological-symbolic codes: hygienic imagery which connected them to Christian morality, an ethic of hard work and responsible domesticity, as well as to the civilized manners and bodies supposedly the epitome of modernity (Burke 156). However, the changed lives represented in *Nervous Conditions* suggest that "exchange" is never merely a metaphor (a figurative transfer of one set of meanings to a separate entity). Whatever their fantasies, neither Nhamo nor Tambu, for instance, can simply shrug off their peasant selves for sophisticated urban identities. If the youthful Nhamo returns to the homestead with soap, toothpaste, and sugar, items which he then reserves for his private use as a defining mark of his superior status as an African versed in the cultures of the modern world, this does not automatically enable him to produce himself, either imaginatively or materially, as an elite individual who is separate from rural poverty and labor. He must still on occasions work in the fields, an activity which demands that through his visceral body (rather than through language or style) he struggle to "re-articulate" the claims which different cultural codes make upon his selfhood. Think also of the event which enables Tambu to continue her education at the Rutivi school near the homestead. It is not difficult to read this through negative theories of commodification. By selling her mielies (maize) on the market in Umtali, Tambu begins her experience of what Marxists call the commercial knowledge of commodities. Her mielies become commodities in that for "them"—in actuality for them plus the added-value of Mr. Matimba's fanciful embellishments concerning Tambu as but one child among the many in a destitute African family— she acquires a previously unimaginable sum of money. The use-value of this cash, in turn, situates her even deeper within the market economy of modernity. From the outset of her story of economic and educational "progress," then, we have embodied in the sale of the mielies a scenario in which the child (dis)associates earnings from labor. Her one morning's work effects an as if magical transformation. It has the mysterious capacity to transform lives. There is no intrinsic "ten pound" exchange-value attached to the mielies, and Tambu's lesson is that the most ordinary object—corn, in this case—may have attributed to it an enigmatic, supramaterial worth through which it becomes something "other" than "itself." (Indeed, in comparison with the labor to which she is put in the fields and in the household, the "work" of standing near the bus rank disclaiming "nice mielies" is itself a small emblem of the bizarre trans-substantiations which capital, in its more systematized form as banking finance, would come to effect upon traditional kinds of production.) As Marx might put it, the money "is the meta-morphosed shape of all [the] other commodities" (88) through which Tambu's life will be altered.

Still, even once I have drafted a negative response to Tambu's maize transactions, it coaxes me to another, less cynical reading. For the maize incident is connected to the young girl's deeply felt longings and desires. It is not money, per se, which is the final object of her desires, but by acquiring money through her creative agency she might then be enabled—through hard work as much as fantastical hopes—to enjoy a degree of freedom from the life which has been planned for her as a rural black woman. Tambu's educational aspirations, on leaving the homestead for schooling at the mission, are inflected with her wish to shed her dull-skinned peasant self for the shininess, freshness and novelty (dare I say "glamour") of what she thinks will be her modern body and identity. Associated with her projected longings for new ways of knowing her "self"—and of knowing how to "produce" this self—is not only the formality of book knowledge and an educational mission that is approved of by her mission educators, but more informal, popularized codes of conduct and expectation as embodied in broadly modern, middle-class behaviors such as internal plumbing, dining, and privacy. In part, the reader might feel uncomfortable that Tambu seeks a metamorphosis into some other body or form, something different from her "previous" self. The dominant metaphors fetishize newness and the as-if magical exchange of one "thing" for another. Yet despite such reifications, another part of the reader might respond sympathetically, for Tambu's projected image of herself and her life at the mission are also, for her, humanizing. Away from the abased authority of Jeremiah, the complex stoicism and hopelessness of her mother and, perhaps most importantly, the hard labor which is the lot of the rural female, she believes she will become a "real" person with a stimulated mind for the first time in her life. The novel itself reveals the limitations of the young girl's dreams, this is true—entrenched racism renders Tambu's entry into the College of the Sacred Heart not as lyrical as she had imagined it would be. Yet by the end of the novel, where she is configured as the putative writer of *Nervous Conditions*, we understand that she has become an agent in determining the action of her own life.

Modernity is most prominently configured in the text as the institution of colonial education, and the confluence of its effect upon family ties, social mobility, and sense of self are subjected to scrutiny. Yet the narrative does not explicitly announce these as markers characteristic of "the modern" black person in Rhodesia, despite recognizing that it is in the intersecting of commercial and ideological vectors that such modernity is fashioned. Consider where Tambu, having just arrived at the Babamukuru-Maiguru home, revels in her new possessions. (Read the passage "'These are your things, Sisi Tambu, your clothes and your washing things,' . . . the toothbrush, here the vaseline and the flannel and a comb" [76]). These things—uniforms, underwear, toiletries, "smart casual dresses"—represent for the youthful narrator her imminent possession of a new sense of self and indeed of self-importance. As the critically-astute adult Tambu might want us to recognize, these commodities are implicated in the bodily surveillance into which a mission education and, beyond that, modern consumer capitalism, encouraged African people. Yet there are also complicated forms of longing and desire which infuse the young Tambu's identification with the goods, and I find myself unable to read this merely skeptically as a sign of the young girl's as-yet-unqualified awe for her generous and successful uncle.

Dangarembga's own sympathies seem to me to be mobile: to what extent does she wish us to read through and beyond Tambu's childish infatuations with upward mobility, and to what degree may we legitimately form emotional sympathies with her, despite sensing that she is being lined up for a fall? Considered diagnostically, the very syntax of the passage undermines any attempt to read it either critically or empathetically: the indexing of items through adjectives and common nouns, for instance, is at once meant to "describe" the goods which are being heaped upon the young Tambu, and to imply that they defy description even for the adult narrator, and the author who is crafting the story. How defy? Not so much because they represent undue excess, I would argue, but because the author is struggling to acknowledge that the dreams, aspirations, and realities of young women such as Tambu were inevitably shaped by new relations to goods. In such a conceptual context, the repeated hyphenation and proliferation of nouns to which Dangarembga must resort signifies her own uncertain response to the situation she describes. She is left searching for words, ways, means . . . something to allow her to know how to conceptualize and convey the volatile place of the commodity in Tambu's changing sense of self. Marx's observations are salutary on this issue: "At the first glance, a commodity seems a commonplace sort of thing. Analysis shows, however, that it is a very queer thing indeed, full of metaphysical subtleties and theological niceties" (43-44). For Marx, the commodity is enigmatic, at once grotesque and wonderful, capable of standing with its feet on ordinary ground, and of a transcendent turning of the everyday object and idea on its head. If Marx is on the one hand referring to the perversely fantastical attribution of meaning to objects, his comments also remind us that commodity relations, being from the outset "not what they seem," cannot unproblematically be made susceptible to analyses premised on brute materialism and manipulation. The recasting of a "useful" object into a fetishized commodity suggests that people have curious relations to commodities, to things, to goods, whether we're thinking in terms of possession, use, or aspirational projection. It follows, then that consumption may entail the production of imaginative human identity rather than necessarily an inert consumption of culturally insidious goods and of ideas. As Burke has observed about post World War II Rhodesia: "Consumption did not just mechanically reproduce a single material repertoire . . . for each class or social group in Zimbabwean society. The consumption of commodities was also shaped by individual acts of will and imagination, engagement and disinterest" (10).

Dangarembga most consciously and dramatically expresses the curious power of the commodity and the place of things in social practice in those passages which detail the older Tambu's recollections of her arrival at the mission and her awed progress up the ironically-named "glamour gradient" of the movement from the kitchen, to the dining room and living rooms. Here, we have Dangarembga representing a domestic variant of commodity culture in great detail because the description bears upon her criticism of the self-inflated middle-class lifestyle of Babamukuru, a member of the first African Christian elite. Dangarembga makes clear the power of commodities to win over the African person who is unused to their plenty. Even the young Tambu is shown to know enough about cultural alienation to use her crafty "thinking strategy" in order to avoid being taken in by the symbolic power of the good life which destroyed the cultural being of her brother Nhamo. In a detailed account of the domestic trappings of the mission household and, by extension, of Baba's hubristic status, Dangarembga reconstructs the response of the younger, experiencing self at the same time as she filters this through the knowledge of the mature narrator. We are told of bookcases holding encyclopedia, walls painted in fashionably shaded contrasts, a whole room given over to dining, a fragile flowered tea set that is in daily use, and an elaborate display cabinet holding fine china. Yet we also read of a dulled sink that has been scoured rather than caressed by modern cleaning material. The narrator ironically remarks on the hopelessness of the domestic toil, given the proximity of the filthy bus station, against the dust which might taint the outward, "illusory" (71) signs of polite middle-class "civilization." Clearly, there are limits to the subjectivities which commodification permits black Rhodesians. Dangarembga has the narrator pointedly recollect, for instance, that while her uncle's home was tastefully decorated, the circumscriptions of taste and style were always financial (69). The reader is left to make the connection: whatever appearances to the contrary (Babamukuru's middle-class comfort being an apt case in point), the racist determinants of a colonial economy were geared towards white advancement and black impoverishment. Here is where contextual information is helpful, for although the novel does not spell this out, Babamukuru and others were members of a specifically African "middle class." Their status was provisional rather than secure in that it depended upon the colonial state's determination to create a buffer zone between marginally acceptable black people such as teachers and doctors and a mass of black people which, it was envisaged, would remain mere units of labor.

That this section of the novel is critical of Baba's consumption patterns is unmistakable. The wry description of the glamour gradient of the household directs attention to design and upward mobility as organizers of the domestic space, but it also insists that we read these in relation to the contradictory materialities of class and race. Baba's home is grand—but only when measured against African middle class standards. Despite Baba's hard work (and, we are to discover, that of his wife), his salary cannot buy freedom from the glass ceilings of racist colonial ideologies. In this section of the novel, Dangarembga gives the lie to consumerism as equal opportunity, and to capitalism as freedom of choice.

However, the novel's criticisms are also by no means straightforward. The pages describing Tambu's arrival at the mission house are themselves marked by authorial uneasiness rather than constant censure. Let's take as an example the studied comments concerning the use or not of harsh scourers:

> . . . the kitchen sink gleamed greyly. This lack of brilliance was due, I discovered years later when television came to the mission, to the use of scouring powders which, though they sterilized 99 per cent of a household, were harsh and scratched fine surfaces. When I found this out, I realized that Maiguru, who had watched television in England, must have known about the dulling effects of these scourers and about the brilliance that could be achieved by using the more gentle alternatives. By that time I knew something about budgets as well, notably their inelasticity. It dawned on me then that Maiguru's dull sink was not a consequence of slovenliness, as the advertisers would have us believe, but a necessity. (67-68)

In her review of the novel, Broughton astutely refers to this passage as contributing to the "sociology of detergent" (5). She understands that apparently trivial household commodities are cathected into status and identity. (In this "sociology of detergent" where does Anna fit, given that she is the woman generally responsible for the washing up?) The matter of Dangarembga's authorial stance remains difficult to pin down. It is true that she has Tambu come to a realization about commodities that is independent of the commercial rhetoric of advertising. Tambu begins to comprehend that household management depends on financial resources, and that dirt is not directly a function of "laziness" or even of the extent to which mass mediated advertising has successfully taught a person to be a dutiful consumer. Nevertheless, in working through this passage I cannot easily separate Dangarembga's authorial voice (and credibility) from precisely the advertising jargon from which she seems to want to distance Tambu. In the passage, despite the fact that the insights are offered in the spirit of the adult self-reflexivity that the reader has all along been encouraged to trust, Tambu sounds pretty much like a woman in a detergent ad. Television is both debunked and treated as a familiar, even popularly reliable, source of knowledge. It is through television information, after all, that she comes to reassess her earlier convictions. Further, the time-line of Tambu's "discovery" about kitchen commodities and her consequent extending of understanding, rather than criticism, to her aunt is blurred: "I discovered years later"; "By that time . . . ." The passage at once exonerates Maiguru for her dull sink and implies that she ought to have known better! These tensions are intensified when we remember that in a novel where the mission house is often referred to as Babamukuru's, the kitchen sink in this passage is designated Maiguru's—this without overt authorial intervention in the adult Tambu's account.

Such difficulties suggest that there is still much analysis to be done of Dangarembga's curious combination of outspokenness and inarticulacy about commodities, social status, and gendered identity in *Nervous Conditions*. The point is not to criticize the author for failing to address explicitly all the cultural influences which have a bearing on her representation of black modernity in colonial Rhodesia. Rather, by searching out Dangarembga's express criticisms of commodity culture and relating them to her silences and half-formed expressions, we could learn a great deal about the contradictory nature of the local and global cultural contexts in which she and her characters are placed.

Tensions concerning the commodity emerge elsewhere in the novel's structure. For instance, Dangarembga makes confident, if only occasional, use of brand names such as "Dover stove" and "Fanta." Admittedly, in much of Africa at the time any woodburning stove was liable to be misdesignated a "Dover stove," and any orange-colored fizzy drink was likely to be misnamed "Fanta." Yet even such colloquial reworkings of individual branding imply that new kinds of consumer goods and associated market relations were becoming familiar to African people and that they played a role in the cultural repertoires through which many African imagined themselves to be modern, progressive, up-to-date. (Burke argues that the generic use of brand names illustrates the creative agency of black people in the face of advertisers' insistence on a passive "African market.") At the rural homestead, for instance, Ma'Shingayi inherits the Dover stove which had once been reserved for the sole use of Maiguru during her urban family's visits. After overcoming her initial attachment to the traditional hearth, Ma'Shingayi comes to appreciate the stove as domestic convenience, even though the modern marketplace has not miraculously freed her from the labors expected of a rural Shona woman. Soft drinks figure similarly. Maiguru tries to appease Tambu's fears about arriving at the mission where her brother died (and to quell her own anxieties about this time performing adequately as a substitute family unit for a child from the homestead) by offering the girl not only sadza, the culturally-familiar, traditional everyday food of the poor rural household, but also "Fanta." We might feel inclined to maintain that "sadza" and "Fanta" are the cultural signifiers of two different lexicons, the pre-market subsistence economy of the homestead and the market economy of consumer capitalism which, under the guise of colonialism, drives life at the mission house and the school. Yet the very rapidity (if not quite ease) with which Maiguru moves between the two in trying to establish an intimacy with Tambu implies that what is at issue is less a question of separate cultural codes than of having to formulate an intercultural repertoire which can accommodate both rural and urban experiences.

This said, the oblique, gestural references to brands in *Nervous Conditions* remain difficult to interpret. Have commodities like the Dover stove and Fanta become such a "commonsensical" part of ordinary life in the Rhodesia of which Dangarembga writes that she does not consider them (and the modern commodity culture of which they are emblems) to deserve sustained critical comment in her narrative? Are we to consider them as having been ideologically and imaginatively disappeared in the story, as it were, just because Dangarembga does not choose to give them attention? Or are they paradoxically invested, through her brief sidelong glances, with the auratic power of the commodity as mediator of human wants, dreams, and fears? I am unsure, especially since it is impossible to reconcile such authorial "inattention" with the sustained analytical focus to which the commodification of black bourgeois life is subjected at other points in the novel (as in Tambu's arrival at the mission house). Still, I find myself testing the following, bifurcated hypothesis: when commodities play an obvious role in the formation of her characters' identities, Dangarembga is confident in commenting on commodification; but even beyond her express focus in the novel, commodity culture is part of the bigger picture of the narrative, whether Dangarembga sees it well or not. Sometimes, issues which have to do with commodities slip unbidden into her peripheral vision when she intends to focus on something else, and then she is uneasily ambivalent about attributing agency to commodities. She is unsure about whether they have meliorative or malevolent capacities: can they affect her characters' life histories for the better, or for the worse? As I have already said, perhaps it is not surprising that Dangarembga cannot

speak with certainty. Her erratic treatment of the role of the commodity in the formation of a black Rhodesian middle class may be
linked to the very trickiness of the commodity as an entity. Sometimes it is actively used by the individual or the group in the negotiation of emergent identities, class positions, and imagined status
distinction. Sometimes it verges on a form of neo-colonialism which
trashes valuable (indigenous) cultures and co-opts individuals into
elite patterns of leisure and consumption that serve the abstracted
economic imperatives of colonial capital's need to manufacture a
wider market for goods. Once again, then, it must be said in any
investigation of *Nervous Conditions* and consumption that the point
is not to dismiss Dangarembga for failing to address
commodification thoroughly or coherently through the narrative
voice which she chooses for her novel. It is more interesting to
admit from the start that the commodity is inherently a slippery
customer.

Let us think a little about patriarchy and commodity.
Dangarembga's novel takes issue with patriarchy in a variety of
familiar manifestations: as racist colonialism, traditional indigenous
hierarchy, and as the gender inequality that persists even under
modernity. Nyasha's failure to negotiate a sustaining selfhood is
attributed to something fairly vague: the difficulty of discovering a
role for the educated, modern, young black woman in late 1960s
Rhodesia. Yet it seems to have been difficult for Dangarembga to
find an appropriate "voice" in which to address the evidence, which
she herself incorporates into the novel, of the burgeoning capitalist
market economy and consumer culture that informs the stories
which Tambu tells. Why this difficulty? Perhaps because to admit
commodity relations into the story as a major plot dynamic would
have been greatly to problematize the nature of the "choices" which
the protagonists make. What does it mean, for instance, to be a
modern black woman in colonial Rhodesia? How is this subject
position inflected through consumption and constrained by racist
policy?

The agonistic relationship between Nyasha and

Babamukuru, by way of example, could be clarified by referring to the discourses of gender and commodity. In Rhodesia in the late 1960s and early 1970s, Burke observes, a burgeoning consumer culture made commercial "toiletries" and beauty aids more widely available to black women. These new subjectivities, while they were not evolved completely independently of traditional patriarchy, highlighted contradictions in the status of black women, and intensified many African men's fears about women's independent sexuality. In both popular conversation and the media, African "women were often depicted as sexually powerful, able to marshal commodities like clothing and toiletries to control men through desire" (158). Whatever the limited nature of the personal freedoms promised by the consumption of goods and the participation in fashionable trends (they do not after all, provide Nyasha with a finally sustaining sense of self), they do represent outlets that enable Nyasha to explore her female identity beyond the designation of dutiful Shona daughter. It is hardly surprising, then, that Babamukuru wishes to marshal his daughter's access to the commodities of "liberated" womanhood, be these tampons, minis, sexy novels or indeed unchaperoned leisure. It is through this control that he seeks to manage her nascent sexuality away from impropriety towards respectability. He considers this to be a responsible, fatherly concern, but reading through the discourses of commodity and patriarchy, we can analyze his actions as an anxious attempt, when faced with the challenges represented by consumption, to retain cultural propriety and authority over female behavior. Respectability is tied to respect. In his view, she is bound (or ought to be bound) to respect him, as patriarch of their Shona extended family; she ought not to give her allegiance to the passing fashions of consumer culture. For Baba, (as for many patriarchal critics of commodification), this is pseudo independence, a dependence on inauthentic cultural meanings rather than a meaningful rite of female adolescent passage en route to independent womanhood. He cannot see that Nyasha's relation to commodities, as to received notions of her "Shonaness," is questioning, critical.

Nyasha is no passive consumer. While she experiments with the subjectivities that modern market relations make available to her, Nyasha also "questions the whole process of assimilation and makes it clear to Tambudzai that real emancipation means more than education and better economic standing" (Veit-Wild 333). Perhaps this is one facet of Baba's dilemma: he does not really understand his daughter's cultural experimentation yet he does sense that it reflects badly on his own class privilege. He fears that his daughter's iconoclastic relation to the modernity which has produced commodity capitalism, commodity feminism and commodified black people will inevitably prompt her to question her role in a traditional Shona hierarchy and thereby wrest from him a significant part of his patriarchal identity. Thus his actions and approbations situate him within the masculine black culture of the 1960s and 1970s in which black women's participation in the curious freedoms of consumerism was frequently considered a challenge to longstanding African cultural hierarchies. For Baba, the very modernity which he so values for himself and for the social standing of his family, has definite limitations when it comes to the liberties allowed his daughter and the other women over whom both customary law and colonialism give him power. In particular, he needs to control Nyasha's independent entry into those aspects of modernity which bear explicitly upon the female body, since it is this liberated body which threatens the potency of his black masculinity. Baba's behavior, too, contains something of the ambiguities of consumer culture: the consumer is variously imagined as a powerfully self-acting agent, and as a victim of economic-symbolic manipulation. When tied, as in this case, to gender, it leaves us with a scenario in which black men might well have been inclined to restrict their female relatives' entry into modern consumer society, as the new cultural choices represented by the production and consumption patterns of a market economy represented a potential threat to male control over women's behavior and aspirations.

Remember that even Maiguru's earnings are managed by

Babamukuru, supposedly in the service of the extended family. Towards the end of the novel, though, especially when it comes to the cultural and financial extravagances of the Christian wedding, she expresses her anger at Baba's denying her the chance to decide how their joint income is spent. This is an apt reminder: despite enduring figurations in western cultural theory of women as extravagant spenders of capital produced by men, Dangarembga's story hints at a socially and historically particular context in which an educated African woman is repeatedly "produced" by a male authority whose power derives from collusions between traditional and modern ways of life and in which she is nearly "consumed" by her inability to direct the cultural choices which are central to the running of the family. (On her arrival at the mission Tambu recollects that her aunt was resting and that she "hoped it was not illness that had put my aunt in bed at that time of the day" [68]. Was it leisure? Depressive ennui? However we read it, the reference resonates with the odd inertias and exhausting energies which mark the behavior of several other female characters in the novel: Nyasha for one, as well as Tambu on the morning of the wedding, and Ma'Shingayi when she fears that Tambu will be acculturated.) We are also told about Maiguru that she cannot drive. While this is not unusual within the historical context in which *Nervous Conditions* is set, it's tempting to observe that Maiguru cannot steer the purchasing patterns of the family. Baba's consuming labors as head master and educational administrator take precedence over other demands; she must wait until he is free before being able to go grocery shopping. Other routines of this supposedly enlightened family are also dictated by masculine fears about maintaining power over the modern, educated black woman as she comes into increasing contact with modernity. Recollect the rigmarole made about serving dinner before Baba has sat down, and the protracted niceties concerning the order of service. By analogy, too, we could say that Maiguru's own desire to describe and secure her marginally superior female status lies in her willingly forfeiting to Anna, the "housegirl" (60), the major tasks of laboring to produce the domestic space, while she gives herself the task of styling the home and reproducing the phatic forms of infantile, lovey-dovey femaleness which Baba will not find threatening.

There is also more to be said about Nyasha. Part of her trauma is that she is obliged to displace her desire for social good—her hostility at the injustices of racism and patriarchy—into a daily relation with the supposed-satisfactions of consumer goods, colonial education, and a middle-class lifestyle whose unspoken limit is race. Nyasha's actions and criticisms uncover the occlusions of the Babamukuru-Maiguru household: the inequalities premised on gender, as well as the tenuousness of what the parents project, by means of possessions, style, food, the organization of space, as their "arrived" status. In comparison with her parents' attempts to fix boundaries so as to exclude the improper and bolster what they perceive to be their proper social status, Nyasha's search for meaning rapaciously crosses cultural divides. She devours (and spits out) varieties of European book learning; she acquires superficial-competence in traditional Shona practices such as appropriate greetings and clay pot making; she experiments with the rituals of female knowledge popular among her contemporaries: cake-baking, fashion, nail-painting, hair-straightening, the use of tampons. She struggles, unsuccessfully, to shape cultural hybridity into a "whole woman" that she can recognize as herself, Nyasha. Perversely, the hybridity of modernity both gives her wider cultural horizons and makes it difficult for her to set limits to what she chooses in her exploration of self. When she does try to "stop" herself (to find something to close the void that threatens her), it is by refusing to conform to conventional eating patterns. Why? Because she has found no belief system that will sustain her—not Shona culture, or colonialism, neither liberated femininity nor consumption. Her own inquiries have repeatedly revealed the limitations of each of these cultural discourses. (Chapman remarks scathingly that Nyasha's supposedly enlightened Western education "has little coherence of idea, action or consequence. Its minor teenage rebellions and freedoms . . . hardly equip the Western teenager for matters of social or political choice let alone the doubly-displaced Nyasha: the African girl caught up in the complex condition of African/colonial dependencies" [308].) Despite her voracious appetite for novelty, she is also driven by an anarchic will to refuse those forms of consumption (education and conspicuous consumerism) which give a black middle class under colonial rule its comparatively privileged place. When she dismisses her father's success as being merely that of a "good munt," when she urges the servant Anna to stop kneeling in her presence and, most dramatically, when she shreds the history text between her teeth, we understand that she is refusing not only the consumption of tainted things associated with her family's class position, but the very ideas which inform this status. What are we to make of this? Are the wages of this ideological "sin," as it were, her necessary death in the novel? No culture—least of all colonial capitalism—can permit that which she represents: a constant critique by those whom it construes as subjects. Compare this with the more promising future which the plot reserves for Tambu. She learns to criticize, yes, but also pragmatically to make the best of a bad situation. She thereby accommodates herself to the status quo even as she secures for herself a higher position in the hierarchy. It might be pushing matters to search out a moral here, but it is difficult to ignore the awkward point that Tambu's survival as the main protagonist occurs precisely because she is thought (by both the author and the conventions of the novel) to be the more desirable . . .? durable . . .? manageable . . .? modern subject. She survives and Nyasha fades away because modernity is willing to sacrifice its potentially better, more critical self in order to perpetuate its structures.

The speculations in the above paragraph are a little contrived and lack the clarity of proper critical inquiry. But if we are interested in relating *Nervous Conditions* to the powerful contemporary discourses of modernity and consumption, such loose "speculation" is germane, and deserves a little space. We could ask, for instance, whether Nyasha's unwillingness to hold on to what she has consumed, despite being attributed by her to forces of patriarchy, is also implicated in the very processes of consumption and "consumer society" through which she is expected to negotiate her subjectivity. By some critics, Nyasha's "nervous condition," her inability to consume, may be taken to illustrate the fact that consumer needs are in principle unlimited and insatiable, and hence destructive. Work through the conceptual contortions this way: consumer culture is the dominant, even privileged medium for negotiating identity within a post-traditional society; the Rhodesia of which Dangarembga writes is moving conflictingly within both the traditional and the modern, therefore consumption is likely to be emerging as a persuasive subject position for young African women such as Nyasha and Tambu. Yet since commodity culture is premised on infinite consumption, "the self" is never something at which you arrive, never an achieved entity with which one is able to feel satisfied. While a romantic strand of modernity urges individuals to fashion themselves into "better people" through hard work, study, and the acquiring of self-reliance, Nyasha discovers that "the self," especially for a young black woman in her time and place, is in fact an exhaustingly infinite project, one which she finds impossible to sustain.

Some of these speculations are a cynical counter to the more sympathetic reading which I have been trying to generate in this paper. The preceding paragraph, for example, emphasizes commodification (and even "modernity") as negative ideology in relation to Dangarembga's characters. Overall, though, I am more interested in arguing for critical readings of *Nervous Conditions* which address the ambivalence towards commodities which marks Dangarembga's text. (Some theorists, of course, consider ambiguity and ambivalence to be inescapable features of modernity itself. Within this theoretical frame, the very subjectivity which we associate with Nyasha—a questioning, self-reflexivity which is perversely liberating and destructive—is cited as the typically heroic-melancholic modern subject.) Reading both in and through Dangarembga's own authorial interests, it becomes possible to see *Nervous Conditions* as a novel which grapples with the fact that the curious life of the commodity and the associated culture of consumption play an important, if not self-evident role in the fears and aspirations, the identifications and alienations of the Sigauke family as its members learn to conceptualize and to express their modern Rhodesian identities. They contribute to the skein of ill-defined nervous conditions running through Dangarembga's novel.

I have tried to demonstrate something of Dangarembga's ambivalent attitude to commodification and goods as these relate to her characters' negotiation of emergent cultural identities. This has necessitated that I regard the "nervous conditions" of the title as not inevitably denoting traumas and neuroses, but also, on occasions, perversely powerful forms of individual agency that provoke a character to shift beyond culturally-entrenched behaviors and assumptions. Since Dangarembga takes similar license with the phrase "nervous conditions," such conceptual experimentation seems legitimate. Not only does Dangarembga selectively feminize Fanon's ideas, she (and/or her publisher) gives her novel the title *Nervous Conditions*, the plural form of a phrase taken from Sartre's introduction to Fanon's *The Wretched of the Earth* rather than from Fanon's text per se. Conversations with colleagues suggest that this conceptual "slippage" is problematic for some academics who regard it as a marketing ploy which plays on the well-traveled slogan—the famous theoretical phrase—or as a mark of shoddy unconcern for the proper lineage of intellectual ideas. I am less troubled by the slips, slides, and elisions packed into the title, and more inclined to view them as symptomatic of the challenges Dangarembga faces in managing a range of often conflicting cultural confluences. Among these are the alienations, assimilations and agencies of the Sigaukes, as well as of "Tsitsi Dangarembga," "African" writer and film-maker who has the power to provoke questions, extremely revealing of an audience's assumptions, about third-world African femaleness and a writer's claim to "cultural authenticity."

Both in English-speaking Africa and in countries abroad, in high schools and at tertiary level, *Nervous Conditions* is among the most prescribed of novels by an "African" writer. As the very collection in which my own essay appears should demonstrate, the text has also become the close subject of an intellectual industry. One conceptual commodity in which the well-established "*Nervous Conditions*" industry trades is "the African woman." A little aside is needed here. Chapman points out that Zimbabwean publishers refused the manuscript, which was then taken up and championed by Ros de Lanerolle of the Women's Press in London. Without her support, the book would probably not have appeared in print (306-07). Paradoxically, though, it is possible that *Nervous Conditions* attracted foreign interest because it deals with African women, a constituency (often misconstrued as a condition) which western feminists are eager to study. Such attention, of course, does help to introduce new voices into received cultural canons, but it also runs the danger of reducing Dangarembga's text to the representatively "African female" object of inquiry, where figures such as Tambu, Nyasha, Maiguru, Lucia, and Ma'Shingayi are frequently viewed either as having "black African" lives fundamentally different from "our" own modernities or, equally facile, as "exploring human conditions that have a general echo for us all" (Joan Riley, back cover of the 1988 Women's Press edition). Several reprints and translation into twelve languages have ensured that Dangarembga's narrative is widely available for those interested in circulating "African woman" for scrutiny by western audiences, even as the manuscript is reputed to have been edited down from a rambling triple-decker charting the girls' experiences as young black Rhodesian women into something more closely resembling the conventional novel. The awkward cultural vectors are exacerbated by several things, among them the book's marketing and critical reception and a cavalier or indifferent attitude to theorizing Dangarembga "now" in relation to Dangarembga (via Tambu and Nyasha) "then." For instance, Dangarembga the writer is herself produced, as it were, by commodified networks of exchange: a black woman educated in England, Zimbabwe, and Berlin, published in Britain, versed in cultural literacies such as fiction, psychology, and film-making. Her labors and packaged versions of her "self" are successfully distributed on the global markets of film and book fairs, interviews, and other forms of literary-cultural journalism. But the literary grapevine has it that audiences at several writers' festivals have been unsettled by Dangarembga's sleekly stylish (read "western") appearance, and by her sometimes aggressive command over the fray of an audience's ill-informed debate. What might the difficulty be? That she is stepping beyond the preferred bounds of acceptable African femaleness? That audiences would have her appear "more authentically African," rather than so adept at mobilizing a plethora of cultural behaviors? The very uneasiness surrounding such receptions of "Dangarembga" suggests that the forms of culture which are relevant in an analysis of her novel are unstable rather than contained, and that they are not necessarily to be located securely in the conventionally agreed-upon spaces of the *Bildungsroman* novel as a genre, or of "African identity."

Even beyond the signifier "Dangarembga," let me address the cover of my own edition of *Nervous Conditions*, since cover artwork and layout are potentially influential mediators of any "message" which readers might imagine a novel to convey. The front cover illustration gives Tambu's "before" picture, where she features as impoverished African female peasant. Instead of an image which suggests cultural shifts or difficult mobility, the image invites readers to think of this as a story in which "progress" (read "western agency") "makes good the dreams of a poor African girl." The requisite marketing panoply of extracts from reviews, emblazoned on the covers and inside front pages, does not help much either. While some legitimately celebrate Dangarembga's female arrival on the literary scene, en masse they are a hotchpotch of western cultural assumptions about Africa (and indeed of "the good novel"). For instance, with no glance in the direction of Rhodesian-Zimbabwean cultural specificity, Dangarembga's debut is praised as a remarkable and classic novel about African women's experience. "African wom/a/en" becomes a trope rather than a culturally and historically specific person or people. I am not averse to all of us as readers from "other" cultures trying to find connections with an imagined "African self"—this projection of sympathies is largely how fiction works—but conceptual headwork must accompany emotional identification. Also, the book is considered by the Judges of the Commonwealth Writer's Prize to be "a beautiful and sensitive exploration of the plight of an African people subjected to a system calculated to poison and destroy their sense of self" (back cover of the 1988 Women's Press edition). What is this "system" referred to—colonialism? Is the assumption that we—and the judges—occupy a comfortably separate cultural space from the "plight" of Tambu and her relatives? That the book's narrative is so good because it confirms the high opinion which we hold of ourselves as modern people willing to make modernity available to third-world people?

My purpose, with these questions, is of course polemical; I cannot offer answers. But my paper has tried to outline a response to *Nervous Conditions* that takes repeated account of the novel as a product of ambiguous cultural energies, consumerism among them. My effort to situate the more conventional debates about "patriarchy" and "identity" in relation to a discourse of consumption has at least relieved me, as critic, of the burden of explaining the life of the essentialized, cliched "African woman" who occupies the boundary of the tradition/modernity binary. I have been freer, instead, to theorize the narrative of *Nervous Conditions* as one constituted by repertoires of knowledge which variously empower and disempower. I have also made space, I hope, for readers of *Nervous Conditions* to take a more informed responsibility in theorizing the novel as one which deals with the very modern cultures which, in some form or another, shape their own lives. As I have argued, in trying to untangle the women's stories which Tambu narrates and the various female selves which populate the novel, it is as necessary for us to work through women's relation to goods and the imagined "good life" to which Tambu aspires and which Nyasha debunks, as it is for us to foreground overt patriarchal oppression in "an African culture." And it is important to take this issue further than a simple refusal of "assimilation," so as to grapple with the fact that Nyasha's own turbulent attempts to fashion a meaningful subjectivity occur as much through consumption as against it. Indeed, the very mode of address which has made *Nervous Conditions* a successful and academically popular literary text intersects with the registers through which "women's popular culture" presents the spectacle of individual lives. Whether we're thinking magazines, radio dramas, or soap operas, these "women's genres" are characterized by confessional logics, intimate testimonies, and serial self-exploration that are not dissimilar from the techniques which Dangarembga uses to have us empathize with the female experience of Tambu and Nyasha. The adolescent femaleness of these two constitutes a body-centeredness which readers are likely to recognize as much from the true stories and advice columns of women's magazines, as from the narratives of women's struggles for independence contained in the more classic genre of the bourgeois novel. I will not pursue this issue further; yet it is worth grappling with the possibility that in its textures and subject matters *Nervous Conditions* crosses the long-established academic boundaries between high and low culture, and that such "transgressions" also place received notions of Africanness and Westernness in new conjuncture. In trying to understand Nyasha and Tambu, then, we cannot simply respond to them as "African women," or even "Rhodesians/Zimbabweans" who are fundamentally dissimilar from "us." We could consider the intersections and deflections which make their lives both analogous with and different from our own. It is not simply, as Boehmer puts it, that "[t]he anorectic distress of the . . . Anglicized Nyasha reveals that the 'modern' and Western can be as psychologically oppressive for a woman as is traditional society" (228). The case is compounded when western intellectuals acknowledge that their (our) own identity formation derives from the very cultures of modernity to which we ascribe both Nyasha's illness and to which we attribute the educated discourses through which we frame our critique.

In essence, this paper enables me to outline a reading which moves beyond the obvious neuroses depicted in the book, allowing into the mix Dangarembga's struggles to express the awkward intersections of cultural institutions such as colonial education, liberal enlightenment, traditional patriarchy, modernity, and consumer culture. Although I have been able only to outline a few ideas, it should be evident that I am given to produce a reading of *Nervous Conditions* which comments on the shifting presences and absences in Dangarembga's novel of the commodity in the world of 1960s-1970s Rhodesia in which the story is set. Indeed, it seems feasible to argue that the ambivalence in the novel towards consumer culture comprises Dangarembga's authorial "nervous condition" and, importantly, that this is a condition of the global modernities which we are likely to call our own.

Chapter 9:
Women and Food in Tsitsi Dangarembga's *Nervous Conditions*

Kelli Donovan Wixson

Throughout Tsitsi Dangarembga's novel *Nervous Conditions*, women's relationships with food reflect their status in society. Living in pre-independence Zimbabwe, the five women named by Tambudzai, the narrator, are doubly removed from access to power, once by the traditional Shona patriarchy and again by the English colonial system which reinforced that patriarchy even as it subjugated the country to colonial rule. The women's daily tasks that Tambu describes in greatest detail focus on food—growing it, preparing it, serving it—and food (or the refusal of it) is the means by which each woman asserts herself in the course of the novel. One way to read the beginning of the novel is as a measure of each woman's success in establishing her agency. Tambu says that her story is "about my escape and Lucia's; about my mother's and Maiguru's entrapment; and about Nyasha's rebellion" (1). A discussion of other contexts for this description, including the role of education and the various manifestations of the "nervous conditions" of the title, is beyond my scope here. My focus will be the agency each of the women attempts to achieve through her relationship with food.

As suggested by Dangarembga's title and epigraph, the writings of Frantz Fanon provide an important foundation for *Nervous Conditions*. A combination of Fanon's ideas in the chapters "Algeria Unveiled" from *A Dying Colonialism* (*DC*) and "On National Culture" from *The Wretched of the Earth* (*Wretched*) illustrate how food becomes the site of resistance for the women in Dangarembga's novel. In "Algeria Unveiled," Fanon stresses that the natives do not predetermine where they will resist the colonizer, but rather they respond to the colonizer's intent to manipulate cultural elements. Fanon describes this as "one of the laws of the psychology of colonization," in which "it is the action, the plans of the occupier that determine the centers of resistance around which a people's will to survive becomes organized" (*DC* 47). He further states that natives spontaneously adjust their attitudes about these cultural elements once they have become centers of resistance. As with determining where resistance will be organized, such redefinition is in response to the colonizer, not established in advance or out of context.

In *Nervous Conditions*, food becomes the focus of the women's self-assertion because of its importance in the oppressive colonial and patriarchal systems depicted in the novel. Tambu's grandmother tells her that the whites had driven the family from their desirable land and had forced them to establish the homestead on soil "so stony and barren that the wizards would not use it" (18). The poor quality of the soil requires hard work to eke out enough food for the family. The novel alludes to generations of women carrying out these tasks, with only occasional help from men. In fact, men often gather to discuss family issues while the women work in the fields (7) or prepare meals (135-36). Throughout the novel, the men of Tambu's family express what they consider to be women's proper (i.e. traditional Shona) roles. For example, Jeremiah, Tambu's father, is concerned that Tambu's early reading "would fill [her] mind with impractical ideas, making [her] quite useless for the real tasks of feminine living" (34), namely, catering to the men in her family. Tambu recognizes the inequity of such a division of labor, but concedes, "[t]he needs and sensibilities of the women in my family were not considered a priority, or even legitimate" (12). When the various women decide to challenge their circumstances, each turns to food as the resource that is most accessible and most charged with colonial and traditional meaning. The women act independently, which is consistent with Fanon's observation about the spontaneous nature of resistance. Until the end of the novel, there is little sense that each woman's assertion of agency through a redefinition of food affects the others.

Fanon's discussion about the meaning of culture in "On National Culture" is also relevant here. For Fanon, the actions taken in the moment of resisting the oppressor redefine culture. Whatever cultural meaning might have existed prior to colonization cannot serve a colonized people. According to Fanon, "[i]t is not enough to try to get back to the people in that past out of which they have already emerged; rather we must join them in that fluctuating movement which they are just giving shape to" and "[t]here is no other fight for culture which can develop apart from . . . struggle" (*Wretched* 227, 233). Although their struggle is localized and gendered rather than national, the women of Tambu's story redefine their relationships with food in the moments when they refuse to accept its colonial and traditional meanings. Each woman's struggle against the established meanings of food generates her agency, and that agency is effective for as long as she struggles. Although some of the women are unable to sustain their newly asserted autonomy and ultimately resume their places in the colonial/patriarchal double-bind, each experiences the power of asserting her own purpose rather than depending on those imposed by others (colonizers and Shona men).

As useful as Fanon's ideas are for understanding *Nervous Conditions*, Dangarembga's novel also expands Fanon's work by exploring more fully the impact of colonialism and patriarchy on women. Numerous critics have drawn attention to this gap in Fanon's writing. To take only one example, Anne McClintock, in her recent essay in the anthology *Dangerous Liaisons: Gender, Nation, and Postcolonial Perspectives*, notes what she calls a "curious rupture" in Fanon's essay "Algeria Unveiled." She points out that "Fanon's thoughts on women's agency proceed through a series of contradictions" (McClintock 97). McClintock's discussion traces the incompatibility of Fanon's perception that the veil is "open to the subtlest shifts and subversions" with his simultaneous "refus[al] to grant the veil any prior role in the gender dynamics of Algerian society" (ibid). She describes Fanon's account of Algerian women's participation in the revolution as "a *designated agency*—an agency by invitation only" and his view that prior to the revolution, "women's agency was null, void, as inert as the veil" (McClintock 98, original emphasis). Contradictions such as these in Fanon's text result from his globalized assumptions about women. Statements in "Algeria Unveiled" in which Fanon refers to Algerian women's veils as a "formerly inert element of the native cultural configuration," a "dead" element, and an "undifferentiated element in a homogeneous whole" (*DC* 46-47) show that he does not distinguish among the various possible reasons why Algerian women would wear the veil, or even acknowledge that such diverse possibilities exist. Dangarembga avoids this hazard by grounding her characters within specific contexts and showing how they respond to their circumstances. According to the critic Deepika Bahri, in his article "Disembodying the Corpus: Postcolonial Pathology in Tsitsi Dangarembga's *Nervous Conditions*":

The women in [*Nervous Conditions*] are neither simply

victims, nor inherently more noble than the men; rather their stories illustrate the difficulty of separating problem and solution, perpetrator and victim, cause and effect . . . . Dangarembga obliges us to recognize that the power structure is a contradictory amalgam of complicity and helplessness—where colonizer *and* colonized, men *and* women collude to produce their . . . "nervous" conditions. (Bahri para. 6, original emphasis)

The women of *Nervous Conditions* are not generalized abstractions; rather, they are concrete, complicated, and varied, simultaneously using and being used by colonial and patriarchal systems. That the struggle for agency and identity occurs on the most basic level of existence, the need for food, is Dangarembga's achievement in the novel.

Each of the stories of the five women which Tambu tells in *Nervous Conditions* is intricately tied to food, and throughout the novel, most of the family's important scenes take place in the context of a meal. However, only Tambu herself and her aunt Lucia are able to "escape" (in Tambu's phrase) from their society's predetermined roles for women regarding food. Since Tambu's escape is linked to all of the other women's stories, I will return to her story later. At first glance, Lucia's efforts to redefine her relationship with food seem to entrench her further within the familial system rather than liberating her from it. During one Christmas holiday, Lucia initially stays in the kitchen with the other women while the patriarchs of the family (ironically including Aunt Tete) conduct a *dare* session to decide her future at the homestead. Lucia boldly interrupts the *dare* to express her intention to leave the homestead. Later, during a lunch, Lucia asks Babamukuru to find her a job, which he does in the kitchen of the Mission School's girl's hostel. Although Nyasha remains indignant about the fact that Lucia ultimately depended on Babamukuru to get a job, and that she is still cast in a traditional female role by continuing to prepare food, Lucia's refuses to have her fate decided by the elders and invents a creative solution to her predicament. Lucia's food service job has the additional benefit of enabling her to go to school, an opportunity she would not otherwise have had. Lucia's escape is successful both because of her aggressive attitude and because she is able to create new possibilities for herself that are not limited to the family's (i.e. the men's) plans for her.

If Lucia can escape because she gives new meaning to the context of food in her life, then Mainini, Tambu's mother, and Maiguru, her aunt, remain "trapped" by food because they withdraw from their established roles without assuming new ones. Both women perform very similar, traditional functions in their respective families, which consist primarily of preparing and serving food. Maiguru is quite fussy about meals, insisting on serving her husband first, and constantly inquiring if his needs are satisfied. Mainini and Maiguru are also in charge of meals on special family occasions, such as Babamukuru's return from England, and Christmas holidays. In addition to her regular household chores, Mainini sells eggs and vegetables to pay for Nhamo's education because her husband Jeremiah is too lazy to work. However, when Tambu wants an education, Mainini only provides her with seeds to grow in her spare time. Mainini wants to teach her daughter that "some things cannot be done" (17), because she believes that Tambu's efforts to get an education are fruitless. Late in the novel, after Tambu has begun to distance herself from her mother and identify more closely with Maiguru, Mainini defines what each woman has to offer the girl in terms of food. She says to Tambu, "If it is meat you want that I cannot provide for you, if you . . . would betray your own mother for meat, then go to your Maiguru. She will give you meat. I will survive on vegetables as we all used to do" (140-41). The difference between meat and vegetables is both the literal material resources of the mission school vs. the homestead, as well as the opportunities of education vs. a life of farming. In her article "An Apple for the Teacher? Femininity, Coloniality, and Food in *Nervous Conditions*," Heidi Creamer states that Tambu's contradiction "between food and lack of food is much more problematic" than she had originally thought, since she had never gone without food at the homestead (Creamer 354). From Maiguru's perspective, her usual responsibility for meals is greatly magnified by her position as the wife of the provider of the family's Christmas dinner. Although she complains about the workload, "what I object to is the way everybody expects me to spend all my time cooking for them . . . . I end up slaving for everybody" (122), Babamukuru ignores her.

Just as Mainini and Maiguru are defined by their traditional roles involving food, so too are their attempts to withdraw from those roles. Mainini is unable to eat in response to her daughter's increasing education. Her appetite decreases during the week preceding Tambu's start at the mission school, and again even more drastically before she leaves for Sacred Heart. In a similar refusal, Maiguru leaves her home because she is tired of being taken advantage of by others, including her husband, who expect her to fulfill her wifely duties obediently. Mainini and Maiguru withdraw from their established responsibilities because for each, doing so is the only available way to resist the pressure of her family and express her feelings. Insofar as others notice and are affected by their withdrawals from family life, Mainini and Maiguru establish their ability to act in ways outside of prescribed patterns. Moreover, both return to their former roles due only to someone else's intervention. Lucia's willingness to end her sister's independence undermines the value of her own, especially since she offers no indication in the text about why she feels that Mainini needs to be brought back into the family. Maiguru seems to have benefited somewhat from her withdrawal becoming less fussy about meals and voicing her own opinion when Babamukuru asks her. Although Mainini and Maiguru do assert a degree of agency, it is drastically limited by their prompt and relatively unchanged return to their former roles. Nyasha's observation to Tambu about Maiguru applies equally to Mainini: "So where do you break out to? You're just one person and it's everywhere" (174).

Of the various forms of resistance and redefinition of food engaged in by the women of Tambu's family, Nyasha's anorexia is the most extreme, and produces the most ambiguous results. Tambu says that Nyasha's rebellion "may not in the end have been successful" (1). Nyasha stops eating, or else binges and purges, in response to her father's efforts to make her conform to his ideas of what a "good girl" should be like, both as the daughter of an African headmaster in the colonial education system, and as a member of the Shona people. As Bahri indicates, "Nyasha's war with patriarchal and colonial systems is fought on the turf of her own body, both because it is the scene of enactment of these systems, and because it is the only site of resistance available" (Bahri para. 4). Babamukuru controls his daughter through food even before she stops eating, as when he reprimands her for serving rice for herself before he had been fully served his meal. The first time Nyasha obviously refuses to eat a complete meal occurs when her father hides her copy of *Lady Chatterley's Lover* and commands her to finish her food. In Babamukuru's opinion, Nyasha's reading of Lawrence's novel is evidence that she has "no sense of decency" (81). Until this point in *Nervous Conditions*, we have the vague impression that Nyasha has a typical appetite, and at first her reaction seems more like a petulant snit than the beginning of her eating disorder. What this scene does make clear, however, is that Nyasha chooses not to eat in order to avoid giving in to her father's authority. For the most part, Tambu casually reports further instances of Nyasha's loss of appetite while studying for exams and after numerous confrontations with her father in which he demands that she comply with his views about proper behavior for young women.

A drastic scene close to the end of the novel reveals how far Babamukuru and Nyasha's relationship has deteriorated and the corresponding increase in the severity of her illness. Babamukuru is upset that Nyasha returns after the hour that "decent girls" come home, and he orders her to eat all of her dinner. She gobbles her food, and then purges in the bathroom. As she later explains to Tambu, "it's . . . more than just food. That's how it comes out, but really it's all the things about boys and men and being decent and indecent and good and bad" (190). Her anorexia is not a response to a single incident, but to a series of repeated provocations.

Nyasha's illness progresses until she finally suffers a complete breakdown while frantically studying for her "O" level exams. It is interesting to note that "striking . . . intellectual hyperactivity" is one of the characteristics which frequently occurs in someone with anorexia (Vandereycken and van Deth [1994] 2); this observation recalls Nyasha's study habits for her Form Two exams and emphasizes the length of her illness. In a morbid parody of the act she has so long refused, Nyasha "shred[s] her history book between her teeth" (201), simultaneously rejecting the colonizer's official version of history, her father's role in the colonial education system, and his prescripts for her behavior based on traditional Shona standards. Nyasha's parents' ignorance of her illness, and the psychiatrist's denial of her anorexia because "Africans did not suffer in [that] way" (ibid) highlight that her condition is beyond both colonial and patriarchal understanding. Bahri has asserted that Nyasha's anorexia is "ironic" because it is a "stereotypically Western female pathological condition" (Bahri para. 3). However, her illness can be understood as her only available response to the double alienation of being a Western-educated female who has returned to Africa and cannot reconcile those two sets of conflicting cultural values. In addition, recent studies of the causes of eating disorders suggest that eating disorders can have a strong cultural component (see Vandereycken 1992) and that non-Western women of color suffer from eating disorders but were excluded from earlier studies which relied on the standard profile of anorexic women as Western, white, and middle- to upper-class (see Thompson). After Nyasha is hospitalized, we do not learn any additional information about her condition. The ambiguous ending to her story indicates that Nyasha's attempt at independence through food refusal is not a model to be imitated, but rather one to be avoided, a lesson which Tambu absorbs.

Returning, then, to the story of Tambu's own successful

"escape" shows that her ability to redefine the meaning of food generates the most lasting form of female agency, for even Lucia's success is individual, affecting no one other than herself. Tambu's independence goes beyond her own story in that she is able to write the stories of all of the women. Creamer states that "Tambu must understand how [the colonial and patriarchal] systems and meanings of food intertwine with her ideas about liberation so that she can understand and tell the story of her 'escape'" (Creamer 351). Early in the novel, Tambu sees that raising her own maize gives her access to an education she would otherwise be denied. Like all of the other women, Tambu is responsible for extensive food preparation at the homestead, and Babamukuru assigns this chore to her at the mission school as part of her punishment for disobeying him. Both literally and metaphorically, food and education are always markers of Tambu's desire to escape; the two are brought together in the descriptions of Babamukuru as one who "devoured English letters with a ferocious appetite" (36). Throughout the novel, Tambu neither follows Lucia's example of taking a job outside of the family's homestead, nor does she attempt independence by refusing to participate in oppressive systems, a choice made by Mainini, Maiguru, and Nyasha. Instead, Tambu learns more from the examples of all of these women than she does in her formal education (Creamer 358).

The various meanings of food, as escape or entrapment, as resistance or oppression, pervade Tsitsi Dangarembga's novel *Nervous Conditions*. As the locus of the overlapping and intersecting ideologies of colonialism and patriarchy, food is the vehicle through which the women of the novel pursue their agency. In the closing scene of the novel, Tambu uses a final image of food to illustrate the development of her critical awareness. "Seeds do grow," she declares, ". . . this story is how it all began" (203-04).

III

POSTCOLONIALISM AND SUBJECTIVITY

Chapter 10:
"Two Disconnected Entities": The Pitfalls of Knowing in Tsitsi Dangarembga's *Nervous Conditions*

Linda E. Chown

> A woman in a state of indecision put her pencil to the paper,
> made a line or a shape, scratched it out, started again, scratched
> it out: at the end of an evening her sketch pad would be full
> of jagged erasures. And so it was with all of us: we were set
> in modes, by organizers and governors unknown to our con-
> scious selves. Doris Lessing, *African Laughter* (406)

Zimbabwean Tsitsi Dangarembga's compelling *Nervous Conditions* explores a host of tangled divisions— political, social, cultural, and psychological. In addition to being a unique postcolonial *Bildungsroman*, a veritable narrative implosion of colonial oppressions, it also subtly undermines significant colonial epistemological approaches to psyche and language. Differences between what Tambu, the main character/

narrator, calls "two disconnected entities" (167) parallel a division in the novel between a Eurocentric, psychologized written praxis and a less self conscious, oral, epistemic modality, a division which lessens by the end of this novel.

Russian linguist Lev Vygotsky's historically grounded hypotheses concerning inner speech helpfully recontextualize the actions of language and memory as forces shaping the Manichean worlds invasively present throughout this novel. Vygotsky posits a form of Manicheanism in language acquisition noting, "[t]hroughout childhood, there is a ceaseless conflict between two mutually antagonistic forms of thinking" (149). Vygotsky proposes an historical and evolutionary theory of language development in which thinking develops from the social or what he calls "egocentric speech" to become individualized or "inner speech." External speech is, he suggests, "for others" and "inner speech [or endophasy]" is "speech for oneself" (130). Dangarembga's novel dramatizes a struggle between these two directions. Vygotsky's theorizing further analyzes a dialectic between these two modalities: "There is," he writes, "no sharp division between inner and external behavior, and each influences the other" (47). Vygotsky concludes that egocentric talk corresponds to an "egocentricism of the child's thinking and its insufficient socialization" (136). *Nervous Conditions* complexly presents dialogue and monologue, extrospective and inner speech. It narratively explores what Vygotsky had earlier observed: "the relation between thought and words is a living process: thought is born through words. A word devoid of thought is a dead thing, and a thought unembodied in words remains a shadow" (153).

It is essential here to stress that Vygotsky valorizes most a transition from inner to external speech which is "intelligible to others" (148). His studies lead him to consider "participation," that phenomenon observed by Levi-Bruhl and Von den Steinen. Vygotsky argues that Western thinking has, overall, neglected the workings of participation in language formation because thinkers have ignored "the mental operations involved" and failed to view this phenomenon "in the context of the other bonds and relationships" (71). In other words, many previous language studies were ahistoric and essentialist. At a later stage in this paper, Vygotsky's specific theories of vocalized speech or orality as they relate to *Nervous Conditions* will be addressed.

In the contexts of Postcolonial Studies, *Nervous Conditions* subtly executes a significant reversal of colonial epistemological practices in re-shaping fixed assumptions concerning psyche in African literature. *Nervous Conditions* grows in a caldron of "ceaseless conflict." Vygotsky's fluid model of language and psyche development offer a non-reductive and productive way to understand Tambu's complex development in the face of conflict, opposition, and inner polarizations. His studies lead him to conclude that the ability to go beyond the hegemony of external influences can evolve only with the aid of "strenuous mental activity . . ." (85). Inner speech, one of his trademark concepts, is "a thinking in pure meanings," "a dynamic, shifting, unstable thing, fluttering between word and thought," a function in which "words die as they bring forth thought" (149).

With Vygotsky's linguistic constructs as anchor, narrative theory further adds to reading the tensions between "two disconnected entities" by illuminating a Eurocentric thoroughly psychologized, written mode and a less self-conscious, pre-Cartesian and a predominantly oral epistemic praxis (Dangarembga 167). Before the end of the novel, tensions between these conflicted ways of knowing dissolve, with each overwriting and erasing the other.[1] Vygotsky speaks of movement into inner speech as "a differentiation of egocentric speech [which is] incomprehensible to others from the child's primary social speech" (148). Placing herself in the seat of conflict in retrospectively composing her own narrative, Tambu succeeds in bringing these two hitherto separate modes into harmony, rendering the "predicative, idiomatic structure of inner speech into syntactically articulated speech intelligible to others" (Vygotsky 148). The linguistic/narrative success thus engendered marks a movement well beyond her culture's reductive Manicheanism.

In spite of external stalemates and rapid-fire cultural changes, this book's final perspective is radically positive. Zimbabwean-born writer Doris Lessing acclaims *Nervous Conditions*, once titled *Nervous Disorders*, for being "a revolutionary book" (423). Lindsay Aegeter, originally from Zimbabwe, stresses that Dangarembga "allows her female characters to protest the predicament of African women not by positioning themselves in *opposition* to their oppressors, a gesture that . . . serves to reinscribe Manichean dualities, but by depicting African women's identity in terms of *constantly shifting positionality*" (233, emphasis added). These shifting perspectives undermine the counterproductive "Western addiction," to what Homi Bhabha calls the "concept of fixity" (qtd. in Jolly 19). As part of the intensive re-delineations characteristic of Postcolonial Studies, Satya Mohanty challenges theoretically fixed expectations underlying all pre-shaped objective frameworks, concluding that current Postcolonial "theoretical accounts of objectivity depend on explanatory accounts of error and distortion" (115). Dangarembga's novel emphatically contributes to such conceptual reshapings. Readers and Tambu alike have to make new sense of both the novel's expected conflicts and its unexpected resolutions, which occur in the course of Tambu's intense self-encounters. With Vygotsky's research into the faultlines of consciousness, we can better explain Tambu's objective, narrative, and personal ebullience at the end.

Postcolonial reconsiderations of positionality frequently allude to a "postpositivist 'realism,'" a practice engendering multiple, culturally viable and variegated explorations of understanding, texts, and circumstances (Mohanty 115). Indeed, this novel's conclusion underscores the productiveness of such "shifting positionality," so that one can affirmatively discover with Tambu that "it was a long and painful process for me, that process of expansion" (204). That is to say, Tambu's "expansion" entails intensely dwelling-in and making sense of abruptly changing positions, which in turn leads her to greater internal and external free-dom. She discovers the marriage of "inner" and "external" speech as "a rerouting of everything I had ever defined as me" (58). Tambu's radiant "expansion" becomes clearer in nonlinearly con-sidering narrative development, attending both to the narrator's exterior *and* interior speech, and re-contextualizing the culturally given subtexts of her various "conditions."

First, the novel swerves rapid-fire between different nar-rative perspectives. On the one hand, Tambu, the novel's central protagonist, is, in Gerald Génette's terms, an autodiegetic narrator from novel's beginning to end. In other words, she is a narrator **narrating her own story**. Simultaneously, hers is homodiegetic narration in the sense that she is clearly **taking part in the story** of a past she is recalling from an unspecified physical perspective in the present. One of the tensions in the novel involves Tambu's un-certain status to herself as to the word and the deed. Here again, Vygotsky's thinking proves pertinent in his radical overturning of conventional models, "The word," he writes, "was not the begin-ning—action was there first; it is the end of development, crown-ing the deed" (153). Such formulations appropriately describe cul-tures whose origins are not saturated with Cartesian misgivings regarding word and thing, identity and circumstance, personhood and others.[2]

After the novel's plot story concludes, Tambu's decisive, epiphanic moment coalesces;

> Quietly, unobtrusively and extremely fitfully, something in my mind began to assert itself, to question things and refuse to be brainwashed. . . . It was a long and painful process for me, that process of expansion . . . a process whose events stretched over many years and would fill another volume, but the story I have told here, is my own story . . . this story is how it all began. (204)

This unqualified confidence and sureness corroborate her achievement. Inner speech activities have lent her the stamina to reject others' stories and attenuate their pressures. Dangarembga's novel gradually spawns a context other than Gayatri Spivak's well known "the subaltern cannot speak." In contrast, Tambu speaks, remembers; she revels in the story, her story, what she has told, said, thought, and written. This book's closing paragraph is prefaced with sentences revealing that hers is indeed a mature speaking perspective, that this now writing-narrating Tambu is reflectively and perceptively older and surer as a result both of her developing external speech and her intensive development of inner speech and introspection. This perspective becomes evident in phrases like "I was young then," or "Although I was not aware of it then . . ." (203). This novel profoundly reminds a reader of the narrator's linguistic stages and levels of self-acceptance.

This is exactly the kind of narrator I have elsewhere named a "persona narrator," one whose pervasive and lonely trauma induces a special recall, on the part of a narrator who "struggled . . . to order a life threatened suddenly by a late shift in perspective, by the unasked-for traumas of self-revision . . ." (Chown 126-34, Mudge 242). Western Freudian psychology has not infrequently hastily frozen in extrospective terms a series of primarily one-dimensional "conditions" and embraced polarized conflict in the process. The most influential effect of this has been an ego-saturated emphasis on one's psyche, often conceived of as property. Against this, Vygotsky warns of devastatingly isolating features of exclusively egocentric speech (15). According to most dictionaries, "psychology" denotes the science or organized study of the psyche. In practice, many times, psychology may become, ironically, a dangerously non-intimate praxis, a focus concerned primarily with classifications *about*, rather than a dwelling *in* psyche.[3] It helps to recall that, in contrast to Tambu, Nyasha, her double and cousin, finally becomes surrounded by psychiatrists whose cultural obtuseness allows them to assume that "Africans did not suffer in the way we had described" (201). This novel painfully traces and particularizes the often shifting grounds and parameters of a "formalist" psychology.

Nervous Conditions complicates and lyrically experiments with the terms of Franz Fanon's "split subject," found in the epigraph to Dangarembga's novel.[4] Just as Vygotsky's groundbreaking, posthumously published 1934 study sought to interweave thought and word, so does Dangarembga's novel of a psychologically divided, culturally circumscribed young woman. Here, however, instead of referring principally to cultural divisions between colonizer and colonized, divisions which condemn the colonized to live dividedly, this novel introduces a person profoundly "split" in another way—between overly conscious self-awareness and a seamless unselfconsciousness in daily living. South African writer J. M. Coetzee has dwelt at length upon limitations of "hyperconsciousness" which he finds decisively freezes, stalls, and imprisons human initiative and vitality. In her account of passage toward adulthood, Tambu moves from a rigid and frequently passive psychologicalization of reality to a trusting depsychologalization of a reality she finally activates on her own.[5] As this happens, distances between other previously fixed polarities also diminish.

Vygotsky posited that intellectual Manicheanism negatively influences everything. One such polarity that he identified was between intellect and affect, arguing that such a separation seriously undermines formulation of personhood. From a Eurocentric context, Elaine Showalter and Judith Ryan have considered unsettling effects of an unfamiliar ambiguous self in a context saturated by hierarchically based divisions. Concretely, in *The Female Malady* Showalter focuses on cultural causes of neurasthenia, that ubiquitous nineteenth-century condition. Specifically, she examines its invasive effects, particularly upon women. She explores links between madness or mental instability and women, concluding, "Women were believed to be more vulnerable to insanity than men, to experience it in specifically feminine ways, and to be differently affected by it in the conduct of their lives" (7). There was, Showalter posits, a significant shift in the social status of madness around 1800, at which time "the symbolic gender of the insane person shifted from male to female" (8). Showalter's study emphasizes culturally inscribed links between women and nervous, psycho-logically affiliated "conditions:"

> At the end of the nineteenth century, hysteria, the classic female malady, became the focal point for the second psy-chiatric revolution, the emergence of psychoanalysis. It was in dealing with hysterical women, after all, that Freud first developed his theories of the sexual origin of neurosis, and his techniques of dream analysis and free association. (18)

The beginnings of the nineteenth century also coincided with the beginnings of the Industrial Revolution and the nearly complete differentiation between public and private worlds. It was, significantly, a time of sweeping change much like that faced by Tambu in her increasingly fluid late twentieth-century world. Vygotsky's conclusions continue to be pertinent here and define some parameters and difficulties of these times of change, suggesting that "psychology has until recently depicted the matter in an oversimplified way" (7).

Nervous Conditions particularizes and criticizes the well-springs of Western neurasthenia in women in African contexts. *Nervous Conditions* draws in bold type the voracious contagious-ness of the female malady in two women protagonists who, it be-comes clear, have virtually no preparation to deal either with their own "condition" or their uniquely powerful, perceptive intelligence. The novel's explicit criticism of stifling hyperconsciousness cor-responds to the understanding that literature is the appropriate site for commentary on the twisted positions spawned by colonialism.[6] Specifically, Nyasha suffers from an eating disorder while Tambu becomes obsessed with and fearful of what is to her a thoroughly uncharted mental life. For instance, thinking to herself, Tambu, observes in one of her most telling reflections:

> He did not know how my mind had raced and spun and ended up splitting into two disconnected entities that had long, frightening arguments with each other, very vocally, there in my head, about what ought to be done, the one

half maniacally insisting on going, the other half equally maniacally refusing to consider it. (167)

Tambu's recognition of this conflicted realm in herself demonstrates the intensity of her encounter with the thoroughly unexpected world of her psyche. Tambu's doubts about attending her parent's wedding become a moment ripe for the type of study that Vygotsky urges that considers "practical dealings with the real world," something with which Tambu and Nyasha acutely struggle (22).

Similarly, Judith Ryan addresses the self in modernist texts in her work *The Vanishing Subject.* In tracing the development of the new psychology and perceived loss of a clear-cut concept of self at the end of the nineteenth century, Ryan finds that "levels of consciousness and degrees of attention began to fascinate thinkers and writers alike" (9). Correspondingly, in this period "the very notion of self" began to change radically (9). One major result of this shift meant that "developing a single, consistent point of view no longer appeared to be a faithful way of representing reality" (19), recalling Vygotsky's warning about the dangers of an "antihistorical," prematurely unifying model (153). An extension of the changing view regarding language in the times of modernism brought about an eerie breakup of traditional modes of self. As individual constructions of reality became increasingly fluid, so too, Ryan argues, did any sense of the certainty for the perceiver as sole constructor of an organized, unified world.[7] For instance, in 1905 Austrian Hermann Behr wrote an essay tellingly called "The Unsalvageable Self." Although emerging Freudian versions of a possibly unified self eventually "gained wide acceptance" in Europe (Ryan 22), Dangarembga's novel explores some immediate effects of an ambiguous life without sure selfhood in twentieth-century Zimbabwe through the unsettledness impelling Tambu's recall and her chaotically ambivalent understandings. *Nervous Conditions* foregrounds the tensions inherent in the Manichean cultural world that sustain divisions between thought and language, word and deed, inner and exterior speech.

These two new constructs, the "female malady" and an unexpected new selfsense, enter decisively into Dangarembga's novel, making the novel a significant document for postcolonial attention. Since Zimbabwe was undergoing radical changes not unlike those described by Showalter and Ryan, Dangarembga's book introduces an encounter with an unsettled cultural issue— namely the locus, function, and reliability of knowing in post-Cartesian communities.

Tambu's account, then, needs to be read in two ways simultaneously: both as that of the young girl experiencing first hand psyche-threatening changes in her life overall and simultaneously as that of an older person reflecting upon her earlier responses during dramatic times of change. Vygotsky provides a way of clearly differentiating between these levels through his theories of monologue, represented by the written and inner speech, and dialogue or oral speech (142). He finds that inner speech omits subjects. More interestingly, he argues that inner speech and oral speech alike "function as a draft" (144). Such hypotheses illuminate Tambu's constant linguistic, psychic struggles. At one point, Tambu will say about one of those changes, "my going to the mission was such a drastic change that it unnerved me" (110). The key word here is "unnerved." Many heroines in European fiction, among them characters in Gilman's *The Yellow Wallpaper*, Brontë's *Jane Eyre*, James' *The Turn of the Screw*, and Plath's *The Bell Jar* fall into fits of "unnervedness" which render them "hysterical" and "unnerved" in the public eye. In these moments, they correspond perilously closely to definitions of the "female malady." In a telling moment in the prologue of Henry James' the *Turn of the Screw*, Douglas readily dismisses the governess as "young, untried, nervous . . ." (8). Dangarembga metamorphosizes this trope of the frazzled and "nervous" woman by contrasting it with Tambu's subsequent mental reach, confidence, and agility. This novel subtly swerves between and makes room for both dialogue and monologue, selfhood and solitude, and the oral and the written. Uninterrupted change which brusquely and traumatically impinged **upon** Tambu's childhood induced **in** her a process of extensive and actually clawingly, dangerously unfamiliar, self-inspection. The title of the book suggests the extent of the internal impacts of changes which set in motion a plethora of overt or covert "nervous conditions." Tambu's narrative recall of this agitated period necessarily inflects and interweaves present and past, inner and external speech, individualistic and collective turns of attention which finally interfuse, abet, and activate each the other.

In developing what he calls "inner speech," Vygotsky points to its positive social results. In a distinction helpful for reading African fiction, Vygotsky concludes that "In inner speech, the 'mutual' perception is always there, in absolute form . . ." (145). His definition thus takes the other and the communal densely into account. For Vygotsky as for Dangarembga, speech does not necessarily equal only the overtly spoken or said. "The flow of thought," Vygotsky writes, "is not accompanied by a simultaneous unfolding of speech" (85). Likewise, Tambu's knowing is not always smoothly particularized and spelled out. There remain gaps, absences, and fragments. Vygotsky's theories attend to those silent distinctions, inner promptings or voicings, and external utterance, both written and oral. To this iconoclastic Russian who knew the effects of oppression, censorship, and dichotomies, "Inner speech is to a large extent thinking in pure meanings. It is a dynamic, shifting, unstable thing, fluttering between word and thought . . ." (149). He appreciated its potential for growth.

In applying Vygotsky's theory to Dangarembga's novel, a reader may question the pertinence of these distinctions between "external" and "inner" speech. For Vygotsky as for Tambu, people can develop in language from dependence on the externalized speech of a child to a teenager's sometimes brooding submersion in inner speech alone, to a language experience which discovers a *triadic* relation between thought, word and deed. Quite directly, Vygotsky maintains: "In the beginning was the deed. The word was not the beginning—action was there first; it is the end of development, crowning the deed" (153). This triadic understanding theoretically undoes the binary or Manichean oppositions which Dangarembga's novel so eloquently presents and ultimately derails. In this novel, finally Tambu finds ways to develop within each of her own conditions.

Coming back to the novel with these contexts in mind, then, a reader finds that in addition to an objective account of cultural change and its bitter consequences, there are a host of binary tensions: between the older and younger narrator, and also between a highly lyrical, chaotically individualistic, emotional Tambu and that more experienced narrator's more orderly narrative direction. These tensions saturate the novel in three areas: relations between Nyasha and Tambu, Tambu's struggles with individuality, and Tambu's uncertainties concerning knowing.

First, one of the most important tensions develops in the personally tense friendship between the "obstinately idealistic" (179) Nyasha and the more fervently controlled Tambu. There are many instances in which the two young girls do not mesh freely. For instance, Tambu faults Nyasha for being "skeptical," for her fascination with gray areas and ambiguities, for her "strange disposition that hinted at shades and textures within the same color" (164). Many conflicts derive from economic differences. Tambu somberly declares that Nyasha "could afford it, being my affluent uncle's daughter. Whereas I, I had to take whatever chances came my way" (179). In another instance, Tambu sadly discovers that Nyasha's "attitude was disappointing, though: I needed her moral support" (161). Tambu quickly explains to herself, "[p]ersonally, I thought Nyasha was a little unbalanced not to be distressed by being abandoned so abruptly. Nyasha, though, didn't know what I was talking about" (173). Their jagged relationship becomes a barometer for changes in their communal world and for Tambu's fluctuating levels of self-acceptance. It also magnifies tensions between self-consumed and collectively aware frameworks.

A second clash occurs not between people but within one. Tambu obsessively recalls and re-presents the increasingly modern self-awareness which besets her. "I was," she bashfully admits, "always aware of my surroundings. When the surroundings were new and unfamiliar, the awareness was painful and made me behave very strangely" (110). To make things worse, she finds herself symptomatic, "anxious and sleepless without knowing exactly why" (150). With some apprehension, she notes that these changes "were too complex for me to think my way out of" (151). Returning to Vygotsky, he posits a chain of development in language acquisition wherein "egocentric speech is a stage of developing preceding inner speech . . . egocentric speech disappears at school age, when inner speech begins to develop. From all this we infer that one changes into the other" (132). Similarly, Tambu moves out of immersion in egocentric speech which is a "transitional function . . . splintered off from general social speech" (Vygotsky 19). She gradually recognizes that what she had previously believed to be objective reality might only be illusory. She faces this possibility rather passionately:

> It stung too saltily, too sharply and agonizingly the sensitive images that the women had of themselves, images that were really no more than reflections. But the women had been taught to recognize these reflections as self and it was frightening now to even begin to think that, the very facts which set them apart as a group, as women, as a certain kind of person, were only myths . . . (138)

She soon feels all the weight of a disjunctive world remembering, "during that holiday I realised that some things were not as they should have been in our family, though I call it a holiday when actually it was not" (133). All of these recognitions constitute the "process of expansion" and movement into collective rather than nervous action.

Thirdly, Tambu grapples with her culture's preconceptions about knowing, especially in the light of neo-Freudian hyper-consciousness. Ngugi wa Thiong'o has insisted upon the imperative of "decolonizing the mind." Such "decolonization" is at the heart of the work of this novel. Tambu quite obsessively overconceptualizes about the nature of thinking. She dedicates considerable energy to comparing HOW people think. For instance, she says of Lucia, "thinking was a slow painful process for her because her mind had not been trained by schooling to do it quickly" (153). Or, as noted before, she refers to her mind as out of control: "my mind had raced and spun and ended up splitting into two disconnected entities that had long, frightening arguments with each other, very vocally, there in my head" (167). Nyasha, who "offers the postcolonial perspective" (236) according to Aegerter, has something intriguing and often incomprehensible for Tambu because of "her multi-directional mind" (*Nervous Conditions* 151). In contrast to Nyasha's baffling multi-directionality, in her reflections on her own development, Tambu recognizes that "deep in the less accessible areas of my mind, although outwardly I would have hotly denied it, I was ashamed of what to me was a pervasive and enervating vagueness" (151). Here is Tambu on the verge of developing the inner speech, which enables her to compose her story.

In an extremely pertinent conclusion, Vygotsky considers that "verbal thought is not an innate, natural form of behavior but is determined by a historical-cultural process and has specific properties and laws that cannot be found in the natural forms of thought and speech" (51). In an insight that may directly enlarge readings of *Nervous Conditions*, he argues that "Only a historical theory of inner speech can deal with this immense and complex problem. The relation between thought and word is a living process; thought is born through words" (153). Dangarembga's novel fully explores the difficult juncture between public and private, external and inner speech, thought and language. In the process, it dramatizes Tambu's individualized growth into insight, into language and perspective of her newly complex condition.

Aegerter emphasizes "the dialectic of autonomy and community characterized by the cousins' friendship" in this novel (238). Accordingly, Nyasha and Tambudzai "are simultaneously inside and outside the ideologies of colonization and sexism, as such they are the pulse and pressure point of resistance as they maneuver between the margins" (Aegerter 238). Consonant with the novel's title, Tambu has succeeded in developing a chart of her own for those shapeless, "multi-directional" areas which she had previously thought a part only of Nyasha's life. In spite of the difficult newness of this living, however, Dangarembga's explosive novel is itself also multidirectional *because of* its richly blended narrative interplay between lyric (or subjective) and narrative (or relational) focus, *because of* its own acutely active positionality.

Finally, at the end, perceived tensions erode in the moment Tambu headily affirms, "something in my mind began to assert itself . . . " (204). At this juncture, formerly uneasy tensions between self and other, lyric and narrative, fade away. The novel naturally becomes one: the history and the story both of others and also the story of self, of lyric and narrative impulses in that suddenly confident "asserting mind" of an unexpected narrator. Tambu has come to command and encourage both her lyrical impulse toward feeling AND a narrative drive to relate and classify. This moment gives rise to a temporary symbiosis between oral and written impulses.

This novel narrates the uneasy collapse of traditional village life via the recall of a highly perceptive and socially identified, rather than neurotically nervous and estranged, young narrator. *Nervous Conditions* celebrates the inherent nexus between individual consciousness and social conditions. Paraphrasing Antonio Gramsci, artist-persons attain completeness to the degree in which they know themselves as part of a community context. Lindsay Aegerter emphasizes: "it is . . . within community rather than individuality that African women's autonomy is fully realized" (234). All along, Vygotsky has posited a community affiliated linguistics: "the conception of word meaning as a unit of both generalizing thought and social interchange is of incalculable value for the study of thought and language" (7). Vygotsky's approach thus invites attention to a more differentiated critical response to African literature's complex oral traditions.

One of the prime elements of language entails sound. Vygotsky observes that written language is speech in thought and image only, lacking the musical, expressive, intonational qualities of oral speech (98). Studies of orality in non-Western cultures are currently discovering the key roles of intonation, music, gesturing, and physical expressivity in language studies. For instance, in the novel, when Nhamo forgets how to speak Shona, his words were "strangely accented" (32). There are multiple references to the sound-accent of Nhamo's speech in this novel. Similarly, the sound of a grunt readily becomes the semantic designator of a person's state of mind. Vygotsky's awareness of the many links between tactile word, intangible thought, and kinetic motion helps illuminate key struggles in *Nervous Conditions*, a novel which must be read in its own historical contexts. The structure of the book demonstrates shiftings between dialogic and monologic, semantic and phonetic, external and internal speech modes of recollection and conversation. At one significant moment in her recall of herself in the events, Tambu speaks as she does often of her own speech, "I talked to him [Mr. Matimba] as though he were just another person and not an adult and a teacher. I felt myself recoalesce" (24). This moment is a radiant example of what Vygotsky calls the "transition from inner to external speech," the "transformation of the predicative, idiomatic structure of inner speech in syntactically articulated speech intelligible to others" (148).

Nervous Conditions introduces a new kind of individualism based on a way of knowing which moves beyond indecision into a richly affiliated certainty. In an observation directly pertinent to Tambu's course throughout this novel, Judith Ryan observes, "By questioning the most fundamental categories of our thought, the notion of subject and object, empiricism effectively demonstrated the fragility of the entire complex structure, individual and social, that rest upon them. For sheer radicalness it was one of the most daring theories of the modern age" (232). The voice which emerges at the end of this novel makes choices on community-shaped grounds, of independent, but not brainwashed, thought, of personally initiated expansion into the area that Tambu can now confidently consider "a sunrise on my horizon" (203). At the novel's opening, one reads, "Therefore I shall not apologise but begin by recalling the facts as I remember them that led up to my brother's death, the events that put me in a position to write this account" (1). The tenor of her final confidence about writing what she knows reveals her enormously positive growth.

Elaine Showalter has warned of dangers "when women are spoken for but do not speak for themselves" (250). In contrast to "subaltern" passivity, here the auto-homo-diegetic narrator speaks for and to herself in an affirmative, thoroughly unexpected, clarity. In adult thought, Tambu unselfconsciously, non-nervously and non-psychologically knows and names, "[t]he river, the trees, the fruit and the fields. This was how it was in the beginning. This is how I remember it in my earliest memories" (3). Here is no easy-to-dismiss, nervous, uncertain, introspective, psychologically tortured voice, but rather a cleansed, definite, newly self-assured woman who has earned individual eloquence in the interstices of various communities, families, selves, and shadows. In an article on African fiction, Edward Sackey has suggested that since "The African oral tradition is not integrated into the written oral tradition, the tradition may be lost to posterity" (405). In the written and oral shapes of draft, memory, and introspective encounter, Tambu, Dangarembga, the novel, and its readers can bountifully and complexly reinvigorate African oral traditions.

Notes

1. This is a movement away from a perpetuation of binary thinking for the undermining and rendering invisible all props which support such distinctions.

2. Rimmon-Kenon re-contextualizes the fine narratalogical distinctions

in the following statement: "The narrative level to which the narrator belongs, the extent of his participation in the story, the degree of perceptibility of his role, and finally his reliability are crucial factors in the reader's understanding of and attitude to the story" (94).

3. Fernando Salvater definitively criticizes "formalist" psychology, saying, "Really, psychology is that from which innerness is totally absent, precisely because it aspires only to confine that innerness" (11).

4. Fanon has persuasively presented various effects of the cultural dichotomy which he termed a "manicheanism delerium," an illness out of control (qtd. in Ashcroft 124-25). Fanon's work seeks in part to demystify the workings of binary oppositions in order to overturn stereotypical stultifications.

5. David Miles has noted that in the nineteenth century there was a "gradual internalization or psychologicalization of reality . . . in practically all areas of thought" (989). In my book, *Narrative Authority and Homeostasis in the Novels of Doris Lessing and Carmen Martín Gaite*, I have proposed a term connoting the converse—depsychologicalization (72). Coetzee considers the "hyperconscious man" the "antithesis of the normal man. Feeling no basis in certainty, he cannot make decisions and act"؍ (Coetzee, *Doubling* 275). The term "inhabit" in this sense I learned from the celebrated Spanish novelist, Carmen Martín Gaite, who said that "she wanted people to learn to live with themselves, to inhabit their time" (Villán 23).

6. Writing particularly of African literature and criticism, Ashcroft notes "the emergence of a criticism which sees the text as the site of activity and 'decolonization' as a political action and not as an independent, aesthetic manifestation of some ideal or recovered authentic African literature . . . "(132).

7. In Eurocentric literatures, the permeability of the self predates of course the late nineteenth century. One finds evidence of a similar lonely fear haunting Cervantes' *Don Quixote*, in Moratin's *El Sí de las Niñas*, in America's solitary Rip van Winkle's desperate fears upon waking from his long sleep that he might have permanently and terrifyingly lost any sense of who he is.

Chapter 11:
Trapped and Troping: Allegories of the Transnational Intellectual in Tsitsi Dangarembga's *Nervous Conditions*[1]

Biman Basu

Postcolonial writers have consistently produced a group of fictional texts in which the narrator or protagonist stands in as the figure of the writer or the transnational intellectual. The embeddedness of this figuration in these texts is fraught with the material conditions of the very production and publication of these texts. That is, post-colonial intellectuals inhabit the "structures of violence"[2] which define their situatedness and serve as the site of production for this discourse. In such a position, these intellectuals are particularly susceptible to the possibilities of resolution offered at the level of transcendent categories. They shift grounds and refer themselves to the category of consciousness and subjectivity even if consciousness of the material conditions that structure their existence does not necessarily alter those conditions and may in fact serve to elide the materiality of this contradictory position.

Tsitsi Dangarembga's *Nervous Conditions* is meticulous in its attention to physical space, both geographical and bodily. The text relentlessly details the process of enculturation as a material process. Yet, equally insistently, it deploys the category of a transcendent consciousness and refers to a liberated subjectivity. This ultimate gesture of reconciliation at the level of consciousness and its tortured syntax, read as an instance of postmodern reflexivity, remains unconvincing. And it may appear as a moment of narrative failure only if we exclusively invoke some rather arbitrary aesthetic criteria. It may be read, instead, more instructively, as a textual transaction, a cultural document that maps the institutional spaces through which the shifting positions of the transnational intellectual must be plotted. A formal problem, a specifically narrative difficulty, rises out of the materiality of the intellectual's position.

Frantz Fanon pays particular attention to the materiality of this position,[3] to the spaces that intellectuals inhabit, and even to their bodily constitution. In *Black Skin, White Masks*, he observes that, for the "man of color," the colonial encounter is marked by "difficulties in the development of his bodily schema," that is, "[a] slow composition of my *self* as a body in the middle of a spatial and temporal world."[4] The "difficulties" arise out of a "corporeal malediction" that the colonizer inflicts, the colonizer "who had woven me out of a thousand details, anecdotes, stories" (111). Conversely,[5] "the Negro, because of his body, impedes the closing of the postural schema of the white man" (160). Here, then, is a figure of the colonial agon in the form of two interlocked bodies.

Fanon's perception that discursive formations proliferate around the body, that the density of "a thousand details, anecdotes, stories" impinge on the "bodily schema" underscores the materiality of his analysis of power. This power, moreover, is also directed toward the organization of space. Emphasizing both colonized bodies and colonized space in the opening pages of *The Wretched of the Earth*, he observes that "[t]he colonial world is a world divided into compartments," a world "cut in two." An analysis of this rigorous demarcation, Fanon asserts, will "reveal the lines of force it implies," "its ordering and geographical layout" (37-38). The effects of discursive power, then, are both somatic and geographic.

In addition to the materiality of power, Fanon recognizes that a specific modality of power operates at the metropolitan center. He notes that in developed countries, certain disciplinary formations—such as education, religion, and the family—produce what he calls "aesthetic expressions of respect for the established order." These institutions as well as "a constellation of postulates, a series of propositions that slowly and subtly—with the help of books, newspapers, schools and their texts, advertisements, films, radio—work their way into one's mind and shape one's view of the world of the group to which one belongs" (*Black Skin* 152). In other words, power operates as discipline and insinuates itself through a multitude of banal mechanisms and induces "respect for the established order." This discipline, however, is not limited to the center and becomes, with colonialism, a planetary project and infiltrates the peripheries. As Benedict Anderson points out, on a global scale, through nineteenth-century map-making practices, "the entire planet's curved surface had been subjected to a geometrical grid" (173). Further, colonial cartography "put space under the same surveillance which the census-makers were trying to impose on persons" (173). Disciplinary power proliferates globally through the casting of a "totalizing classificatory grid" (184) which places both land and people under surveillance.

In *The Wretched of the Earth*, Fanon acknowledges that in an early phase of colonialism, "the agents of government speak the language of pure force" (38). With the first anti-colonial uprisings, however, "the more brutal manifestations of . . . [colonialism] may perfectly well disappear. . . . But such a disappearance will be paid for at a high price: the price of a much stricter control of the country's future destiny . . . a servitude that is less blatant but much more complete" (142). Although Fanon is addressing colonialism, his perception of the shift from "pure force" to a power "less blatant" clearly anticipates what Michel Foucault describes as the shift from punishment as the spectacular vengeance of the sovereign to the more efficient bureaucratic administration of discipline. Foucault observes that punishment is replaced by a "technology of reform" (48) which penetrates the body and inserts it into the "circuit of bio-power." This shift in modalities of power, Fanon observes, turns out to be "a saving of expense to colonial power" (142). His remark that a number of postulates and propositions "shape one's view of the world" through the technological and institutional minutiae of everyday directs our attention to what Foucault calls "subjugated knowledges," ones that are "low-ranking" or "disqualified" (82).[6]

While Fanon does, at times, appeal to a "people's consciousness," a "collective consciousness," his work demonstrates that colonialism primarily constitutes a material intervention. He repeatedly refers to land and labor as the primary objects of colonialism, and, accordingly, he continually draws our attention to a specific conceptualization of space and a rigorous administration of the body. Fanon and Foucault are helpful in defining both the object of study and the method of analysis.[7] Their emphasis on the body directs our attention to the materiality of power and disentangles us from a web of discursivities where "progress" and "freedom" are always projected in terms of a subjectivity invested with consciousness. Foucault points out that when "power takes hold on the body, this isn't through its having first to be interiorized in people's consciousness." Rather, it operates through "a network or circuit of bio-power, or somato-power" (186). The point here is not to dismiss consciousness but to displace it strategically from its privileged status as a category for analysis. With such a displacement, and the consequent deflation of a series of exalted categories, we are better equipped methodologically to turn to the "subjugated" and "disqualified," to the realm of the banal.

Contemporary postcolonial fiction has responded to colonial cartography not only by questioning the adequacy of its classificatory grid but also by demonstrating that surveillance is a technique through which power operates as a positivity. It is not limited, negatively, to objectification, but more positively, through processes of subjectification, through technologies of self, it produces subjects. Consciousness of these processes, moreover, is not effective as a means of resistance. While Dangarembga herself speaks of "the consciousness of being a woman," for example, she adds that this consciousness must be situated in "a wider context" (Veit-Wild 105). Further, she is wary of the benefits of a specific type of education, particularly as it is presented in its liberal aspect as a consciousness-raising project. Commenting on one of her characters, Maiguru, she observes, "[h]er education enables her to see, to become conscious of it [colonialism], but it really doesn't enable her to do anything about it." She points out that "consciousness always has a very great individual cost," hopes that, someday, consciousness will provide "a basis for action" (Petersen 346). While the narrator of *Nervous Conditions* invokes the exalted categories of consciousness, emancipation enlightenment, and such, the text is steadily corporalized, the narrative moves into the space of the banal, and language itself is represented in its materiality.

Decolonized space, though especially dense, consists not of a spectacular density, but a uniform, dispersed density. This space is a corporalized space in which the technologies of discipline proliferate and attach themselves to the body, hence its density and its banality.[8] The exercise of disciplinary power must be apprehended not at the level of the subject endowed with consciousness but in the space of the banal. Disciplinary mechanisms are not aimed at the transformation of consciousness, and discipline is not internalized at the level of consciousness. These mechanisms are aimed at bodies, and discipline is epidermized. In the process, bodies are trained, bodily functions regulated, gestures are acquired, postures cultivated, styles are adopted, and attitudes assumed.

In *Nervous Conditions*, Dangarembga articulates a tertiary space of the homestead, the mission, and the convent, and the relations between the three spaces are fluid. The spaces, traversed by lines of force carrying their own intensities, are subject to constant and repeated deterritorializations and reterritorializations.[9] Tambu moves through all three spaces as a figure of the transnational intellectual in the making; Nyasha, caught in the intermediate space, has traveled in the Western space and occasionally visits the "native" space of the homestead. Nhamo's movement from the homestead to the mission, though a relatively minor movement, anticipates these larger movements and their finely calibrated differences. Because of "something that he saw at the mission" (7), he "refused to come home" (6). A year later, "no longer the same person" (52), he was not only "several tones lighter in complexion," but "he had forgotten how to speak Shona" (52). These details, like skin color and mother tongue, serve metonymically to signal the process of expatriation which is a central concern of the novel. Although we are informed rather humorously that Nhamo has not really forgotten Shona, we are told that "he did not speak to [his mother] very often any more" (52). Only his father is impressed: "the more aphasic he became," "the more my father was convinced that he was being educated" (53). Whatever the "something" is that Nhamo sees at the mission, at his death, his mother is uncompromising in her indictment of it: "First you took his tongue so that he could not speak to me. You bewitched him and now he is dead. . . . You and your education have killed my son" (54).

This movement from the homestead to the mission, however, is enfolded in a simultaneous movement, that of Nyasha, from the mission to the homestead. Her return to the homestead is exacerbated, moreover, by a long stay in England: "I missed the bold, ebullient companion I had had who had gone to England but not returned from there" (51). And Nyasha, too, has forgotten Shona, as Tambu registers rather indignantly: "Shona was our language. What did people mean when they forgot it? . . . I remembered speaking freely and fluently before they went away. Now they had turned into strangers" (42). Even though Nhamo is disposed of fairly early in the novel and Nyasha's movements are mapped in detail, the same "something" that Nhamo sees is deployed in a series of statements both from and about Nyasha. Tambu, for example, tells us, "I could not help wondering what my cousin had seen that I had not" (96-97) and, "Nyasha gave me the impression of moving, always moving and striving towards some state that she had seen" (152). Nyasha herself insists that "when you've seen different things you want to be sure you're adjusting to the right thing" (117).

"Something," "some state," "different things," "the right thing," these are the only expressions the text offers by way of explanation for certain severe disjunctions in the narrative. This is because the something that Nyasha has seen does not show itself clearly in its objective existence. It is a movement, a relation of power, power in a granular consistency that courses through an intricate and compelling network. In order to escape, to elude this network, Nyasha, as we have seen, is "moving, always moving and striving." "You have to keep moving," she explains, "Getting involved in this and that, finding out one thing and another. Moving, all the time. Otherwise you get trapped" (96). A little more explicitly, perhaps, she asserts, "You've got to have some conviction, and I'm convinced I don't want to be anyone's underdog. But once you get used to it, well, it just seems natural. . . . You're trapped. They control everything you do" (117). Further, the narrator observes that Nyasha is "experimental," always insisting on "alternatives" (178). Always engaged in the "probing of this and that and everything" (97), Nyasha "thrived on inconsistencies" (116) and was "at times stormy and turbulent" (151).

Nyasha, above all, is mobilized against being "trapped," against "something," against "it." The text does not simply oppose mobilization and fixity, the dynamic and the static. Rather, it is one type of movement and another, movement and counter-movement.

While the "it" in the above passage may arguably have a direct reference to "being an underdog," the progress from "it" to "They control everything" suggests a larger referential framework. What "seems natural" is the individual's subjection, the disciplining of the subject and the normalization routinization of disciplinary power. What "you get used to" is the "stricter control," and the subject's internalization of discipline results in a "more complete servitude." The novel documents the ways in which the body is implicated in the mechanisms of power, and to this end, it maintains a level of materiality, of corporality. The site of the most furious contention between Nyasha and her father, Babamukuru, is precisely the body. It often has to do with what she wears, how she talks, what she eats (or does not eat), whether or not she dances, and so on. The body is also the site on which Nyasha enacts her resistance. She wears short dresses, smokes cigarettes, and goes dancing. When forced to eat, she withdraws to the bathroom, "gagging and choking," using her toothbrush to disgorge (190).

In the schizophrenic language of the climactic passage of the novel (200-01) the referential framework is completely dissipated. In spite of this referential slide, however, the moment is entirely lucid. If we extract a series of statements, represented in direct discourse, as Nyasha's speech, we have the following:

> I don't want to do it.
>
> They've done it to me.
>
> They did it to them too.
>
> Why do they do it . . . to me and to you and to him?
>
> Do you see what they've done.
>
> They've taken us away.
>
> They've deprived you of you, him of him, ourselves of each other.
>
> They've trapped us. They've trapped us.

Look what they've done to us.

I'm not one of them but I'm not one of you.

In spite of the rigid polarization between "they" and the progression, me-you-him-us, there is no identification between "me" and "you": "but I'm not one of you." Rather, the sliding of references throughout the passage and the substitutions of pronouns serve as a mapping of the micropolitics of power. The disappearance of the "brutal manifestations" of power leaves only its circulation, the lines of which are marked along a series of innocuous pronouns. Even if there are certain moments of ostentatious brutality in the novel, Nyasha's resistance is directed not at the individual agent ("it's not his fault"), but at a structure of relations. Earlier in the novel, she says, "'[i]t's not really him, you know. I mean not really the person. It's everything, it's everywhere'" (174). The lexicographical diffuseness in general and the referential obscurity suggest the nebulousness of agency and only trace the circuits of power by marking out its effects.

As technologies of discipline are implanted on the body and power courses through its network of bodies, in this scene, literacy as a technology provokes a violent reaction on the site of its implantation. In fact, as we shall see, the syntax of the narrative simultaneously deploys the body and the book, food and literacy, eating and reading. The novel, ostensibly, is about Western education, even Christian education, specifically. Throughout the novel, education is associated with "emancipation" (56) and "progress" (147). It is concerned with "developing" (151) backward sectors of the community and, perhaps more grandly, with "freedom" (183). While education is, to be sure, consistently perceived as a means out of economic deprivation, the language through which it is articulated unmistakably invokes the grand narratives of emancipation and enlightenment. These are the narratives that Nyasha questions relentlessly. While Tambu is "[p]lunging into these books," "everything from Enid Blyton to the Brontë sisters," Nyasha, although herself absorbed in her reading of D.H. Lawrence at one time, is more interested in "history" and thinks that Tambu is "reading too many fairy-tales" (93). She prefers to read about "the condition in South Africa," about "Nazis and Japanese and Hiroshima and Nagasaki," about the "Jews' claim to Palestine," and so on.

The climactic passage of the novel must be understood in such a context. The violent image at the center of this scene is the culmination of the relentless interrogation that Nyasha directs at the processes of colonization:

> She rampaged, shredding her history book between her teeth ("Their history. Fucking Liars. Their bloody lies."), breaking mirrors, her clay pots, anything she could lay her hands on and jabbing the fragments viciously into her flesh, stripping the bedclothes, tearing her clothes from the wardrobe and trampling them underfoot. (201)

Colonialism attempts to discipline the "native," and the technologies of reformation are applied at diverse points. The most tenacious point of implantation, however, the point of deepest penetration, is the colonized body. As Foucault remarks, "nothing is more material, physical, corporal than the exercise of power" (57-58). We are reminded that in her unswerving judgment, Ma'Shingayi is quite clear about what the mission at Umtali did to her son: they "took his tongue." The points of implantation of colonial technologies of discipline define a logic and syntax which culminate in Nyasha's bizarre "shredding [of] her history book between her teeth." If colonialism mutilates the native body, if they "took his tongue," Nyasha mutilates "Their history," takes the pages of colonial history "between her teeth" and shreds the process in an unanswerable corporalization of that history. In this scene of violent and carnival degradation,[10] while "stripping," "tearing," and "trampling," she is also "jabbing the fragments viciously into her flesh."

While Nyasha's movement is from the West, from the "outside" into the native, into the inside in the form of an "immersion," Tambu moves from a native interior increasingly toward a Western

exterior, in the form of an "emergence."[11]   In the hybridized, intermediate space of the mission, Tambu undertakes "A slow composition" of a bodily schema in response to the technologies of discipline directed at her body. In the only instance of her resistance to
the authority of Babamukuru, Tambu, caught between conflicted
claims, experiences the destructuration of a bodily schema most
acutely, the "splitting into two disconnected entities" (167)— "The
body on the bed" and "the mobile, alert me" which "had gone somewhere where he could not reach me" (166). In this space, however,
a post- and neocolonial space, a "capillary form" of power constitutes the lines of force, encircles the subject, and produces docility
(Foucault 39). A specific regime of discipline saturates the space
and directs its attention to a meticulous management, a thorough
administration, of the body. This form of power, as Foucault puts
it, "reaches into the very grain of individuals, touches their bodies
and inserts itself into their actions and attitudes, their discourses,
learning processes and everyday lives" (39).

The homestead and the mission, however, are not strictly
"compartmentalized." The first chapter of the novel, in fact, offers
a semiotics of colonialism by presenting a topography of the native landscape. The prominent signs are "The river, the trees, the
fruit and the fields" (3). On either side of the road, we have "Aca-
cia, lantana, msasa and mopani" (2). The river, Nyamarira, has a
special place in the life of the village, particularly that of its women.
There the women collect water, wash clothes, bathe, and sun themselves. The riverbank is their gathering place: "the women had their
own spot for bathing and the men their own too" (3). The landscape, however, is disrupted, first, by "District Council Houses"
built "to enable administration" (3), then by the more banal signs
of metropolitan encroachment: "Fanta and Coca-Cola," "a
gramophone," and, of course, "a beer-hall" (4). As a result, "In the
interests of decency bathing was relegated to further up the river"
(4).

The prevailing signs in the semiotics of the intermediate
space are those of technology, a technology that relentlessly

"reaches into," "touches," "inserts itself into" the bodies and everyday lives of those in the "contact zone." Tambu thus experiments with the "paneled toilet" (79), discovers "bedclothes" (91), and delights in "The joy of that bath!" (90). She is impressed by the "glossy and dark" dining table, "its shape and size": "No one who ate from such a table could fail to grow fat and healthy" (69). She marvels at the way her cousin "work[s] her way daintily through egg and bacon and tea" (91), but after some initial trouble, learns to use knife and fork (82). Tambu's growth in this environment produces the expected result: "I grew quite plump."[12] The statement is followed immediately by, "I began to menstruate" (95). She is anxiety-ridden, not because of her menstruation, but because she might be "making a mess" in the "white bathroom" (95). Nyasha offers her a tampon, and after an initial hesitation about the consequences of "pushing the offensively shaped object into my vagina," she "nervously inserted a tampon with minimum discomfort" (96).

Even before Nhamo's death, that is, before the prospect of "emancipation" presents itself to Tambu, she has what she calls "complex, dangerous thoughts that I was stirring up, not the kind that you can ponder safely but the kind that become autonomous and malignant if you let them" (39). When Nyasha has a violent confrontation with her father, Tambu is able to "leave tangled thoughts knotted, their loose ends hanging. I didn't want to explore the treacherous mazes that such thoughts led into" (116). What Tambu does is deploy a strategy to impede the momentum of a movement which threatens to erupt into action. To subdue "malignant" and "treacherous" thoughts is to safeguard her complicity with authority, with her benefactor, Babamukuru. She must subdue these thoughts which "if considered too deeply would wreak havoc with the neat plan I had laid out for my life" (76). Once Tambu is induced into the circuitry of banality, once seduced by, and invested in a specific libidinal economy, she adopts a posture of "greater virtue" (88). Her complicity with disciplinary authority and reverence for the emancipatory project, the text informs us, "had stunted the growth of [her] faculty of criticism" and "It had happened insidiously" (164). Thoroughly enmeshed in the lines of force that traverse the terrain and the body of the intermediate space, Tambu turns docile, even if it is a docility performed with "masochistic delight" (169).[13] Tambu, as figure of the transnational intellectual in the making, yields to the seduction of power and seeks desperately to assert a vestigial agency in masochistic complicity.

The novel begins with Nhamo's and Nyasha's alienation from their community and Tambu's disapproval of, and anger at, their alienation, her own pain of "exclusion" (39). Tambu, however, repeats precisely these movements. And even though the adult narrator may position herself at a distance and observe Tambu's complicity, the narrator herself can only remove herself, through a relatively safe aesthetic device, to a self-ironizing subterfuge. The experience of this distancing, this alienating, in spite of the mitigating intervention of the narrative voice, is inevitable,[14] particularly in relation to her mother and to Nyasha. Tambu is rapidly assimilated into life at the mission: "I always hated leaving the mission and all my friends and Nyasha" (108). When she does go home for Christmas, as she listens to her mother talk about her illness, her "mind drifted away from my mother and her suffering" (129). At a gathering of the women at the homestead, Ma'Shingayi is characteristically direct and perceptive, if somewhat strident. She tells Tambu, "'You think your mother is so stupid she won't see Maiguru has turned you against me with her money and her white ways? . . . If it is meat you want that I cannot provide for you, if you are so greedy you would betray your own mother for meat, then go to your Maiguru" (140-41).

The movement, homestead-mission, is augmented by the second movement, mission-Convent. The mission, as intermediate space, serves as the grounds for recruitment into the Convent. It produces "good Africans" (107). When Tambu's departure for the Sacred Heart Convent is imminent, her mother's health breaks down completely. Tambu knows that she can restore her mother's health "by not going to Sacred Heart. But this was asking too much of me" (184). Nyasha's response to Tambu's selection for the Convent is also clear. To Tambu's musings about what an opportunity it would be, she says "It would be a marvelous opportunity. . . . To forget who you were, what you were and why you were that" (178-79). She calls the "recruitment" a process of "assimilation" in which those "who might prove a nuisance if left to themselves" are accommodated in "an honorary space" in which "they could make sure that you behaved yourself" (179).

The intermediate space, marking a stage in the process of discipline, is a space of seduction. Tambu's mother and Nyasha apprehend her selection for the Convent, at some level, as a process of expatriation. Although Nyasha's response may seem to imply conspiracy, it cannot be read at the level of intentionality. Rather, she examines the structure of this process and comments on its effects. Those who demonstrate the greatest potential are selected for the Convent. As a result, they are removed from both the native and intermediate spaces and contained in "an honorary space." Their selection serves simultaneously as their containment. Thus the elect few enter the Sacred Heart Convent where they are the only "natives": "I looked and looked and searched carefully through the crowd, but I could not find a single black face which did not belong to our party, except of course for the porters." We also learn that the Sacred Heart is a segregated domain: "And the Africans live in here," a nun explains to the family (194). The movement into this third space may thus be read as a movement into Western space.

Once at the convent, Tambu practically repeats the movements she has rehearsed when she moved from the homestead to the mission. She finds that "reading took up so much of my time that there was none left in which to miss Nyasha" (195). If Tambu does feel "a pang of guilt," it is "dissolved quickly in the stream of novelty and discovery I had plunged into" (197). When Nyasha has a nervous breakdown, Tambu "felt Nyasha needed me but it was true: I had to go to school" (202). Tambu is disturbed by "guilt," but "the thought of returning to Sacred Heart filled me with pleasure. The books, the games, the films, the debates—all these things were things I wanted" (203). In the intermediate space of the mission, discipline insinuates itself through everyday physiological processes signaled in the series toilet-bedclothes-bath-egg and bacon-tampon. Here, in the space of the Convent, the series is constituted by the activities of literacy: reading-discovery school-books. The two series, however, are not contradictory, but, in fact, complementary. The "joy of that bath" has its counterpart in "the stream of novelty" that "filled me with pleasure."

In *Nervous Conditions*, there are moments of physical confrontation, eruptions of violence, but the prevailing procedure of the narrative is one in which the body is caught in a continual process of encirclement, a process in which a "technology of reform" impinges directly on the body. It is not so much an internalization in consciousness, but rather, an epidermalization of discipline. It involves acquiring certain styles and attitudes, assuming a posture, in short, the performance of discipline. Discourse, as an emblematic instance of the productions of technology, is thus corporalized. Literacy is represented in its materiality. Utterance is tied to its physical coordinates, and these physical coordinates describe the syntax of the narrative. The "tongue" finds its syntactical coordinate in "meat," and tongue and meat describe this syntax. So too, books are "devoured," or more precisely, Babamukuru is described as "having devoured English letters with a ferocious appetite" (36) and Tambu as "eat[ing] the words that come out of her [Maiguru's] mouth" (140). And, as we have seen, Tambu "plunge[s]" into books (93), "plunge[s]" into a "stream of novelty" (197). Ma'Shingayi identifies this enthusiasm as "greedy."

Against this steady corporalized discipline, we have an incipient insurrectionary mobility, thoughts that are "stirring," that are "loose," thoughts that are "distracting" and "treacherous," that would "wreak havoc." But this mobility is stilled by nothing as profound as "progress," "emancipation," or "freedom." Rather, this rebellious mobility is weighted, this non-productive expenditure of energy is disciplined and directed into productive circuits entirely at the level of the banal. This discipline is achieved at the level of the body, as a meeting of corporal need, a fulfillment of appetite. The body is the prioritized site for the implantation, for the attachment of technologies of discipline, and this attachment occurs almost imperceptibly with a surreptitious complicity, "with minimum discomfort." At the first remove, homestead to mission, the series toilet-bath-egg and bacon-tampon culminates in "I grew quite plump." At the second remove, mission to convent, discipline is achieved at the level of "novelty and discovery" and "pleasure" derived from "things."

If Tambu, as adult narrator, adds a dimension of self-consciousness, and thus of irony, to the narrative, the last paragraph of the novel does not suggest irony but confession. After the precise and meticulous depiction of the movements we have observed, the final paragraph tells us, "Although I was not aware of it then, no longer could I accept Sacred Heart . . . my mind began to assert itself, to question things and refuse to be brainwashed" (203-04). The narrator, then, claims an "aware[ness]," a consciousness, even if projected beyond the narrative time of the text. This appeal to consciousness as a strategy of resistance, however, seems to contradict the dominant mode, the prevailing syntax of the narrative, one that relentlessly documents the process of colonialism as a material, corporal one.

In spite of the narrator's early assertion that this "story is not after all about death" (1), Tambu's movement in the syntax of the novel is punctuated first by death, then by her mother's illness which requires a "shock treatment" (185) and finally by Nyasha's "nervous condition." Only the figure of rebellion and the moment of revolt are violent. Nyasha, periodically disgorging, ejecting that which is forcibly inserted into her body, initiates a counter-movement to the prevailing syntax of the narrative. She launches this counter-movement, this resistance, precisely from the contested site, the body that would be disciplined. She shreds the book with "her teeth," "plunges into" and jabs "viciously into her flesh" in a carnivalesque and schizophrenic deterritorialization of her body. In spite of the introductory paragraph's assertion that this story is about the narrator's "escape," other characters' "entrapment," and Nyasha's rebellion, a "rebellion [which] may not in the end have been successful," it is Nyasha's violent rebellion that initiates the "lines of escape," the "lines of flight," from the territorialized body of the colonized native. A central trope of the text, then, is "entrapment," "rebellion," and "escape." Nyasha rebels against the naturalization of the trap: "once you get used to it, well, it just seems natural." Whether Nyasha's rebellion is "successful" or not, she accurately registers the workings of a disciplinary regime in general and the potential for discursive violence in the project of literacy in particular. The narrator, however, is careful to distinguish between Nyasha's resistance, which she considers less than successful, and her own "escape." And her escape, as we have seen, is predicated on an appeal to the category of consciousness which "really doesn't enable her to do anything about" her subjection. In fact, the narrator's assertion of awareness may be read as her subjection to a micropolitics of power, that is, as her subjectification in a process of discipline. If power is apprehended, not negatively as repression, prohibition, or objectification, but positively as producing subjects, the narrator's rhetoric of consciousness signals this subjectification and serves to elide the materiality of her contradictory position.

The reader, to be sure, cannot overlook Tambu's "escape" from the brutalizing patriarchy and dehumanizing poverty of the "native" space, but the bulk of the narrative is enacted once she enters the intermediate space, and from then on, in the making of a post-colonial intellectual (the postcolonial artist as a young woman), she is increasingly consolidated in a specific economy, subjected to a specific regime of discipline, that of the western intellectual enterprise. And the postcolonial and transnational intellectual is peculiarly prone to submit to a corporalized and banal regime of discipline, but then, to escape this normalization and neutralization by deploying the category of consciousness as a mechanism of escape. The intellectual attempts to escape his/her neutralization by asserting, questioning, refusing, all the while, inhabiting the very structure s/he questions and refuses. In other words, the text, with its narrator, trapped and troping, inhabiting a western intellectual structure and engaging specific discourses, may be read as an allegory of the postcolonial and transnational intellectual.

An exacerbated issue in postcolonial studies has been the centrality of discourse[15] and a particular type of postcolonial fiction has been produced in which the narrator or the protagonist serves as a figure of the intellectual. These texts, directly implicated in the "structures of violence," need to be read, not as instances of postmodern auto-referentiality, but as texts with a narrative and critical difficulty arising from a specific historical circumstance. To read texts such as *Nervous Conditions,* and others like it, as allegories of the transnational intellectual is to plot the proliferation of the technologies of discipline in the tertiary spaces of the transnational and to acknowledge that the intellectual is particularly prone to the blandishments offered at the level of the banal and simultaneously to elide this position by an appeal to a unique subjectivity endowed with consciousness. These texts remind us that as intellectuals trapped in powerful institutional structures, we may in practice be desperately troping.

Notes

1. This is a revised and expanded version of an essay that was published in *Ariel* 28.3 (1997): 7-24.

2. The term is Gayatri Chakravorty Spivak's (138-51).

3. Although Fanon is sometimes caustic about the "facile internationalism" of a cosmopolitan position (*Wretched* 83), his strenuous efforts to establish a relationship to "the masses" are themselves indicative of his ambivalent position. Thus when he asserts that "[t]he peasant's cloak will

wrap the militant nationalist around with a gentleness and firmness that he never suspected" (126), and that intellectuals must "bury themselves" in "the hearts of the people" (187), perhaps he tells us more about himself than about the peasant. It is perhaps equally important to note, however, that he also underscores the "fluctuating movement" of the people, "this zone of occult instability where the people dwell" (227). While "occult" may still suggest a distance from the people, his emphasis on fluctuation and instability remove him from the essentialism of "[t]he peasant's [maternal] cloak," from the desire to be wrapped and buried.

4. He continues with a graphic representation of this composition of a bodily schema: "I know that if I want to smoke, I shall have to reach out my right arm and take the pack of cigarettes lying at the other end of the table. The matches however, are in the drawer on the left, and I shall have to lean back slightly" (111).

5. Strictly speaking, according to Fanon, the converse is not true—that the white man is constituted in relation to the black man—because "The black man has no ontological resistance in the eyes of the white man" (110). Nonetheless, the appearance of the black body within the parameters of this bodily schema does have some effect. Generally, there is an "influence exerted on the body by the appearance of another body" (160). The effect is that the body "experience[s] a destructuration" (161).

6. In a different context, Toni Morrison says that if her work is to confront a "Third World cosmology as [she] perceives it," she "must centralize and animate information discredited by the West" (388). What is interesting here is the notion of discredited knowledges and of a hierarchy of knowledges.

7. For a review of the "successive appropriations" of Fanon in postcolonial theory, see Henry Louis Gates (457).

8. I do not use the term "banality" here in precisely the same way as Achille Mbembe does in the celebrated essay, "The Banality of Power and the Aesthetics of Vulgarity in the Postcolony." Ostentatious public display is one aspect of banality, but another is its almost imperceptible regularity, not only in the postcolony but in the hybrid space of the transnational.

9. On territorialization, deterritorialization, and reterritorialization, see Gilles Deleuze and Felix Guattari.

10. "Carnival degradation" in the sense that Mikhail Bakhtin uses the term.

11. Signifying on the dynamic of immersion and ascent that Robert Stepto identifies in African American texts, Paul Gilroy observes a simultaneous movement of immersion and emergence in, for example, W.E.B. Du Bois' *The Souls of Black Folk* (137-38).

12. Using a psychoanalytic framework, Sue Thomas offers some interesting comments on the novel's emphasis on food and the body (28). See also Heidi Creamer.

13. For example, she is "masochistic" in using her sense of inferiority and shame as a "fine lash of guilt to whip myself on with" (89). For not attending her parents' marriage, Babamukuru decides that she must be "punished" and she receives "fifteen lashes" (169). He decides that she has to be disciplined (172) by taking over the maid-servant's work for two weeks. She performs these "chores grimly, with a deep and grateful masochistic delight" (169). When she insists that Nyasha should not help her with these chores, Nyasha in fact retorts, "I'm sorry to deprive you of the pleasure" (170). The entire narration is, in fact, tinged with this masochism. While it is not the purpose here to explore the implications of this, it must be said that the masochist is not entirely powerless and, in fact, may often be the one in control in S/M (McClintock 226).

14. It is, of course, important to note the distinction, as does Heidi Creamer, for example, in the article noted above, between the naïve and the informed narrator. The novel, as we shall see, particularly in its ultimate paragraph, suggests that this distinction may be the most compelling motivation, the central conflict that informs the structure of the novel. It is the reconciliation of these voices, or more precisely their irreconciliation, that is of interest here for the novel's representation of the fraught position of the postcolonial and transnational intellectual.

15. Henry Louis Gates Jr. foregrounds this preoccupation when he comments, "[y]ou can empower discursively the native, and open yourself up to charges of downplaying the epistemic (and literal) violence of colonialism; or play up the absolute nature of colonial domination, and be open to charges of negating the subjectivity and agency of the colonized, thus textually replicating the repressive operations of colonialism." (462)

Chapter 12:
Tsitsi Dangarembga's *Nervous Conditions*: An African Woman's Revisionist Narrative[1]

Mary Jane Androne

Tsitsi Dangarembga's 1988 novel *Nervous Conditions* deconstructs the female novel of development as it records a young girl's growing disillusionment with the compromises she is forced into at a colonial mission school and her despair over her position as a woman in pre-revolutionary Zimbabwe. As such, it is a first-person retrospective narrative that shares many qualities with what Caren Kaplan and Kenneth Harrow refer to as "outlaw genres" or "literature of revolt"—*testimonio, temoinage,* renegade autobiography and resistance literature. Kaplan sees *testimonio* as a genre that challenges the implicit patterns in Western subjective narratives that present individual, singular accounts of experience and Harrow defines "*temoinage*" as "literature that bears witness to social, cultural, and historical realities" (x). What Dangarembga's novel has in common with these other genres which resist formal classification is an underlying ideology that questions the validity of liberal, humanist concepts of self-discovery revealed in a linear plot which records the triumphs and victories of an individual woman struggling against impossible odds. In presenting her protagonist Tambu's story of her transition from her rural homestead to the mission school where her uncle is headmaster, Dangarembga questions the values inherent in those genres intent on presenting what Patricia Waugh refers to as "the achieving, rational, autonomous, transcendent successful self" (26). The form Dangarembga creates also challenges those assumptions underlying literary forms which function in reinforcing the hegemony of colonial values through celebrating individual achievement within a "progressive" economic and political environment (Beverley 103). Like the *testimonios* of South American women which represent the collective suffering within political regimes which are oppressively sexist as well as elitist, *Nervous Conditions* is a text which destabilizes the idea of progress and individual achievement in such societies. In demonstrating the deformation and truncation of women's lives, Dangarembga's narrator, Tambu, subverts the very notion of "development" as she acknowledges how "the generations of threat, assault and neglect" batter the negative myths of women into beliefs about themselves that African women internalize (138).

Implicit in *Nervous Conditions* are two plots and two paradigms of selfhood. The first is the story of Tambu's uncle, Babamukuru, the headmaster of the mission school she attends, and is the model on which she would like to pattern her own life. The second is the collective, collaborative plot of all the women in her family, which subverts the first plot and eventually takes it over. At the end Tambu says, "[t]he story I have told here is my own story and the story of four women whom I have loved" (204). The story then shifts from a plot centered on individual achievement and development to a narrative of collective consciousness and collaborative effort.

The classic plot of individual achievement is epitomized in the stories Tambu hears of her successful uncle, Babamukuru. When she is a young girl her grandmother recounts the myth of his struggle to achieve:

> She walked, with my uncle, with Babamukuru, who was nine years old and wearing a loin cloth, to the mission where the holy wizards took him in . . . he was educated in their wizardry . . . He surprised the missionaries by performing exceptionally well at school . . . He was diligent, he was industrious, he was respectful. (19)

Tambu concludes after hearing her grandmother's tale that "this indicated that life could be lived with a modicum of dignity in any circumstances if you worked hard enough and obeyed the rules . . . the message was clear: endure and obey, for there is no other way" (19). When Babamukuru offers her the chance to be educated at the mission school where he presides (but only after her older brother's untimely death) she determines to follow her uncle's example—"I will be like Babamukuru straight as an arrow, steely and true" (88). The quest she sets out on is one where she will "do it alone" as her uncle had before her and where she would avoid all the denaturalizing pitfalls her brother fell into. Before his death Tambu claims her brother, Nhamo, had become a stranger to her as he was assimilated into the culture of the mission school forgetting his language, rejecting his family and rural roots, and cultivating western ways. So she sets her course as one that will emulate her uncle who "was God" but also as one that will not allow her to be seduced by the distracting splendors of a richer, wider world. Finally, though, Tambu follows neither of these courses. Dangarembga's narrative makes it clear that her protagonist must suspend her reason, her moral judgment and her sense of political justice if her plot is to be her uncle's plot-that of the triumphing, assimilated, unified self complicitous with the colonial power structure: "Through hard work and determination he had broken the evil wizards' spell. Babamukuru was now a person to be reckoned with in his own right . . . He didn't need to be bold because he had made himself plenty of power . . . Plenty of Money. A lot of education. Plenty of everything" (50). Her description here suggests the extent to which she has internalized a Western trajectory of achievement and success.

Dangarembga's narrative, however, reveals an ever widening split that suggests a disjunction between the narrating "I" with the narrated "I" and also within Tambu's self as she tells the story. Again, Dangarembga subverts the integrity of an autobiographical or first-person initiation novel which assumes the unity of the self as she challenges the system that would erase her identity as an African and subordinate her as a woman. Kenneth Harrow discusses the ways literatures of revolt foreground "dialogism" in the sense that they demonstrate the "contradiction between formalist and deconstructionist viewpoints" (xi). In ironically juxtaposing the "idealized" plot of the *Bildungsroman* where the protagonist progresses in a predictable pattern with the trajectory of disillusionment Tambu ultimately must acknowledge to be her plot, Dangarembga demonstrates the ways in which traditional narrative structures cannot accommodate the specific oppressions her female protagonist experiences in this particular colonial setting. Dangarembga structures Tambu's telling her story not to suggest two voices but to expose how fragmented her "self" is and to hint at the disintegration of the imagined "self" she hoped to become in following her uncle's example. Looking back on this period in her life, she reconstructs that earlier self who admired her educated aunt, pitied her mother who "suffered from being female and poor and uneducated and black," and considered Babamukuru "nearly divine." This observing present self admits she forced herself into unnatural postures as she resisted ambiguity and avoided the "treacherous mazes" that independent thinking tempted her towards and "took refuge in the image of the grateful poor female relative" (116). These two selves reveal the split in consciousness of the narrating Tambu and suggest the folly of her willingness to be developed in the way Babamukuru saw fit. Throughout her story, Tambu refers to her various selves: the self she leaves behind at the homestead, the "new" self she expects to find at the mission, and the very fragmented and divided self she finally has to recognize once she's left. This fragmentation is also reflected in her cousin, Nyasha, who sees herself as "hybrid" because of her British education and her loss of her language and culture, and who envies her cousin her connection with her past. Tambu insists, though, that "[s]he did not know what essential parts of you stayed behind no matter how violently you tried to dislodge them in order to take them with you" (173).

At other times, however, she disapproves of her Anglicized cousin's rebellion against her father and resists Nyasha's warning because her example calls into question her own obedient compromises: "Everything about her spoke of alternatives and possibilities that if considered too deeply would wreak havoc with the neat plan I had laid out for my life" (76). In order to function, and survive at her uncle's school Tambu suppresses her political consciousness as she single-mindedly applies herself to her studies and finds herself drawn into all the culturally alienating habits she so disapproved of in her brother, Nhamo. Toward the end of her narrative she acknowledges:

> Above all, I did not question things . . . I was not concerned that freedom fighters were referred to as terrorists, did not demand proof God's existence nor did I think that the missionaries, along with other Whites in Rhodesia, ought to have stayed at home. As a result of all these things that I did not think or do, Babamukuru thought I was the sort of young woman a daughter ought to be. (155)

What disrupts this plot and wakes Tambu from her sleepwalking is her involvement with her female relatives who chafe under Babamukuru's rule and eventually rebel. Early on Tambu realizes that her position as a "female" will make it impossible for her ever to realize the goals she's set for herself: "But what I didn't like was the way all the conflicts came back to the question of femaleness. Femaleness as opposed and inferior to maleness" (115-116). The double oppression of African women under a colonial system which employs the tenets of western patriarchy to reinforce women's subordination is, perhaps, Dangarembga's central political insight. Neil Lazarus speaks of African women writers as being "differently political" because of their experience of the twin scourges of colonialism and sexism (Lazarus 211). Dangarembga's text bears this out. When Tambu finally disobeys her uncle she gets fifteen lashes and is forced into domestic servitude as punishment. Babamukuru's message is clear: "Anyone who defies my authority is an evil thing in this house, bent on destroying what I have made" (167). The ideology underlying Tambu's abandoned quest for success and autonomy is the psychological phenomenon which results from the dual repression of political and gender constraints alluded to by Lazarus. As Dangarembga's plot shifts from Tambu's individual, assimilationist rise to collective effort and collaboration with all her female relatives and friends, she acknowledges "[i]f I forget them, my cousin, my mother, my friends, I might as well forget myself" (188). In recording these women's resistance to patriarchy, Dangarembga suggests that the strongest, most resilient females are not the women educated and "liberated" in the West and privileged within their societies, but the women who emerge from rural Africa and are shaped by agricultural labor and live within communities where women support and work with one another. In an interview in which she discusses *Nervous Conditions*, Dangarembga mentions the contrasted cultural experiences of Nyasha and Tambu as crucial differences which are psychologically determining:

> I personally do not have a fund of our cultural tradition or oral history to draw from, but I really did feel that if I am able to put down the little I know then it's a start . . . I think the problem of forgetting—remembering and forgetting— is really important. What is interesting is that Nyasha as an individual does not have anything to forget: she simply

doesn't know. . . . She obviously feels some great big gap inside her and that she ought to remember it because this is her heritage . . . Tambudzai on the other hand is quite valid in saying that she can't forget because she has that kind of experience Nyasha is so worried about forgetting because it's not there for her to remember. Tambudzai is so sure that this is the framework of her very being that there is no way that she would be able to forget it. (Wilkinson 191)

Perhaps the most daring, if not the most powerful, woman in *Nervous Conditions* is the unmarried Lucia, the African woman with the least education who lives on the margins of society. When the men of the family meet to deliberate Lucia's fate—the male family members designate her "vicious," "unnatural," and "uncontrollable," because she acts out her sexuality as she pleases—Lucia interrupts their council and takes her fate into her own hands when she demands employment in the nearest town and the freedom to live on her own. Maiguru, Babamukuru's Western-educated wife who has a Masters degree, not only refuses to intervene with the men on Lucia's behalf—"I don't want to intrude into the affairs of my husband's family. I shall just keep quiet and go to bed" (138)— but later fails in her own rebellion against her husband. After Maiguru runs away, Nyasha, her daughter, and Tambu speculate on what she might do with her life: "She'll go back to study for another degree. She'll teach at the university. She'll become a doctor. She'll start her own business" (174). Instead Babamukuru collects her from her brother's house and returns her to her privileged position as wife of the Mission school's headmaster.

Nyasha's ill-fated rebellion is perhaps the most ominous. Hospitalized in a clinic in Salisbury and suffering from anorexia nervosa, Nyasha is unable to benefit from her intelligence and insight. Dangarembga's narrative implies that not having a language and a culture and finding herself unable to accept her father's absolute authority, Nyasha cannot free herself from those internalized values and pathological behavior patterns which all too often shape Western women's consciousness. It is because she sees and understands so clearly what is happening to her that Nyasha is such a poignant victim. Lamenting her loss of Shona and her ignorance of the "old ways" and rural African culture, Nyasha tells her cousin: "[i]t's bad enough when a country gets colonized, but when the people do as well! That's the end, really, that's the end!" (147). And she knows very well the fate Tambu is heading for when she goes off so enthusiastically to the European convent school at the novel's end. She warns her of the price that her compromises will force her to accept in return for the library, the instruction, and the green haven Tambu yearns to escape to: "The process was called assimilation, and that was what was intended for the precocious few who might prove a nuisance if left to themselves . . . So they made a little space . . . an honorary space in which you could join them and they could make sure that you behaved yourself" (179).

But despite all her consciousness, Nyasha is unable to save herself as she drifts into madness and breakdown at the novel's conclusion. Dangarembga's text seems to suggest that consciousness is not an end in itself and that individual struggle and insight are merely that in a society where women's lives are circumscribed by sexist, racist institutions that determine them psychologically as well as politically. Dangarembga's plot, though, offers alternatives to the "ideas" of liberation and sexual equality Nyasha and Maiguru learn through their Western education. Tambu tells us in the beginning of the novel that she and Lucia "escape," her mother and Maiguru are "trapped," and Nyasha "fails" in her rebellion. But the moments of collaboration and collective effort these women enact are what John Carr refers to as "moments of resistance and affiliation" which typify testimonial accounts. It is significant that Nyasha's breakdown claims Tambu's attention and takes her away from school when she insists on making the trip to Salisbury with her cousin—"I could not leave my cousin in that state" (198). Tambu's journey to selfhood and success is disrupted, but her connection with other women exemplifies the possibility of political agency when women join their efforts.

Ironically, Dangarembga encloses Tambu's story by two events. Her opening sentence—"I was not sorry when my brother died"—announces the circumstances that gave her a chance for an education. In the end her mother gives birth to her younger brother whose existence undercuts her academic future, since, as Babamukuru tells her, "I feel that even that little bit of money could be better used. For . . . there is now the small boy at home . . . and you will be in a position to be married by a decent man and set up a decent home" (180). Fortunately for Tambu, an emboldened Maiguru intervenes on her behalf and persuades Babamukuru to allow Tambu to escape. Her arrival at the convent school opens rather than closes her story. This retrospective novel ends with bitter consciousness as Tambu finds her prospect of "her new wide life" narrowed to a small room shared by six African girls segregated from the rest of the school: "It was a long and painful process for me, that process of expansion. It was a process whose events stretched over many years and would fill another volume . . ." (204).

In commenting on the influence of oral African folktales in her writing, Dangarembga speaks of places in those works where the reader must respond and is hence drawn into the tale. The open-ended, unresolved ending surely accomplishes this in *Nervous Conditions*. The absence of narrative closure leaves the reader to speculate on the relation of contemporary African women to the power structure that has evolved in Zimbabwe since the late 1960s. Choosing "nervous conditions" for a title as an allusion to Fanon's phrase in *The Wretched of the Earth*—"The condition of native is a nervous condition"—Dangarembga clearly means to foreground gender as the category which determines African women's lives and keeps them "natives" in relation to the dominant and controlling power structure. And finally, "nervous conditions" is also an ominous metaphor for those internalized definitions of femaleness that shape from within women's private and public lives.

Notes

1. This essay was first published in Charles Cantalupo, Ed. *Ngugi wa Thiong'o: Texts and Contexts*. Trenton, NJ: Africa World Press, 1995. 323-331

Chapter 13:
Reading "The Letter" of a Woman: Narrative Strategies in Dangarembga's Story of Apartheid South Africa

Jacqueline Wigfall

Depicting South African women political prisoners, Tsitsi Dangarembga masterfully coordinates a network of narrative strategies in "The Letter." This short fiction uncovers the effect of (neo)colonialism on a South African woman who is held as a political prisoner. Anonymous, yet singularly foregrounded, the protagonist insurgently narrates her past and present experiences under apartheid.[1] At times, the narrator expresses her desire to represent other South Africans who cannot be heard but whose struggles she witnesses. She is, therefore, a Black woman into whose body multiple experiences of colonized women are collected. Her multiplicity is one aspect of her potentially universal appeal for a variety of readers. During passages that represent long stretches of the narrator's memory, we also experience her idiosyncratic subjectivity. In this capacity, the narrator mediates several ideological realms ushered into the text by way of (epistolary) letters and shifting geographies, tropes that consistently circulate in postcolonial and postmodern literatures. Of particular significance is the sense of the narrator's personal agency through her own body, voice, and political vision. Tsitsi Dangarembga's contemporary, South Asian-American writer Meena Alexander has written that "[w]oman is a fault line between worlds" in her poetic autobiographical memoir "Fault Lines" (1996).[2] Alexander has resided on different continents, and is fluent in many languages. She describes her identity as "the condition of being fractured . . . multiple beings locked into the journeys of one body." Utilizing "the corrosive magic of the first person singular," Alexander insists upon "writ[ing] the truth of the body, pitted, flawed, unfinished." Alexander's multifaceted subjectivity—and theory of women of color's autobiography—brings to mind the full-bodied humanity Dangarembga invests in the narrator of "The Letter." Neither this narrator nor Alexander owns disembodied voices; both textualize identity as sexual, maternal, domestic, public and political. Their stories indicate that acts of inscribing female experience(s) do achieve personal resistance to (neo)colonial regulation. The breaks in their texts indicate their struggles to survive or change. Alexander speaks of the fractures that mark sites of contention and resistance in her text. In Dangarembga's short story, textual rifts take the form of interstices [3] or casually rent openings lacking the "corrosive" edges of "fault lines." All the same, textual breaks and twists in "The Letter" indicate places where the narrator strategically complicates her story in ways easily missed by the unassuming reader. In particular, her story contains two levels to discover: a "safe," domestic memoir and a harrowing political subtext that climaxes towards the end. The subtext fractures the memoir and "The Letter" transforms from personal story to prison letter. This strategy relocates readers of "The Letter" to a political realm in which their own complicity in (neo)colonialism is questioned. Readers may find themselves alternately seduced or duped by the narrative charisma of the woman's account, but never outside of her purview.

Dangarembga's unveiled critique of apartheid, conflation of the stereotypes which envelope African women, and construction of interstices as forms of call and response, locate her work within discursive traditions established by African women. While this essay endeavors an African-centered, exploratory approach to reading "The Letter," it primarily discusses a selection of narrative strategies that regulate the reading experience and escalate the plot leading to the dupe. In addition to its authorship in English, several aspects of "The Letter" are European, an eurocentrism Jill Conway introduces in her globalizing anthology of women's memoirs. Like the mid-eighteenth century memoirs she describes of Western Europe, 'The Letter" records for progeny important state affairs, particularly how the apartheid state regulated and terminated the lives of Black South Africans. Conway explains that Jean Rousseau (1712-1778) shifted autobiographical purpose from the rarefied and élite political or religious chronicles, to the memoir of self-creation. The quotidian details of an individual's social life characterized "the modern tradition of romantic individualism" inscribed in European autobiography. We see evidence of Rousseau's concept in "The Letter" narrator's use of personal markers (mother, lover, teacher, wife, and daughter) that socially locate her. The palimpsest, the political letter, and the memoir—narrative structures found in "The Letter"—evidence Dangarembga's contribution to traditions of writing in the first-person designed and sustained by English women writers, political prisoners, and women autobiographers of color. Furthermore, for its multi-dimensional quality, this analysis appreciates that Dangarembga's short story contributes to several literary traditions, the first of which is Zimbabwean literature by women.

A number of post-independence achievements historicize Dangarembga's short story. Individual women entered the canon of Zimbabwean literature during the mid-1980s. The archaeology of individual professional careers spans over a decade. Kristina Rungano published *The Storm is Brewing* in 1984, half a decade before her participation in the Zimbabwe Women Writers Collective (ZWW).[4] In 1986, several women authors were anthologized in *Short Stories for Zimbabweans by Zimbabweans*, published out of a competition sponsored by the Lion's Club. But the boon for Zimbabwean women writers came in 1988 when Tsitsi Dangarembga won the Commonwealth Writer's Prize for literature for *Nervous Conditions*, her first novel. In 1992, Margaret Busby anthologized ZWW members Barbara Makhalisa and Kristina Rungano, in addition to Tsitsi Dangarembga and Sekai Naenza, in *Daughters of Africa: An International Anthology of Words and Writings by Women of African Descent*. The following year, Flora Veit-Wild's interview of Tsitsi Dangarembga was published in Carole Boyce Davies' *Moving Beyond Boundaries, vol. 2: Black Women's Diasporas*. Prior to the explosive critical acclaim Tsitsi Dangarembga earned for *Nervous Conditions* (1989), she wrote "The Letter" (1985), first published within *The Sound of Snapping Wires: A Selection of Zimbabwean Short Stories* (1990), edited by T.O. McLoughlin. Despite these individual achievements, publishing has been a difficult arena for women to enter during the first two decades of Zimbabwean independence.

The superficial nature of critics' regard for this canon reflects Zimbabwean women writers' struggles to gain a wide and attentive audience. In the introduction to *The Sound of Snapping Wires*, McLoughlin couples "The Letter" with "The Spirit," another anthologized short story which offers "a facet of the war." McLoughlin describes the characters in both texts as "victims, but they have more spiritual room to move in than those entangled in the action of the war." McLoughlin's review of "The Letter" concludes with a final remark about protagonists, "free to fight back from their isolation, to act against submission or despair, and to give their hopes a tangible framework" (xix). Although his point is not further explicated, McLoughlin's suggestion that Dangarembga's protagonist faces isolation and despair provides a germane point of departure for analyzing narrative strategies in "The Letter." Apartheid history is the backdrop for Black, female experience in "The Letter."

As Leonard Thompson describes in *A History of South Africa*, by 1985,[5] South Africa experienced waves of political resistance and violent backlash as "clashes between township residents and security forces" took the explosive forms of school and bus boycotts, residential relocations, work stayaways, physical attacks and murder (Thompson 229). Sebokeng, as painted by the narrator of "The Letter," is a meager home—a nesting place for despair. In recounting her parents' hard lives in Sebokeng and Pretoria, the narrator remembers that her father is assaulted for "daring to walk over the land of his heritage without the baas' permission" and that her mother could scarcely feed her children despite her employment as a domestic like numerous other Black mothers, who "wipe[d] the feces hourly from the plump buttocks of an overfed Boer baby while her children scavanged [sic] dustbins in the shanty town" (237). In their world, violence threatens all members of Black society. The narrator observes that gang fights are common among the frustrated adolescents, mothers are beaten when they protest the arrest of their daughters, and "my uncles and sisters . . . were shot down at random by Boer policemen for so much as whispering that there is life after Botha" (237). Her family's experiences are clearly based upon social reality. The correspondence between South African political history and the narrator's experiences lend the story social and historical depth.

Reflecting a pattern of unreasonable arrest and detention, Themba, the narrator's husband, is abducted under state suspicion that he is a subversive. This episode was all too common under apartheid. The army as well as the police controlled the townships. Thousands of people were being detained in solitary confinement, without being brought to trial and without the knowledge of their families, friends, or lawyers. In addition, in spite of much vague official talk about including Africans in national decision-making, President Botha and his colleagues were adamant about retaining the racial structure of government institutions and rejected any suggestion that Africans should participate equally with whites (228).

In his work on the psychological ramifications of apartheid, Frank Talk explains that South Africa's climate of Black powerlessness bred an insidious cycle of fear, denial, and mute resistance in which fearful Blacks complied with the state's ritual stereotyping: "One frequently hears people say of someone who has just been arrested or banned—'there is no smoke without fire' or if the guy was outspoken—'he asked for it. I am not surprised.' In a sense this is almost deifying the security police; they cannot be wrong . . ." (337). Although "The Letter" never discloses any occasion where the narrator and her husband publicly criticize Botha or the government, neither does the text reveal fear on the part of the narrator or any of her family members. Indeed, in closing her account, the narrator coolly, pragmatically articulates her uncertain fate as a political prisoner: "I have had ample time to get used to the aberrations of people in the grip of totalitarian fervor. I do not know what is going to happen to me. I may be charged with an act of treason . . . or they may hold me here to abuse me physically and mentally for a while" (243-44). The narrator's perspective not only feminizes the "guy" who has just been arrested or banned, but also modifies the "terrorist" status of the Black detainee. The narrator's testimony as a wife and lover exposes the humanity and typicality of Black people unreasonably targeted by the state.

Consistent rationale and spirited resilience (signified by a Black person's show of overt resistance) threatens Boer officials who regulate apartheid. The narrator explains her and her husband Themba's transformation from politically covert to overt resistors. "Together we saw the tension that dissects South Africa quite clearly disclose to us our only course of action—we became political people," she explains, to counter the genocide and nonexistent "recourse to justice" faced by their people (238). It is a costly personal empowerment for each of them, and their marriage is permanently destroyed. After Themba is considered "a major security risk" and abducted, the narrator begins her vigil and waits for a sign that he is still alive. Each day she walks to the post office to check for the arrival of a letter from him. After seven years of mind-numbing waiting, she takes a lover and bears her second child, Thandi. When Themba's letter arrives five years later, the joyous narrator keeps it (against her mother's advice that she destroy it) in order to repeatedly savor its materiality. The narrator's happiness explodes upon reading that Themba urges wife and daughter to join him in Botswana where he resides in exile out of harm's way. Before the narrator can strategize how she will explain to Themba the birth of Thandi, whom she also desires to take with her to Botswana, she is arrested by Boer soldiers who mysteriously arrive at her home and arrest her on the pretense of being a terrorist. They implicate Themba's letter as evidence of her subversive associations. Her arrest shifts time and structure in the narrative: "Searching the house," says the narrator, "it did not take them long to find my letters [sic] and decide that they were subversive. I was bundled into the jeep and brought here to the police station" (243). With this statement, the narrator reveals that she has not been telling her story from the privacy of her home, but from "here," a prison cell. Unlike her physical location which shifts from home to cell (so that one location cancels the other), her maternal and political subjectivities conflate. The narrator is suddenly both wife/ mother and detainee. Thus, in her text, paired characterizations parallel doubled narratives.

A prison narrative picks up where the domestic story ends: "they threatened to shoot my children to make me confess to my terrorist activities" (243). We see that up until this point the plot is merely the palimpsest, or "cover story," behind which the prison story waits. Originally referring to a document inscribed on parchment that bears traces of previous writing, a palimpsest is literally a literary artifact from which lost Greek discourse has been recovered.[6] Anglo-American feminist critics have adapted palimpsest to name a literary theory of textual duplicity. Sandra Gilbert and Susan Gubar first discussed women's creation of palimpsests as a narrative strategy whereby nineteenth-century English women writers communicated "taboo feelings."[7] In agreement with Gilbert and Gubar's assessment that the subtext withholds a feminist critique, Nancy K. Miller proposes that conventional narratives circulate through the palimpsest layer of English women's writing (Childers and Hentzi 218-19). These theories suggest that the narrator of "The Letter" erases her "domestic" memoir of raising a family and checking the mail to make room for the story of her arrest and detainment under the Terrorist Act.[8] At the moment of her arrest, the climax ruptures the palimpsest and "The Letter" takes on multiple meanings. Themba's letter, the marital response Themba's letter invites, and the letter of South African law are decentered by the unsolicited letter the reader "receives from" the detainee. "The Letter" thus privileges the African woman's political experience.

Carol Boyce Davies and Anne Adams Graves outline six themes which generally characterize African women's literature, including: contradictions of motherhood and precariousness of marital relationships; the nature of social power relations; the struggle for economic independence; and the politics of (neo)colonialism and its effect on society and women. As developed through themes of loneliness and waiting, the African woman's relationship to (neo)colonial realities is central to "The Letter."[9] However personal the narrator's specific testimony of waiting and loneliness appears, the narrator also recognizes that she is politically representative of any life trapped in a world devoid of security: "I am not unique—there are many families here in the village who have a father, a son, an uncle or a nephew who has not been heard of for many years, who has been imprisoned . . . reported missing or dead" (237). "The Letter" fulfills an African feminist purpose by staging the testimony of a female protagonist who tells an implicitly political story on behalf of detained, exiled, silenced, or murdered African women and men who have experienced the nightmare as well. Moreover, the narrator's story discloses aspects of living in a society organized to destroy a South African woman and anything or anyone she values. In her story, the (neo)colonial state annihilates the maternal core of the Black South African family.

In the face of such catastrophic power, the narrator's voice sounds clearly and idiosyncratically throughout the story. "The Letter" remains a woman-centered, first person narrative before and after its climax. Although dialogue is absent from the text, the narrative does not map stale, flat territory. Dangarembga's different types of discourse produce a multi-dimensional story, representing multiple voices: "My single solitary and individual life is like the lives of the tribe; it differs in these specific ways, but it is a balanced life because it is both solitary and representative." This voice reflects Toni Morrison's theory of the creative and cultural forces that molded autobiography into a classic form of Afro-American literature (339). Morrison's explanatory potential in the continental African context suggests that "The Letter" shares with diasporic kin a literary structure in which individual and collective representations are balanced. As mentioned previously, the text engages in political ethnography and, prior to the narrator's climactic arrest, ethnographic touches nuance the domestic realm of her rural environment as well.[10]

The narrator remembers, for example, that each morning she drew water from the outside tap, "waiting for fifteen minutes until the trickle of water that escapes when the tap is turned on full had filled the drum" (235). This detail of her mornings at home is made even more specific; in an aside, the narrator explains that "(There is a drought this year and the water pressure is low)" (235). Also parenthetically she references for the reader's attention noteworthy objects in her environment, including "tuck-shops and kiosk" which function as stores (239). The narrator describes water and make up as ritual materials of personal hygiene. Poured into an enamel washing bin or heated on the paraffin stove, available water was used for daily washing (236). A "little lipstick" was used on her shopping days, "since anything heavier is out of place in the village and apt to make people stare and whisper behind [her] back about [her] morals" (236). Although less ethnographic in kind, we further note that "The Letter" features colorful details which simply and clearly paint the narrator as "real." For example, while reading Themba's letter, she recognized "the familiar style" of Themba's hand, "with the t's crossed so heavily." Laughing aloud at the good fortune of receiving his letter, the narrator's thoughts were joyous during her final walk from the Post Office to her home:

> I wanted to hug my mother, to kiss Busi and throw Thandi into the air and catch her as I used to do when she was a baby. Instead I forced myself to walk even more slowly than usual and as I walked, I recited to myself the names of each pupil in my class in order to restore some balance to my mind (239).

I quote the passage at length to privilege the whole moment as it appears in Dangarembga's text. The scene captures both the internal excitement the narrator wished to externalize as physical energy, and the psychological means she engaged to mask joy behind a reserved facade. Apparently, Dangarembga's facility in creating authenticating detail places her in the vanguard of African writers. According to Mineke Schipper's evaluation, "the striving for the illusion of authenticity in fictional first-person narrative genres is very much en vogue in African literature" (125).

Writing as a woman is clearly another example of Dangarembga's vanguard status among African writers. Davies and Graves explain that like Dangarembga, African women writers "bring specific perspectives to the evaluation of their societies;" African women writers engage in different discourses that voice many realities (311). In "The Letter," the narrator's social identity signifies how an African woman's subjectivity is relational. The narrator is the meeting point for five different people. As mother, she is the stitch that binds Thandi and Busi as half sisters. As daughter and wife, the narrator sutures the distance between mother and son-in-law who are unrelated without her presence in the family. Finally, as a lover, the narrator stands in for the gap between the men who fathered her children. Whether we perceive her as a point of rupture, the "fault line" Alexander names of the woman of color located between worlds, or a crucial stitch, the narrator embodies the connective capacity to unify several people into a family. Overall, she seems to occupy a center equidistant from each member; she is no more partial to one member than another. Yet one aspect of her maternity suggests this is not absolutely the case.

When specifically speaking of her relationship with Thandi, the narrator credits her daughter born out of wedlock with preventing her from "deceiv[ing] myself into believing that I am a more virtuous woman than I actually am" (235). Thandi, short for Thandiwe, means "Beloved" in Shona (Asante 15). Dangarembga's correlation of daughter's name and mother's sexuality suggests that "Beloved" signifies the narrator's ability to transgress. Nonconformity is arguably a personal attribute the narrator appreciates about herself, for she divulges the secret affair very early in her memoir. The narrator only suggests a wrinkle in her amusement for Thandi's striking phenotypic dissimilarity from Busi when "we meet uncompromising strangers. . . . But on the whole," she concludes, "it is good" (235). Through her self-determination in the form of sexual freedom, the narrator transcends societal indictment of her immorality. Moreover, unlike Alexander, who "had to be secretive about the writing that came out of my own body," the narrator discloses the experience of her maternal and sexual body— "pitted, flawed." The narrator's spangled individuality ironizes the location from which she writes. Even a prison—meant to dehumanize her and mark her indistinguishable from other detainees—fails to erase her memories and silence her creative message.

From a literary perspective, the narrator represents a particular blend of female African subjectivities. She is the result of four (of six) overlapping stereotypes first outlined by sociologist Kenneth Little: "girl-friends and good-time girls," "wives,' "free women," "mothers," " 'political' women and workers," and "courtesans and prostitutes" (qtd. in Davies and Adams). The narrator is neither portrayed as courtesan or prostitute, nor as a girl-friend/good-time girl, but she does embody the remaining types of women. She is both Themba's wife, and as the lover of Thandi's father, a free woman. Moreover, she freely travels unaccompanied in Sebokeng and Pretoria, and happily describes the household she shares with Thandi, Busi, and their grandmother, "quite a colony of women . . . self-sufficient" (236). Consequently, the subjective result of her characterization is not wholly Zimbabwean or South African. As Stephanie Newell explains, the narrative strategy of conflated stereotypes is also recognizably West African:

> West African women's writing tends to focus on specific societies' treatment of the female body. In so doing, women writers might be seen to humanize the female archetypes that signify men's nations, and replace the static Mother Africa symbol with kinetic images of women. (7)

In this way, "The Letter" shares narrative strategies found in African women's writing from the West Coast, particularly Ghana and Nigeria.

Writing of the intertexts shared by West African and African American women's writing, Karla Holloway raises a point about "shifting," as a textual motion in Black women's narratives, which applies to the change from memoir to letter in "The Letter":

> [T]hese works are often characterized by the presence of a translucent flux and identified by a shifting, sometimes nebulous text. The narrative structures in these works force the words within the texts to represent (re)memories in/of events and ideas that revise and multiply meanings. A re-

sult of this revision is that what seems to be ambivalence
is actually a sign of displacement. (56)

In Holloway's hands, shifting indicates a displacement (for example,
of "reality" or history, for memories). Following her lead, we know
that the displacement of something has occurred in "The Letter"
because the detectable representatives of displacement (in this case,
words) have altered. Consequently, shifting also connotes change,
progression and transfer throughout "The Letter." In the relationship
between author and protagonist, we witness Dangarembga's
willingness to transcend national difference, a literary approach
signified by her shift of first person perspective from Zimbabwean
writer to South African narrator. The text's transformation from
memoir to letter and the narrator's progression from (text) consumer
to producer act as subsequent forms of textual progression. Shifting
and displacement function collaboratively during the climax of the
story. When the narrator recounts her arrest, the plot suddenly
changes from past tense to present tense and transfers her location
from home to prison. On the palimpsest level, more subtle
displacements accumulate as the plot unfolds.

The most obvious displacement is that of emotions. When
describing moments of joy or despair, the narrator proceeds ratio-
nally; the pace of her narration is the same during both instances.
There are no grammatical aberrations or disruptions of her linear
thought. Only two interjections of "Ha! Those Boers!" communicate a welling of excessive feeling. An additional, superficial displacement occurs in the domestic context when the narrator displaces Themba for "a man who comforted me during a few hours
of solitude" (235). Themba is oblivious to his wife's affair and
subsequent birth of Thandi. Eventually, guilt undercuts the narrator's
rationalization of her tryst when she reads that Themba has safe-
guarded his end of conjugal fidelity (241). Thus, the text anticipates the narrator's need to confess her extra-marital sexual activity to her husband. How will she justify displacing Themba twice
over—as the recipient of her monogamous affections and as the

father of her children? Finally, the last of the clear displacements occurs during the climax when the narrator is arrested and taken by jeep from her home. The narrator is literally removed from the community where she raises her daughters, cares for her mother, and teaches her pupils. The narrator's detainment humanizes historical disappearances, which raised the statistics of real South African mothers and teachers displaced from homes and schools during the apartheid era of South Africa. The final displacement, of the audience/reader, occurs beneath the palimpsest-plot and is therefore more difficult to discern.

Cast as the narrator's audience, "The Letter" reader is consistently addressed as an intimate from the moment the narrator initiates her story. She readily divulges both the ordinary and the fantastic attributes of the day in the first two lines of her story, pointedly asking her audience, "Can you imagine such a thing?" She proceeds to tell the reader how her day began like any other, with her walk to the Post Office, yet unfolded like none other because "This morning I received a letter from my husband, the first in twelve years" (234). Parenthetical ethnographies also signal moments when the narrator speculatively discloses details which familiarize her environment and lifestyle for the reader. Utilizing the unstated "hypothetical you" as well as second person direct address, the narrator cautions her reader: "[You] Do not misunderstand me. I am not resigning myself to my lot. No, indeed, I am glorifying in it. You see, it was painful for me when I lived in the Township . . ." (237). The narrator invites the reader to identify with her and anticipate her feelings. For most of the text, the narrator addresses the reader as a "listener" worthy of trust. Her endearing tone communicates an awareness that empathetic listening is happening on her behalf: "So imagine my surprise when I saw the post-master waiting for me at the post office door this morning with a letter in his hand. Feel how my heart stopped . . .. Consider how my hand shook" (238-39). Although the narrator sustains her connection to her audience until the end of her story, after her arrest, she changes tone and displaces her audience from a position of casual listening to a tenser realm in which listening is devalued as unproductively passive. The stakes are higher for the narrator and the reader after the narrator's situation dramatically changes.

Following the narrative climax, shifts in textual content and audience location abound. Initially, the narrator force-feeds the reader a violent text of political reality: "I will not tell you how they threatened to shoot my children to make me confess to my terrorist activities, nor will I tell you how they beat my mother when she pleaded for me" (243). The narrator earnestly confesses these horrors even as she claims refusal. We also note that "The Letter" ends in a remarkably different tone from how it began: ". . . I have told you my story, not to arouse your pity, but only so that you may know that these things are happening to us in our country" (244). There are two striking aspects to this statement. The first is that the narrator accosts her reader/confidante as an "other" whose "pity" is not to be confused with her "story." Carefully selected possessives separate the narrator from the reader while simultaneously gesturing toward the shared fate of letter reader and writer in "our country." Perhaps the reader prone to pity is also South African and takes interest in South Africa's future. Perhaps location marks her only difference from the narrator/writer. In this case, the letter reader may exist as the urban counterpart to the letter writer from rural Sebokeng. Thus, Dangarembga's ethnographic references may be seen to intentionally paint a rural landscape that ignites the imagination of the South African reader dwelling in the city. As previously discussed, apartheid contributed to the culture of fear in which denial led many undetained Black South Africans to assume that most detainees were indeed state terrorists. It is likely that the narrator perceives skepticism on the part of her reader whose country she shares but whose political consciousness she seeks to raise.

In absence of an ultimatum, the narrator's assertion, "I have told you my story, not to arouse your pity" ostensibly exempts the reader, whomever she is, from further interaction with the narrator.

Mere consumption of the story requires only pity, which she refuses; there is nothing further for the reader to do, perhaps. On the other hand, the acerbic tone of the statement, and the narrator's refusal to model a range of responses convey her critique of the idle reader. The implication is that the recipient of "The Letter" has consumed an entire testimony and should be moved to action. Unlike the narrator who has no choice but to endure detainment, the letter reader has no excuse for waiting for the narrator's "next letter." The silence following the last line of the "The Letter" resounds loudly. The silence signifies the reader's inactivity and the chilling sound of the narrator's waiting for the reader to activate a response to her plight. Out of her silence sounds a call for further agency on the part of the reader now that speaking, reading, and listening are over.

Although the palimpsest is ruptured at the climax and the narrator's final words complete the plot, the text refuses closure. We are left to independently reconcile any unanswered questions about what happens next: How did her letter reach a public reader in the first place? Will the officials discover Themba's whereabouts and detain him again? What will happen to Busi "who is thirteen . . . and grown into quite a woman" (235)? Will both girls join Themba in Botswana? Will their mother ever be released from prison? The uncertain ending is more disruptive than was the feminist interstice the narrator represented throughout the palimpsest of her memoir. The narrator did not face mortal danger when poised as the connective "space" between family members or the "rupture" between domestic and political subjectivities—wife of a subversive on the one hand, detained subversive on the other. Ironically, "The Letter" does not necessarily communicate futility. Once the reader considers the narrative silence at the end of "The Letter" as an interstice, rather than a conclusion, she can enact a final shift in political consciousness from a reluctant consumer to an active cultural agent.[11]

To do this, the reader must inhabit the uncomfortable space the ending creates and embrace the task of making meaning without the aid of the narrator. As cultural critic, bell hooks champions Black cultural productions which require a reader or film spectator to meditate and think rather than be told what a text means (194). Speaking as a Black woman writer, Toni Morrison explains that she models the textual interstices in her own narrative prose from cultural interstices that manifest along a continuum of Black arts. Indeed, the spaces are necessarily created and reserved for the entry of the reader whose participation in call and response with the artist produces mutual agency:

> There are things that I try to incorporate into my fiction that are directly and deliberately related to what I regard as the major contributions of Black arts, wherever it is. One is the ability to be both print and oral literature . . . . It should try deliberately to make you stand up and make you feel something profoundly in the same way that a Black preacher requires his congregation to speak, to join him in the sermon . . . to accede or to change and to modify—to expand on the sermon that is being delivered. In the same way that a musician's music is enhanced when there is a response from the audience . . . . I have to provide the places and spaces so that the reader can participate. Because it is the affective and participatory relationship between the artist or the speaker and the audience that is of primary importance, as it is in these other art forms. (341)

As a narrative strategy, interstices prompt the reader to continue the work inspired by the artist. The reader who is willing to respond to the call and work through the spaces in "The Letter" has not only exercised her critical thinking, but participated in the tradition of African and Diaspora arts as well. Dangarembga's insertion of interstices invites readers to enter her text reflectively and intimately consider the social and political realities of life for South African women under apartheid.

Overall, it is worth noting that the characterization, which shifts the identity of the detainee from memoir narrator to letter writer (and from free, to detained) also parallels the multiplication of audience perspective(s). These tactics, integral to the detainee's strategic narration, reflect the ultimate political strength of Dangarembga's project. "The Letter" invites readers to "role play," particularly readers who meet Dangarembga's text outside of South Africa and have much to learn, from many vantages, about resistance, complicity and apartheid. The eventual transfer of responsibility from writer to reader performs "The Letter" author's quintessential dupe. Consequently, Dangarembga's international community of readers might yet consider the ways in which her efforts situate her artistry at the intersection of multiple cultural traditions and genres. We might yet appreciate a host of textual strategies in her work, from depicting authentic African detail to the feminist impact of first person perspective, as well as a variety of intertexts and narrative maneuvers: the letter as "contraband" in the reader's hands, and how Dangarembga's construction of this trope compares with the works of other writers[12]; the ways in which the text negotiates binaries of public/private and domestic/political in constructing female subjectivity; the risk of self-expression in state-regulated environments and the role of gender and location in writing[13]; the narrator as a discursive "trickster" in the tradition of African storytelling and diasporic orality; the role of memory in historical fiction. Literary offerings like Tsitsi Dangarembga's undeniably call for many responses.

Notes

1. Anonymity is an important theme in "The Letter." Besides her mother, the narrator is the only member of her family who remains unnamed in the story. Her husband is Themba, their elder daughter Busi, and the younger daughter, Thandi.

2. In *Black Women, Writing and Identity: Migrations of the Subject*, Carole Boyce Davies encourages readers to complicate how the academy names

(or canonizes through naming), literatures authored by residents of neo-colonial countries (81-83). Her proposal and analyses have significant implications for how twentieth-century work by women writers, like Tsitsi Dangarembga's and Meena Alexander's, are read and categorized. In this essay, I refer to the "postmodern and postcolonial" literature of Black authors in order to indicate a network of twentieth-century writers and/or conveniently reference the literary quality of their projects.

3. Introduced by Hortense Spillers and Valerie Smith into discourses of psychoanalytic and cultural criticism on the Black experience, "interstice" often circulates in poststructuralist discussions of African American women's writing and experience. See Spillers' "Interstices: A Small Drama of Words" in *Pleasure and Danger: Exploring Female Sexuality* (Carole S. Vance, ed. 1984). I draw my current use of the term from *The American Heritage Dictionary*: "A space, especially a small or narrow one, between things or parts" from the Latin "to stand in the middle."

4. Zimbabwe Women Writers (ZWW) was one of the first three women's media organizations established following national independence in 1980. ZWW gained non-profit status in 1990 through the informal cooperation of black and white volunteers serving as its steering committee. By 1994, when the Minister of Information voiced his public support of ZWW in "the struggle of women to overcome their oppression," ZWW had established 17 branches and 12 public libraries outside of Harare, published 2 English language anthologies, facilitated numerous public readings and conducted over twenty literary workshops targeting different aspects of literary proficiency and professionalism. The 500 dues-paying members in 1994 were black and white Zimbabwean women of Shona, Ndebele, German, Spanish, Dutch and New Zealand parentage or descent residing in Northern and Southern Zimbabwe centers including Bulawayo, Mutare and Marondera— all of them Anglophone authors of poetry, short stories or novels. Taking initiatives to ensure that as many women in Zimbabwe as possible benefit from literary projects, ZWW flourished artistically despite poor financing and sparse materials.

5. This date is meaningful if we assume the plot of "The Letter" is contemporaneous with the year of its authorship. This could mean that the narrator's arrest occurs in 1985 and her husband's occurred twelve years prior, around 1973.

6. *The American Heritage Dictionary.* Second College Edition. Boston:

Houghton Mifflin, 1982.

7. Moreover, a critical feature of the palimpsest theory is that a "hetero-sexual romance" covers a "deeper, more dangerous story of rage" (Childers and Hentzi 218). Although the even-toned narration of the detainee's let-ter might further mask the rage she harbors for being detained, the do-mesticating palimpsest of her memoir undoubtedly recounts heterosexual pleasures.

8. The Terrorism Act was instituted in 1967: "Repressive legislation es-calated from the mid-1950s onward. . . . The mass of legislation gave the police vast powers to arrest people without trial and hold them indefi-nitely in solitary confinement, without revealing their identities and without giving them access to anyone except government officials" (Thompson 199).

9. Consequently, Dangarembga's themes of loneliness and waiting sug-gest a "famished" happiness, perhaps parallel or approximate to the theme of environmental drought which typifies Zimbabwean prose: "Two de-terminants of our existence as a community, taken up by writers as an integral part of their imaginative vision, are rain and drought, abundance and poverty" (McLoughlin xx-xxi).

10. Dangarembga's use of ethnography in "The Letter" brings to mind the ethnographic travel diaries of South African writer Nontando Jabavu. *The Ochre People: Scenes from a South African Life* (1963) incredibly details three geographic regions (See Busboy 287-97).

11. My reading does not intend to discount the possibility that literature inspires the concrete political action of readers. However, I also regard "The Letter" as fictional and thereby functioning as a highly constructed (if well designed) short story whose value as fiction does not elide the value of the "real autobiography" and prison narratives that prompt orga-nizing, lobbying, protest, and revolution for social change, frequently on behalf of individual people in the world.

12. One example of a fruitful cross-cultural analysis of letter-texts could explore this trope's emergence in works such as Alice Walker's *The Color Purple*, Patricia Powell's *Me Dying Trial*, Mariama Ba's *So Long a Let-ter*, Edwidge Danticat's *Crick Crack*, and "The Letter" in cross-cultural consideration.

13. I thank the editors for bringing to my attention the following interrogations which animate points of departure for thinking about the politics of writing and reading in the South African context: "Why would a South African dissident write letters that they know will incriminate others? What do they gain from such a dangerous act? Is self-expression worth the risks to others? Themba's husband writes from exile, the narrator writes from jail. Does the site of writing create a different relation to politics? Does gender?" Essential international readings for a comparative project on women's (neo)colonial experiences in detainment might include Barbara Schreiner's *A Snake with Ice Water: Prison Writings by South African Women* (COSAW, Congress of South African Writers, 1992) and Kavita Punjabi's "Probing 'Morality' and State Violence: Feminist Values and Communicative Interaction in Prison Testimonies in India and Argentina" (*Feminist Genealogies, Colonial Legacies, Democratic Futures*. Eds. M. Jacqui Alexander and Chandra Talpade Mohanty. New York: Routledge, 1997). Punjabi, for example, explores the careful ways in which women detainees in India and Argentina draw on personal experience to divulge information about their torture and launch "crucial critique of the functionings of state apparatus" (159).

Chapter 14:
Embracing the Shadow: Recognizing Liminality in Dangarembga's Jungian Undercurrents

Kgomotso Masemola

The interview between Tsitsi Dangarembga and Jane Wilkinson in 1989, published in 1992, carries greater significance than has been accounted for. It is here that all questions asked relating to the act of writing as "rewriting," remembering and forgetting, the difficulty of the interface between fact and fiction, and the viability of norms and values, especially in terms of the family constellation, are related to Carl Gustav Jung's archetypes of the soul. When asked about the distinction drawn between fairy tale and romantic stories on the one hand and reality and history on the other, Dangarembga says: " . . . at the end of the day it's like this Jungian idea of embracing the shadow, isn't it? I mean, where you have fact you have fiction as well and sometimes the interface is difficult" (Wilkinson 191). The clear line of divide between binaries disappears in the conditions of anomie that characterize the situation of colonization and decolonization. Writing becomes the rewriting of history from an ambivalent space. Like Homi K. Bhabha elsewhere, Helen Tiffin states that "[p]ostcolonial cultures are inevitably hybridized, involving a dialectical relationship between European ontology and epistemology and the impulse to create or recreate independent local identity" (95).

What is at stake in Dangarembga's *Nervous Conditions,* is the sustainability of silencing women within the family as well as other ways of "othering" them. Nyasha's voyage into English modernity, for instance, challenges the privileged discourses of Shona society. Similarly, Tambudzai finds it necessary to adapt to these patriarchal discourses while at the same time exploring the possibilities offered by "Englishness." Tambudzai's agency exists in an interstitial space structured by ambivalence. For Dangarembga, "We need another set of norms . . . to rethink all these norms and values and customs both traditional and Western" (Wilkinson 194). Accordingly, she responds to the comment on the success of the wedding: "the fact that the wedding was a success makes an important point in that again it's a question of embracing the shadow . . ." (194).

To embrace the shadow is to embrace the colonizer and the colonial edict. This act, however, requires a defiance of what Jung calls the moral complex. I argue here that the moral complex represents the discourse of cultural difference. This is crucial because it is Jung who refers to the two important sources of the shadow complex as cultural indoctrination and familial repression (Stevens 48). The discourse of cultural difference discriminates against women and "the Evil Stranger" (colonizer) and becomes complicated as women construct their subjectivity in relation to the discourses of the "Evil Stranger" and patriarchy. Since the shadow is unwanted and antisocial, it is quite clear that embracing it in effect carries with it the prospect of being rejected by society.

Nyasha and Lucia are subversive in their acts, yet Nyasha's rationality, which symptomizes her English acculturation, does not really or effectively undermine cultural discourse or the moral complex whose recognition actually depends on rationality. Tambudzai's ability to be in a sense oblivious to the negative prospects of "Englishness" makes her "too eager to embrace the 'Englishness' of the mission; and after the more concentrated 'Englishness' of Sacred Heart" (203). Cultural indoctrination, as Jung would have it, would want the moral complex to posit "Englishness" as the archetype of the Predator or Evil Stranger. Nyasha upholds the self/other binaries that typify the discursive ontology and European epistemology that renders subjectivity as the Other: "I won't grovel. Oh no, I won't. I am not a good girl. I'm evil. I'm not a good girl" (200).

Nyasha's less successful subversion stems from her ironic willingness to see men and colonizers as the Enemy or the Predator or, in short, a shadow she will not embrace. In so doing, she unwittingly exercises her subjectivity under and within the tyranny of binary oppositions. Her experience of familial repression, of seeing her mother and Ma'Shingayi living for their husbands and Maiguru's education not being enough for her emancipation, cause her total rejection of males in general. At the peril of reinforcing the false distinctions between masculine and feminine, Nyasha regrets her mother's pandering tendency towards males, even when she (Maiguru) had left Babamukuru to spend some time with her brother and his family: "Nyasha was unhappy that Maiguru had gone to her brother. 'A man! She always runs to men,' she despaired. 'There's no hope, Tambu. Really, there isn't.' Nor did she want her mother to come back soon. It was difficult to say whether she wanted her to come back at all" (175). Tambudzai, however, responds to historical necessity and the question of survival or what Jung earlier on called the principle of adaptation. Tambudzai's personality has to undergo changes—convenient enough to assume her persona as "the grateful poor female relative." Carl Gustav Jung is quoted as saying, "[o]ne could say, with little exaggeration, that the persona is that which in reality one is not, but which oneself as well as others think one is" (qtd. in Stevens 47). This explains why Tambudzai is aware that, in her own words, "I was not the person I was expected to be" (Dangarembga 110). According to Stevens, "through the persona we codify ourselves in a form which we hope will prove acceptable to others. It has sometimes been referred to as the social archetype or the conformity archetype, for on it depends the success or failure of one's adaptation to society" (47). It is interesting that the "self" is not effaced but under erasure. As distinct from its Freudian appropriation, in Jung's use, "the self" means "the center of consciousness and what we refer to when we use the terms 'I' or 'me'" (Stevens 45). Its function is to defend consciousness against unwanted contents arising from the unconscious through repression, denial, projection, and rationalization. To quote Tambudzai: "But in those days it was easy for me to leave tangled thoughts knotted, their loose ends hanging. I didn't want to explore the treacherous mazes that such thoughts led into. I didn't want to reach the end of those mazes, because there, I know, I would find myself and I was afraid I would not recognize myself after taking so many directions" (Dangarembga 116). Tambudzai represses the contents of the unconscious in such a manner as to repress the thought that, she suspects, would lead to premature conflict and sabotage her long-term goal of wholeness and emancipation. When she assumes her persona it is because of the rationalization of ego defense. This in itself indicates that Tambudzai's self-fashioning is ambivalent. In this sense the "I" or "me" that for Jung constitutes the center of consciousness allows the self to exist with the possibility of assuming different personas in order that self may survive. In a different context, Bhabha sees this assumption of a persona as mimicry. In Tambudzai's case, she wants to be "selfed" through education; she wants to be like Babamukuru who had "[p]lenty of power. Plenty of money. A lot of education. Plenty of everything" (50).

Tambudzai's acquisition of education is an act of self-empowerment. For education, albeit negatively mobilized against women by Babamukuru, is important for the proper exercise of women's subjectivity. To embrace it is therefore an act of "embracing the shadow." As in the case of Maiguru, acquiring that education involves assuming a persona that will be convenient for emancipation. Despite Babamukuru's authoritative and domineering tendencies with regard to women, Tambu "felt secure at the mission under Babamukuru's shadow and [she] could not understand why Nyasha found it so threatening" (116). She faces a situation of historical necessities whereby she also has to negotiate the colonial discourse synonymous with the "Englishness" of education. She also has to negotiate the patriarchal discourse that makes possible the alienating circumstances of social marginality because she is already implicated in it as a daughter of Babamukuru's brother. The shadow complex that arises from familial repression also offers possibilities since, projecting herself as the "grateful poor relative", Tambudzai cannot be totally seen as an objectivized other. Once embraced, the shadow can be instrumental for the woman who leads her life as the in-between figure. As such, she cannot have a fixed identity but evinces positive alterity and becomes what Sally McWilliams calls "a composite of shifting selves" (105). At one moment she has to be the obedient niece and at another a cousin who sympathizes with Nyasha's assertiveness, and yet disapprove of Babamukuru's treatment of Nyasha while distancing herself from Nyasha's unstrategic rebelliousness. "Embracing the shadow" allows Tambudzai considerable purchase on the simultaneous subversion of cultural indoctrination and familial repression through the exploration of the pathologies of a traditional discourse that clashes and melds with modernity.

To embrace the shadow in this case is to exercise agency in a liminal space. It is Dangarembga who, as we discussed earlier, insists on the interface between fact and fiction or, put differently, between binarisms, being difficult (Wilkinson 191). If where there is fact there is fiction, the women of whom she speaks throughout the novel will have to negotiate the split forms of familial repression, instead of falling victim to the tyranny of binaries reified by treating men such as Babamukuru as the Enemy or Predator. Having both Predator and provider, fact and fiction, in the same space not only deflates binarisms but also suggests mimicry. As earlier discussed, mimicry is involved in the situation of "embracing the shadow," which indicates the possibility exists for inscribing heterogeneity within an opposition so as to displace it. Tambudzai acts out Babamukuru, by way of exchanging positions with him so that she will have empowerment and simultaneously disempower him. She subverts and mocks the binary structure of male/female by repeating Babamukuru, dislocating him fractionally through mimicry. In the interstice where splits are continuously negotiated, becoming Self and Other or existing as both gives us a clear sense of the ambivalent self-fashioning that is instrumental for meaningful survival. Acquiring whatever "education" Babamukuru has signifies progress.

Yet Sue Thomas thinks of power, education and money as functioning to "sustain the spell of Englishness over [Babamukuru] and the myth that an English education represents progress" (28), emphasizing only the price to be paid in the course of acquiring education. Of course, education has fashioned Babamukuru into "a good boy, a good munt. A bloody good kaffir" (200) who has to use that English education to give Nyasha and Chido a glimpse of the English values that influence Nyasha's desire to resist traditional patriarchal discourse. As a result of the selfsame education, Nyasha is able to be sufficiently critical about history, consciousness, and colonialism which, if she had not been to England, would not have been possible. Besides, the interest that she has in traditional history of the Shona as well as the "old ways" (147) bears testimony to her embracing of the very culture that inscribes her position as inferior to men on the basis of gender.

One of the greatest dangers of the argument such as Thomas's, which singles out progress as if it is enunciated in the manner in which the colonial edict articulates it, is its unproblematized critique of the notion of progress. Granted, Babamukuru becomes a much more patriarchal authority who effectively silences his wife regardless of her education, but it is not difficult to recognize throughout Dangarembga's novel a refusal to render Babamukuru, education, Whites, and colonialism as stable categories that can be neatly mapped onto the "either/or" scheme of binaries. Besides, in *Nervous Conditions* education, the West, and its discourse of progress create what is known as an environment of "trust" (Giddens 102). For, in the absence of alternatives, investing in rational constructs is better than operating outside the discourse of equality and emancipation. Thomas does not recognize value in the liminality of colonization and decolonization, the interstitial space of the subject of cultural discourse. Nor does she appreciate that progress is not only to "self" women, or that "selfing" is not moving from the margins to the center. It is also a *process* that is represented in what Bhabha calls a "specific, problematic kind of temporality . . . peculiarly split and doubled in its effective implementation" (Attwell 102). Englishness is therefore not some spell cast on a docile colonial subject who is willing to encounter and be subdued by myths of progress only to later uphold them: liminality's possibilities of mimicry may repeat the myth of associating English education with progress into real progress.

Indeed, if where there is fact there is fiction (in Jungian terms), that myth of which Thomas speaks can be exchanged with factual progress through the exchange of hybridity as well as through parodic doubling. The edicts of English education and language, as well as an external notion of progress, are not imposed on passive colonial subjects, particularly where there is a specific problematic of temporality at work. Since we own that the colonial subject is not passive but finds agency in the split forms of English education, the choices that Babamukuru, Maiguru, and Tambudzai make serve to demonstrate the difficult conditions under which their agency operates. Tambudzai makes a choice that will disallow or reverse the helplessness that Sue Thomas unwittingly expects and projects in her analysis. Tambudzai says that she "banished the suspicion, buried it in the depths of [her] subconscious, and happily went back to Sacred Heart" (203).

Again, let us consider this decision as it was earlier antici-pated: "I did not know because I did not speak English. But, I assured him, I was going to learn English when I went back to school" (28). Tambudzai can master the discourses that constitute her, but she also has to reconfigure them. This is an act of reappropriation of English education and the language itself. This, however, re-quires recognition of the liminality of the position from which such a reappropriation takes place. For it is not a matter of responding directly to an Englishness that is an Enemy on the other side of the binarism: it is more a matter of reconfiguring the subject of cul-tural difference. This transforms the processes of reappropriation at a level that is specific while undermining whatever discourse aspires to claim a primary ontological status for itself in relation to some "othering" education or language. The reappropriation of English education or English as a language is very much a part of undermining the alterity that obtains in the specific and problem-atic temporality of colonization and recolonization.

As far as embracing the shadow is concerned, it is not dif-ficult to discern that, once embraced, English education can be an enabling mode for progress in terms of its access to "re-embed-ding" systems such as the discourse of the liberation of women. Familial repression, the very cause of the shadow complex, engen-ders a lack which is eventually turned into a space for the subver-sion of the other source of the shadow complex, that is, cultural indoctrination. The potential for subversion is limitless because the historical situation of postcoloniality includes displacements and contradictions. This situation's potentialities are hardly sur-prising given that, according to Jungian psychology, irrespective of having familial repression as its source, the shadow complex emerges "out of potentially actuality relations [and], in time, comes to structure those relations" (Brooke 17); and this in itself goes to show that for the putative other to be "selfed," embracing the shadow reconstitutes the particulars of family life. Examples of this are when Maiguru turns her docility into emancipatory activity; when Tambudzai disapproves of her parents' wedding; and when Lucia recognizes her potential for agency as an unmarried woman without totally rejecting marriage.

Dangarembga is acutely aware of the vulnerability of the "dominant discourse." This discourse, thoroughly patriarchal and coinciding with colonialism, encounters counter-hegemonic discourse in the account of a woman who will not compromise her self as she encounters conflicts that are discursively positioning femininity as a marginality. Tambudzai says, "now I began to see that the disappointing events . . . were serious consequences of the same general laws that had almost brought my education to an abrupt, predictable end . . . I did not want my life to be predicted by such improper relations. I decided I would just have to make up my mind not to let it happen" (38). Nyasha also confesses that "it's not virtue that keeps me so busy! I think, though, that your uncle is pleased with the quieter environment and I have discovered that it is restful to have him pleased, and so these days I am doing my best not to antagonize him. You can imagine how difficult that is. Impossible, it seems" (196-97). The interstitial space is difficult but somehow uncannily necessary. Thus the view that "[t]he oppressed are victims of social injustice; their significance, however does not reside in the fact of their victimization but in the possibility that their agency will transform their fixed relations" (Hitchcock 8). That Nyasha was taken to England was not deleterious but in some ways fortunate in that she was soon to find herself in conditions of hybridity, the very conditions that give her energy, "at times stormy and turbulent, at times confidently severe, but always reaching, reaching a little further than I thought of reaching" (151-52). This is a benefit of what Bhabha in a different context describes as "a willingness to descend into that alien territory [a means for the] recognition of the split-space of enunciation [which] may open the way to conceptualizing an international culture based . . . on the inscription and articulation of culture's hybridity" ("Difference, Discrimination" 22). As earlier pointed out, the possibilities for mimicry are legion in hybridity. Female subjectivity may be exercised positively although initially appearing to be split in a process through which they "self" themselves from what seems to be marginality. Tambudzai learns from Nyasha that "there were other directions to be taken, other struggles to engage in besides the consuming desire to emancipate [herself and her] family. Nyasha gave [her] the impression of moving, always moving and striving towards some state that she had seen and accepted a long time ago. Apprehensive as [she] was . . . [she] wanted to go with her" (152). Tambudzai's development includes "having to cope with [Nyasha's] experimental disposition, her insistence on alternatives, her passion for transmuting the present to the possible" (178). This experimental disposition characterizes the conditions of the problematic temporality of liminal space.

In Jungian psychology complexes such as the shadow "are not isolated entities but tend to be related to each other, particularly in polarity: for example child and mother, mother and old wise woman, woman and death, mother and father, hero and father, hero and maiden, victim and victor, or trickster and wise old woman . . . [they] tend towards conflict and resolution" (Brooke 17). Although a victim of the patriarchal discourse that constructs female subjectivity in Babamukuru's family and a person whose radical behavior leads to her loss of appreciation for values of respect, Nyasha becomes important for Tambudzai:

> Nyasha was something unique and necessary for me. I did not like to spend too long without talking to her about the things that worried me because she would, I knew, pluck out the heart of the problem with her multi-directional mind and present it to me in ways that made sense, but not only that, in ways that implied also that problems existed not to be worried over but to extend us in our search for solutions. (151)

Elsewhere Attwell and Bhabha describe the tendency of arguing for a psychic need to "make up for the lack" as unprogressive. According to them the lack that metropolitan accounts are always suggesting, is part of a disseminatory negotiation with the colonial or its shadow (106). In my mind, this disseminatory negotiation corresponds closely with hybridity. At times, Nyasha acts and speaks of herself in a tone that is nothing short of regret, but Dangarembga hails the condition that Nyasha laments. Nyasha describes her situation thus: "We shouldn't have gone. . . . They should have [packed us off home]. Lots of people did that. Maybe that would have been best. For them at least, because now they're stuck with hybrids for children. And they don't like it" (78).

Tambu on the other hand regrets and mimics. She considers it an opportunity to be hybrid and chooses the image of the "poor female relative" who depends on the mercy and patriarchal design of Babamukuru. When Tambudzai voices her dissatisfaction, it is with the intention of a strategic engagement that will involve no spectacular conflict but still salvage victory and authority: "The most I could do was ask in a small, timid voice to be allowed to stay, with Nyasha, I specified, for a few more days. Nobody was more surprised by my audacity than I was. Babamukuru did not answer, but I was not taken home. I did not take it as a victory though I took it as proof that Babamukuru was good" (199). What good is it recognizing the good of an oppressive patriarchal figure such as Babamukuru? In the order of (interstitial) things, victim and victor, related to each other in putative polarity (Brooke 17), are as much exchangeable as repeatable when splitting and doubling occur in the specific temporality of the colonial situation. Babamukuru becomes reinscribed so that parodic doubling effects a relation of alterity between women (as the same) and men (as the other). In *This Sex Which Is Not One* (1985) Luce Irigaray invokes a sense of mimicry whereby we have the same as that which it simulates but necessarily also different from the same, until the woman being the same mimes herself without being herself. Tambudzai mimes herself as a disempowered adolescent female without being disempowered; she stands more to benefit as she takes refuge in the image of "the grateful poor female relative" (116). In other words, in terms of both Jung and Irigaray, Tambudzai repeats the patriarchal relations that she finds without actually reinforcing them.

Tambudzai finds herself in an interstitial situation at Sacred Heart where the problem is not really one of identity but of inferiorization and a production of lack through the differential discourses that *at the same time* give Tambudzai access to the values of humanism, enlightenment, and so forth. We read that in a school in Rhodesia, a country with more Africans than Whites, the Sister remarks: "We have more Africans here than usual this year and so we had to put them all in here" (194). Tambudzai is therefore to be reduced to the Same through institutional processes of categorization. All this while we bear in mind that the Jungian Self has individuation as its *raison d'être* (Stevens 45). Tambudzai is not only a subject produced spectacularly in a plane of difference but finds herself "in-between," so much so that her identity is best accounted for in terms of liminality. Being in a position of in-betweenness, Tambu accrues more chances for the productive undermining, exchanging, repeating, and mimicking with a privileged self-assured presence until she can live "with and within difference" (Minh-ha *Woman* 84). Tambudzai, unlike Nhamo, does not find it necessary to repudiate her family background as she pursues her emancipation. She lives instead in "two worlds," ensuring that she does not grow aphasic like Nhamo (53) or anorexic like Nyasha when she feels the need to, in her own words, "discipline my body and occupy my mind" (197). Tambudzai suffers terribly and is forced into a position of introspection, concluding that "Babamukuru could only be so charitable to our branch of the family because [they] were so low. He was kind *because of the difference*" (65, emphasis added). Difference is thus used to forge a new interstitial position. For it is only in such a position that the lack of individual identity effected by the "Same-ing" of Tambudzai by the nuns can be turned into a space of emancipation.

Albert Memmi uses the term "depersonalization" for the "mark of the plural" embossed on each individual colonial subject, implying a systematic creation of an anonymous collectivity (85). This process is effectively disavowed by the individuation essential to, often concomitant with, the personal adjustment that underscores the reconciliation of opposites and tensions within the psyche of the (Jungian) Self as well as within the archetype of the shadow (Brooke 17). It therefore becomes part of the adjustment and the psychic totality of the Self that difference with regard to Europe be reconciled without losing sight of individuation. The site of the actualization and/or reconciliation is interstitial and, accordingly, the self-fashioning is ambivalent. That should better explain why Tambudzai will not be deterred by any of the alienating circumstances, saying, ". . . I was ashamed of my weakness in succumbing so flabbily to the strangeness of my new circumstances . . . I reaffirmed my vow to use the opportunity my uncle had given me to maximum advantage" (89). It is not a matter of "embracing the shadow" for her emancipation and only that: Tambudzai affirms her place in the hybridized scheme of things: "[Nyasha] was not very explicit about these consequences beyond assuring me that they would follow, and I did not push her because, in spite of the warning, I would still have liked to go to a multiracial school, and I liked the feeling of ambition and aspiration that went with this desire" (105). There are two chief points that need to be made about this passage. Tambudzai anticipates the benefit of being in a situation of difference, where her hybridity and individuation are possible. For her, embracing difference seems to be part of the subject of cultural difference. The second point follows directly from this. Her encounter with the differential discourses at the mission enables her to resist being fashioned into the knowable other, a White ontological identity. She is therefore seeing the opportunity of a liminal space, where the master narratives of the European civilizing mission are both to be embraced and commensurately tested and contested. Hence embracing the shadow is a deliberate choice.

Of key interest is that the space which is designated as the one occupied by a "subject peoples" does not actually belong to the "subject peoples." It is a site of objectification which is designated to make Tambudzai unhappy and desperate. Being the object of certain stereotyping and depersonalizing, there might be a misrecognition on the part of the colonial subject, invoking delusions of self-knowledge when the subjectivity of females continuously divides and splits. Yet the persona that assumes the image of an inferior other can mislead (and somehow disrupt the consciousness of) the colonizer or Shona patriarch.

Tambudzai's quest for education is not an act of wholesale adoption of values that are dangerous for her. The colonial stereotypes show the colonizer's incapacity to exercise the virtues of christianity/enlightenment/humanism. When Tambudzai arrives at the convent she faces inhumane and marginalizing ways of greeting, ways that underscore objectification: "At the door a nun, smiling beatifically, made us welcome by shaking our hands and asking us 'Which one is this?' before taking us up and down corridors to a room at the end of a long hallway" (194). Tambudzai, always determined to learn the English language, might internalize the stereotypically naturalized address of Africans as regarding her to be one amongst others that are the same. The Comaroffs explain the situation thus: "Colonizers in most places and at most times try to gain control over both the material and semantic practices through which their would-be subjects produce and reproduce the very basis of their existence" (236). If Tambudzai has all along been seeing the earlier difficulties as a result of "[f]emaleness as opposed and inferior to maleness" (116), it would make sense to forge links with other females such as Nyasha in order that they may share an identity as oppressed women. Jung's influence on Dangarembga counters generalizing Tambudzai into Sameness by presenting her instead as the ego that emerges out of the fragments which gradually cohere. One reason why the reconfiguration of the subject of cultural discourse cannot be distanced from Jung's archetypes is that it more or less duplicates the conditions under which differential discourses can be simultaneously embraced and undermined through a disseminatory negotiation that renders the journey emancipatory. One might add that Tambudzai appropriates the violence of naming by categorizing the nuns, paying particular attention to their vices as well as insisting on difference in order that she may make discriminatory choices: "There were nuns to be observed and classified according to whether they were human or not, lay-teachers whose idiosyncrasies had to be identified so that you did not fall prey to them. The white students needed careful study to decide whether they were different or similar to me, whether they were likeable or not and what their habits were" (195). It is in and through such a restaging of values that her identity and individuality will be assured. Also, the agency or reconfiguration of the subject of cultural discourse is shown to necessarily involve the transposition and substitution of the subject of cultural difference, culminating in an alterity that bears testimony to what the Comaroffs designate as the "long history of symbolic struggle" (235). Tambudzai is engaged in the kind of struggle mentioned here, not only constituted but also constituting (in an ambivalent mode of self-fashioning) discursive conditions of possibility.

Tambudzai, like Lucia later, finds the mission crucial in the symbolic struggle that later culminates in the wholeness or "selfing" of women, albeit that their subjectivity has to undergo divisions that render them "unnatural" in relation to traditional and colonial discourses. "Unnaturalness" indicates the new enunciative position that emerges when mimicry turns the discursive conditions of dominance into grounds of intervention. I use "unnatural" as a term that signifies a deliberate and conscious effort by females such as Nyasha in her rebellious rantings or Tambudzai in her resistance to culture's call (or, in fact, cultural discourse's claim) for a woman's subservience, or even Lucia's forthright, confrontational character. That is to say, being unnatural is in a sense affirming the subjectivity of women. I nominate here this condition as an ironic unnaturalness, particularly because it brings to view the real unnaturalness of men. This explains why it takes Nyasha, in a moment of ironic unnaturalness, to show the extent to which Babamukuru misrecognizes the symptoms of difficult existence in hybridizing conditions. But she understands that Babamukuru is himself a victim of what Nyasha explains to Tambudzai as a process: "The process . . . was called assimilation, and that was what was intended for the precocious few who might prove a nuisance if left to themselves, whereas the others—well really, who cared about the others? So they made a little space into which you were assimilated, an honourary space in which you could join them and they could make sure that you behaved yourself" (179). As I earlier pointed out, Nyasha does not sympathize with Maiguru; she thinks Maiguru silences herself despite her qualifications; she cautions Tambudzai of the disadvantages of *being* in the nun's school. What is more striking here is her disavowal of possibilities for reconstituting the subject of cultural difference. Tambudzai recalls Nyasha's warning: "they made a little space into which you were assimilated . . . into which you could join them and they could make sure that you behaved yourself. I would be comfortable in such a position, she remarked nastily, because look how well I had got on with Babamukuru. But, she insisted *one ought not to occupy that space*" (179, emphasis added). Rejecting that space, Nyasha disavows ambivalence; but that ambivalence is being staged when Tambudzai rationalizes the "Englishness" that her mother laments and resolves to affirm the subject of cultural discourse within the realities of interstitial positioning in the history of divided subjectivities. Tambudzai, then, will speak symptomatically and exercise her agency as she engages in a disseminatory negotiation with the colonial edict. Her position, like Maiguru's later, relates more to the undecidability of a discourse whose central ambivalence reflects the historical contingencies attending interstices. Her residence in such a space is amenable to her differential representation of the liminality of cultural knowledges, ambivalent as they are in modernity. She embraces modernity and its social pathologies in order that she may re-inscribe her difference in a fashion that lends authority to her marginal articulation of her selfhood. The shadow Tambudzai embraces is thus shown not to possess the quintessential properties of the predator but rather propensities to undecidability. It is her undecidability that, according to Bhabha's "Freedom's Basis in the Indeterminate," is "built into the factual processes of mutual understanding" (50).

Jung similarly speaks of the reconciliation of opposites in the quest for wholeness *qua persona*. To "embrace the shadow" is in Bhabha's terms, a form of subversion, "founded on that uncertainty that turns the discursive conditions of dominance into the grounds of intervention" ("Signs" 173). It is this uncertainty, to which a Jungian reading of Dangarembga's narrative alludes as it refers to the "grateful poor female relative" (116), that reveals the liminality of cultural knowledges on a differential and contingent scale.

Bibliography

Chapter 1: "The Nervous Collusions of Nation and Gender; Tsitsi Dangarembga's Challenge to Fanon" (Heather Zwicker)

Bahri, Deepika. "Disembodying the Corpus: Postcolonial Pathology in Tsitsi Dangarembga's *Nervous Conditions*." *Postmodern Culture.* 5.1 (September 1994). Online. Internet.

Bordo, Susan. *Unbearable Weight: Feminism, Western Culture, and the Body.* Berkeley: U of California P, 1993.

Bray, Abigail. "The Anorexic Body: Reading Disorders." *Cultural Studies* 10.3 (1996): 413-429.

Buchan, T. and L.D. Gregory. "Anorexia Nervosa in a Black Zimbabwean." *British Journal of Psychiatry* 145 (1984): 326-330.

Creamer, Heidi. "An Apple for the Teacher? Femininity, Coloniality, and Food in *Nervous Conditions*." *Kunapipi* 16.1 (1994): 349-360.

Dangarembga, Tsitsi. *Nervous Conditions*. Seattle: Seal Press, 1989.

"This Year, Next Year . . .". *Women's Review of Books.* 8: 10-11 (1991): 43-44.

Ellerman, Ellen. "The Literature Bureau: African Influence in Papua New Guinea." *Research in African Literatures* 26.4

(1995): 206-215.

An Editor's Manual. Compiled by The Literature Bureau. Gweru, Zimbabwe: Mambo Press, 1992.

Fanon, Frantz. *The Wretched of the Earth.* Trans. Constance Farrington. NY: Grove Weidenfeld, 1963.

Garner, D. M., P. E. Garfinkel and M. P. Olmstead. "An Overview of Socio-Cultural Factors in the Development of Anorexia Nervosa." *Anorexia Nervosa: Recent Developments.* Ed. P. Darby *et al.* NY: Alan R. Liss. 1983. 65-82.

George, Rosemary Marangoly and Helen Scott. "An Interview with Tsitsi Dangarembga." *Novel* 26.3 (1993): 309-319.

Gordon, Lewis R. "Fanon's Tragic Revolutionary Violence." *Fanon: A Critical Reader.* Eds. Lewis R. Gordon, T. Denean Sharpley-Whiting and Renee T. White. Oxford: Blackwell. 1996. 297-308.

Hooper, Malcolm S.H. and David M. Garner. "Application of the Eating Disorders Inventory to a Sample of Black, White, and Mixed Race Schoolgirls in Zimbabwe." *International Journal of Eating Disorders* 5.1 (1986): 161-168.

Jameson, Fredric. "Third-World Literature in the Era of Multinational Capitalism." *Social Text* 15 (1986): 65-68.

Lazarus, Neil. "Disavowing Decolonization: Fanon, Nationalism, and the Problematic of Representation in Current Theories of Colonial Discourse." *Research in African Literatures* 24.4 (1993): 69-98.

Mohanty, Chandra Talpade et. al., eds. *Third World Women and the Politics of Feminism.* Bloomington: Indiana UP, 1991.

Moore-Gilbert, Bart. "Frantz Fanon: En-gendering Nationalist Discourse." *Women: A Cultural Review* 7.2 (1996): 125-135.

Mowitt, John. "Algerian Nation: Fanon's Fetish." *Cultural Critique* (1992): 165-186.

Musandireve, Chigango. "Tsitsi Dangarembga : Woe unto bossy man!" *Moto* 136 (May 1994): 20.

Ngugi wa Thiong'o. *Decolonizing the Mind.* London: Heinemann, 1986.

Petersen, Kristen Holst. "Between Gender, Race and History: Kirsten Holst Petersen Interviews Tsitsi Dangarembga." *Kunapipi* 16.1 (1994): 345-348.

Probyn, Elspeth. "The Anorexic Body." *Body Invaders: Panic Sex in America.* Ed. Arthur Marilouise Kroker. Montreal: New World Perspectives, 1987. 201-211.

Seidman, Gay. "Women in Zimbabwe: Postindependence Struggles." *Feminist Studies* 19 (1984): 419-440.

Sugnet, Charles. "*Nervous Conditions*: Dangarembga's Feminist Reinvention of Fanon." *The Politics of (M)Othering.* Ed. Obioma Nnaemeka. London: Routledge, 1997. 33-49.

Sylvester, Christine. " 'Urban Women Cooperators,' 'Progress,' and 'African Feminism' in Zimbabwe." *differences* 3.1 (1991): 39-59.

Thompson, Becky Wangsgaard. " 'A Way Outa No Way': Eating Problems Among African-American, Latina, and White Women." *Gender and Society* 6.4 (1992): 546.

Uwakweh, Pauline Ada. "Debunking Patriarchy: The Liberational Quality of Voicing in Tsitsi Dangarembga's *Nervous Conditions*." *Research in African Literatures* 26.1 (1995): 75-84.

Veit-Wild, Flora. "'Women write about the things that move them': Interview with Tsitsi Dangarembga." Special issue of *Matatu (Black Women's Writing: Crossing the Boundaries.* Ed. Carole Boyce Davies) 6.3 (1989): 101-108.

Whyte, Beverley. "No Need to Feel Nervous." *MahogaNY* (1989): 12-14, 48.

Wilkinson, Jane. "Tsitsi Dangarembga." (Interview) *Talking with African Writers: Interviews with African Poets, Playwrights and Novelists.* London: James Currey, 1992. 189-198.

Wright, Derek. " 'More than Just a Plateful of Food': Regurgitating Colonialism in Tsitsi Dangarembga's *Nervous Conditions.*" *Commonwealth* 17 2 (1995): 8-18.

Chapter 2: "Tradition, Modernity and the Family as Nation: Reading the *Chimurenga* Struggle into and out of *Nervous Conditions*" (Susan Z. Andrade)

Abel, Elizabeth; Marianne Hirsch, Elizabeth Langland. *The Voyage In Fictions of Female Development.* Boston: UP of New England,1983.

Beverley, John. "The Margin at the Center: On *Testimonio* (Testimonial Narrative)." *De/Colonizing the Subject.* Eds. Sidonie Smith and Julia Watson. Minneapolis: U of Minnesota P, 1992. 91-114.

Boumhela, PenNY. "Realisms and the Ends of Feminism." *Grafts: Feminist Cultural Criticism.* Ed. Susan Sheridan. NY: Verso, 1988. 77-91.

Camara, Laye. *L'enfant noir.* Paris: Plon, 1953.

Chinodya, Shimmer. *Harvest of Thorns.* Harare: Baobab Books, 1989.

Creamer, Heidi. "An Apple for the Teacher?: Femininity, Coloniality, and Food in *Nervous Conditions.*" *Kunapipi* 16.1 (1994): 349-60.

Dangarembga, Tsitsi. *Nervous Conditions.* Seattle: Seal Press, 1988.

De Beauvoir, Simone. *The Second Sex.* Trans. H. M. Parshley. NY: Knopf, 1953.

Dubey, Madhu. "The True Lie of the Nation: Fanon and Feminism." *differences* 10.2 (1998):1-29.

DuPlessis, Rachel Blau. *Writing Beyond the Ending: Narrative Strategies of Twentieth Century Women Writers.* Bloomington: Indiana UP, 1985.

Fanon, Frantz. *Wretched of the Earth.* Trans. Constance Farrington. NY: Grove Press, 1963.

_____. *Black Skin White Masks.* Trans. Charles Markmann. NY: Grove Press, 1967.

Felski, Rita, *Beyond Feminist Aesthetics: Feminist Literature and Social Change.* Cambridge: Harvard UP, 1989.

Hove, Chenjerai. *Bones.* Cape Town: David Phillip, 1988.

Macheray, Pierre. *A Theory of Literary Production.* Trans. Geoffrey Wall. London: Routledge, 1978.

Ogot, Grace. *The Graduate.* Nairobi: Uzima, 1980.

Petersen, Kirsten Holst. "Between Gender, Race and History: Kirsten Holst Petersen Interviews Tstsi Dangarembga." *Kunapipi* 16.1 (1994): 345-48.

Radhakrishnan, R. "Nationalism, Gender, and the Narrative of Identity." *Nationalisms and Sexualities.* Eds. Andrew Parker, Mary Russo, Doris Sommer, and Patricia Yaeger. NY: Routledge, 1992. 77-95.

Sembene, Ousmane. *Xala.* Paris: Présence Africaine, 1973.

Soyinka, Wole. *Ake.* London: Rex Collins, 1981.

Stratton, Florence. *Contemporary African Literature and the Politics of Gender.* London: Routledge, 1994.

Sugnet, Charles. "*Nervous Conditions*: Dangarembga's Feminist Reinvention of Fanon." *The Politics of (M)Othering: Womanhood, Identity and Resistance in African Literature.* Ed. Obioma Nnaemeka. London: Routledge, 1997. 33-

49.

Vance, Carole. "Pleasure and Danger: Toward a Politics of Sexuality." *Pleasure and Danger: Exploring Female Sexuality*. London: Routledge, 1984.

Chapter 3: "Modernity, Alienation and Development: *Nervous Conditions* and the Female Paradigm" (Ann Elizabeth Willey)

Achebe, Chinua. "The African Writer and the English Language." *Morning Yet on Creation Day*. Garden City, NY: Doubleday, 1975.

Dangarembga, Tsitsi. *Nervous Conditions*. Seattle: Seal Press, 1989.

Irele, Abiola. "In Praise of Alienation." *The Surreptitious Speech; Présence Africaine and the Politics of Otherness 1947-1987*. Ed. V.Y. Mudimbe. Chicago: U of Chicago Press, 1992. 201-224.

Rodney, Walter. *How Europe Underdeveloped Africa*. London: Bogle-L'Ouverture Publications, 1972.

Chapter 4: "Strategic Fusions: Undermining Cultural Essentialism in *Nervous Conditions*" (Jeanette Treiber)

Dangarembga, Tsitsi. *Nervous Conditions*. Seattle: Seal Press, 1989.

Fanon, Frantz. *The Wretched of the Earth*. Trans. Constance Farrington. NY: Grove Press, 1963.

JanMohamed, Abdul R. "The Economy of Manichean Allegory: The Function of Racial Difference in Colonialist Litera-

ture." *"Race," Writing, and Difference.* Ed. Henry Louis
Gates, Jr.. Chicago: U of Chicago P, 1986. 59-87.

Lavie, Smadar and Swedenburg, Ted. *Displacement, Diaspora, and
Geographies of Identity.* Durham, NC: Duke UP, 1996.

Narayan Uma. "Essence of Culture and a Sense of History: A Feminist Critique of Cultural Essentialism." *Hypatia* 13. 2
(1998): 87-106.

Ogundipe-Leslie, Molara. *Recreating Ourselves. African Women
& Critical Transformations.* Trenton, NJ: Africa World
Press, 1994.

Ross, Kristin. *Fast Cars, Clean Bodies. Decolonization and the
Reordering of French Culture.* Cambridge, MA: MIT
Press, 1996.

Taiwo, Oladel. *An Introduction to West African Literature.* London: The Trinity Press, 1967.

Chapter 5: "Indexing Her Digests: Working Through *Nervous Conditions*" (Brendon Nicholls)

Bahri, Deepika. "Disembodying the Corpus: Postcolonial Pathology in Tsitsi Dangarembga's *Nervous Conditions.*"
*Postmodern Culture: An Electronic Journal of Interdisci-
plinary Criticism* 5.1 (Sept. 1994): 26 paras. Online.
Internet. 2 June 1997.

Bardolph, Jacqueline. "'The Tears of Childhood' of Tsitsi
Dangarembga." *Commonwealth Essays and Studies* 13.1
(1990): 37-47.

Bhabha, Homi. "Of Mimicry and Man: The Ambivalence of Colonial Discourse." *The Location of Culture.* London:
Routledge, 1994. 85-92.

Booker, M. Keith. *The African Novel in English: An Introduction.* Portsmouth: Heinemann, 1998.

Bosman, Brenda. "A Correspondence Without Theory: Tsitsi Dangarembga's *Nervous Conditions.*" *Current Writing* 2.1 (1990): 91-100.

Creamer, Heidi. "An Apple for the Teacher? Femininity, Coloniality, and Food in *Nervous Conditions.*" *Kunapipi* 16.1 (1994): 349-60.

Doke, C.M., D. McK. Malcolm and J.M.A. Sikakana. *English-Zulu Dictionary.* 1958. Johannesburg: Witwatersrand UP, 1988.

Duval, Alain and Marr, Vivian, eds. *Collins Robert Comprehensive French English Dictionary Volume 1.* Glasgow: Harper Collins, 1995.

Fanon, Frantz. *Black Skin, White Masks.* Trans. Charles Lam Markmann. NY: Grove Press, 1967.

_____. *Les Damnés de la Terre.* Paris: François Maspero, 1961.

_____. "Medicine and Colonialism." *Studies in a Dying Colonialism.* 1965. Introd. A.M. Babu and Adolfo Gilly. Trans. Haakon Chevalier. London: Earthscan Publications, 1989. 121-45.

_____. *The Wretched of the Earth.* 1961. Introd. Jean-Paul Sartre. Trans. Constance Farrington. London: Penguin, 1990.

Flockemann, Miki. "'Not-Quite Insiders and Not-Quite Outsiders': The 'Process of Womanhood' in *Beka Lamb, Nervous Conditions* and *Daughters of the Twilight.*" *The Journal of Commonwealth Literature* 27.1 (1992): 37-47.

Foucault, Michel. *Discipline and Punish.* 1977. Trans. Alan Sheridan. Harmondsworth: Penguin, 1991.

Jardine, Lisa. "Who, Now, is the Reader?" Raymond Williams Memorial Lectures. Corpus Christi College, Cambridge. 31 Oct. 1998.

Hill, Janice E. "Purging a Plate Full of Colonial History: The *Nervous Conditions* of Silent Girls." *College Literature* 22.1 (1995): 78-90.

Holst Petersen, Kirsten. "Between Gender, Race and History: Kirsten Holst Petersen Interviews Tsitsi Dangarembga." *Kunapipi* 16.1 (1994): 344-48.

McWilliams, Sally. "Tsitsi Dangarembga's *Nervous Conditions*: At the Crossroads of Feminism and Post-Colonialism." *World Literature Written in English* 31.1 (1991): 103-12.

Miller, J. Hillis. "Ariadne's Thread: Repetition and the Narrative Line." *Critical Inquiry* 3 (1976): 57-77.

Mkize, D.L. "*AmafufuNYane*--Is It a Culture-Bound Syndrome?" *South African Medical Journal* 88.3 (1998): 329-31.

Nair, Supriya. "Melancholic Women: The Intellectual Hysteric(s) in *Nervous Conditions*." *Research in African Literatures* 26.2 (1995): 130-39.

Ngubane, H. *Body and Mind in Zulu Medicine: An Ethnography of Health and Disease in* NY*uswa-Zulu Thought and Practice*. London: Academic Press, 1977.

Pentolfe Aegerter, Lindsay. "A Dialectic of Autonomy and Community: Tsitsi Dangarembga's *Nervous Conditions*." *Tulsa Studies in Women's Literature* 15.2 (1996): 231-40.

Plasa, Carl. "Reading 'The Geography of Hunger' in Tsitsi Dangarembga's *Nervous Conditions*: From Frantz Fanon to Charlotte Brontë." *The Journal of Commonwealth Literature* 33.1 (1998): 35-45.

Rooney, Caroline. "Re-Possessions: Inheritance and Independence in Chenjerai Hove's *Bones* and Tsitsi Dangarembga's *Nervous Conditions*." *Essays on African Writing 2: Contemporary Literature*. Ed. Abdulrazak Gurnah. Oxford, UK: Heinemann, 1995. 119-143.

Spivak, Gayatri Chakravorty. "Displacement and the Discourse of Woman." *Displacement: Derrida and After*. Ed. Mark Krupnick. Bloomington: Indiana UP, 1983. 169-95.

Sugnet, Charles. "*Nervous Conditions*: Dangarembga's Feminist Reinvention of Fanon." *The Politics of (M)Othering: Womanhood, Identity and Resistance in African Literature*. Ed. Obioma Nnaemeka. London: Routledge, 1997. 33-49.

Swartz, Leslie. *Culture and Mental Health: A Southern African View*. Cape Town: OUP, 1998.

Thomas, Sue. "Killing the Hysteric in the Colonized's House: Tsitsi Dangarembga's *Nervous Conditions*." *The Journal of Commonwealth Literature* 27.1 (1992): 22-36.

Uwakweh, Pauline. "Debunking Patriarchy: The Liberational Quality of Voicing in Tsitsi Dangarembga's *Nervous Conditions*." *Research in African Literatures* 26.1 (1995): 75-84.

Veit-Wild, Flora. "'Women Write About the Things that Move Them': An Interview with Tsitsi Dangarembga." *Matatu: The Journal for African Literature and Culture* 3.6 (1989) 101-08.

Vizzard, Michelle. "'Of Mimicry and Woman': Hysteria and Anti-colonial Feminism in Tsitsi Dangarembga's *Nervous Conditions*." *Span: The Journal of the South Pacific Association for Commonwealth Literature and Language Studies* 36 (1993): 202-10.

Woodward, Wendy. "The Powers of Discourse: The Identity of Subaltern Women under Colonial Law in *Nervous Conditions* and *Daughters of the Twilight*." *Journal of Literary Studies* 9.1 (1993): 80-91.

Chapter 6: "Moving Forward From Death: Cultural Autopsy as a Guide to the Living" (Jeffrey L. Geller)

Achebe, Chinua. *Things Fall Apart.* NY: Fawcett Crest. 1959.

Cavell, Stanley. *Pursuits of Happiness: The Hollywood Comedy of Remarriage.* Cambridge: Harvard UP, 1981.

Dangarembga, Tsitsi. *Nervous Conditions.* Seattle: Seal Press, 1988.

Fanon, Frantz. *The Wretched of the Earth.* NY: Grove Press, 1963.

Geller, Jeffrey and Vela, Richard. "Happiness Through Insanity." *Film and Philosophy* IV (1998): 58-65.

Kemedjio, Cilas. "The Curse of Writing: Genealogical Strata of a Disillusion: Orality, Islam, Writing, and Identities in the State of Becoming in Maryse Conde's *Segou"* *Research in African Literatures* 27.4 (1997): 124-143.

Scott, John. *Africa: World's Last Frontier. Headline Series.* Foreign Policy Association. No. 135, May 20, 1959.

Chapter 7: "Dangarembga's Dirty Work: Acting Up and Speaking Out, "Good Medicine" for Africa" (Giuliana Lund)

Arnold, David. *Colonizing the Body: State, Medecine and Epidemic Disease in Nineteenth-Century India.* Berkeley: U of California P, 1993. Ed. Imperial Medicine and Indigenous Societies. Manchester: MUP, 1988.

Association pour l'Etude des Litteratures Africaines. *Litterature et maladie en Afrique: image et fonction de la maladie dans la production litteraire.* Actes du Congress de L'APELA, Nice, September 1991. Paris: Harmattan, 1994.

Bernheimer, Charles and Claire Kahane, eds. *In Dora's Case: Freud--Hysteria--Feminism.* NY: Columbia UP, 1990.

Bhabha, Homi. *The Location of Culture*. NY: Routledge, 1994.

Brantlinger, Patrick. "Victorians and Africans: The Genealogy of the Myth of The Dark Continent." *"Race," Writing, and Difference*. Ed. Henry Louis Gates, Jr. Chicago: U of Chicago P, 1986. 185-222.

Celine, Louis Ferdinand. *Journey to the End of the Night*. Trans. Ralph Manheim. London: Calder, 1988.

Césaire, Aimé. *The Collected Poems*. Trans. Clayton Eshleman and Annette Smith. Berkeley: U of California P, 1983.

Cixous, Helene and Catherine Clement. *The Newly Born Woman*. Trans. B. Wing. Minneapolis: U of Minnesota P, 1986.

Comaroff, Jean. "The Diseased Heart of Africa: Medicine, Colonialism, and the Black Body." *Knowledge, Power, Practice*. Eds. S. Lindenbaum and M. Lock. Berkeley: U of California P, 1993. 305-329.

Conrad, Joseph. *Heart of Darkness: An Authoritative Text, Criticism, Bakgrounds, Sources*. Ed. Robert Kimbrough. NY: Norton, 1988. 3rd Ed.

Curtin, Philip D. *Death by Migration: Europe's Encounter with the Tropical World in the Nineteenth Century*. Cambridge, UK: Cambridge UP, 1989.

_____. *The Image of Africa: British Ideas and Action, 1780-1850*. Madison: U of Wisconsin P, 1964.

Dangarembga, Tsitsi. *Nervous Conditions*. Seattle: Seal, 1988.

_____. *Everyone's Child*. Zimbabwe, 1996.

Diawara, Manthia. *African Cinema: Politics and Culture*. Bloomington: Indiana UP, 1992.

Douglas, Mary. *Purity and Danger: An Analysis of the Concepts of Pollution and Taboo*. NY: Ark, 1966.

Fanon, Frantz. *Black Skin, White Masks*. Trans. Charles Lam

Markmann. NY: Grove, 1967. *Peau noire, masques blancs.* 1952.

_____. "Medicine and Colonialism." *A Dying Colonialism.* Trans. Haakon Chevalier. NY: Grove, 1965. 121-145.

_____. *The Wretched of the Earth.* Trans. Constance Farrington. NY: Grove, 1963.

Feierman, S. and J. Janzen, Eds. *The Social Basis of Health and Healing in Africa.* Berkeley: U of California P, 1992.

Foucault, Michel. *The Birth of the Clinic: An Archeology of Medical Perception.* Trans. A. M. Sheridan. NY: Vintage, 1973.

Freud, Sigmund. *Dora: An Analysis of a Case of Hysteria.* Ed. Philip Rieff. NY: Collier, 1963.

Garett, Laurie. *The Coming Plague: Newly Emerging Diseases in a World Out of Balance.* NY: Farrar, 1994.

Gilman, Sander. "AIDS and Syphilis: The Iconography of Disease." *AIDS: Cultural Analysis, Cultural Activism.* Ed. D. Crimp. Cambridge: MIT P, 1988.

_____. "Black Bodies, White Bodies: Towards an Iconography of Female Sexuality in Late-Nineteenth Century Art, Medicine, and Literature." *"Race," Writing, and Difference.* Ed. Henry Louis Gates, Jr. Chicago: U of Chicago P, 1986. 223-261.

Haggard, H. Rider. *She.* 1887. Bloomington: Indiana UP, 1991.

Jordanova, Ludmilla. "Nature Unveiling Before Science." *Sexual Visions.* Madison: U of Wisconsin P, 1989. 87-110.

Fox Keller, Evelyn. *Reflections on Gender and Science.* New Haven: Yale UP, 1985.

MacKenzie, John J. *Imperialism and the Natural World.* Manchester: Manchester UP, 1990.

MacLeod, Roy and Milton Lewis. *Disease, Medicine and Empire:*

Perspectives on Western Medicine and the Experience of European Expansion. NY: Routledge, 1988.

Miller, Christopher. *Blank Darkness: Africanist Discourse in French.* Chicago: U of Chicago P, 1985.

Miller, N. and R. C. Rockwell, Eds. *AIDS in Africa: the Social and Policy Impact.* Washington, D.C.: Ntl. Council for Intl. Health, 1988.

Mouralis, Bernard. *L'Europe, l'Afrique et la folie.* Paris: Présence Africaine, 1993.

Sartre, Jean-Paul. "Preface." *The Wretched of the Earth.* Frantz Fanon. Trans. Constance Farrington. NY: Grove, 1963. 7-31.

_____. *La Nausee.* Paris: Gallimard, 1938.

Showalter, Elaine. *The Female Malady: Women, Madness and English Culture, 1830-1980.* London: Virago, 1985.

Sontag, Susan. *Illness as Metaphor* and *AIDS and Its Metaphors.* NY: Penguin, 1991.

Sugnet, Charles. "*Nervous Conditions*: Dangarembga's Feminist Reinvention of Fanon," *The Politics of (M)Othering: Womanhood, Identity, and Resistance in African Literature.* Ed. Obioma Nnaemeka. NY: Routledge, 1997. 33-49.

Swanson, Maynard. "'The Sanitation Syndrome: Bubonic Plague and Urban Native Policy in the Cape ColoNY, 1900-1909." *Journal of African History* 18 (1977): 387-410.

Vaughan, Megan. *Curing Their Ills: Colonial Power and African Illness.* Oxford: Blackwell, 1991.

Verges, Francoise. "'Chains of Madness, Chains of Colonialism: Fanon and Freedom." *The Fact of Blackness: Frantz Fanon and Visual Representation.* Ed. Alan Read. London: Institute of Contemporary Arts, 1996. 46-75.

Watts, Sheldon. *Epidemics and History: Disease, Power and Imperialism*. New Haven, CT: Yale UP, 1997.

Young, Robert. *Colonial Desire: Hybridity in Theory, Culture and Race*. NY: Routledge, 1995.

Chapter 8: "Some Very *Nervous Conditions*: Commodity, Culture and Identity in Dangarembga's Novel" (Sally Ann Murray)

Boehmer, Elleke. *Colonial & Postcolonial Literature*. Oxford: Oxford UP, 1995.

Broughton, Treva. "Adolescent in Zimbabwe." *Southern African Review of Books* October/November (1988): 5.

Burke, Timothy. *Lifebuoy Men, Lux Women: Commodification, Consumption, & Cleanliness in Modern Zimbabwe*. London: Leicester University Press, 1997.

Chapman, Michael. *Southern African Literatures*. London: Longman, 1996.

Chennells, AnthoNY. "Authorizing Women, Women's Authoring: Tsitsi Dangarembga's *Nervous Conditions*." *New Writing From Southern Africa*. Ed. Emmanuel Ngara. London: James Currey, 1996. 59-75.

Dangarembga, Tsitsi. *Nervous Conditions*. London: The Women's Press, 1988.

Fanon, Frantz. *The Wretched of the Earth*. Harmondsworth: Penguin, 1961.

Marechera, Dambudzo. *The House of Hunger*. London: Heinemann, 1978.

Marx, Karl. *Capital*. London: William Dent, 1930.

Veit-Wild, Flora. *Teachers, Preachers, Non-Believers: A Social*

History of Zimbabwean Literature. London: Hans Zell, 1992.

Chapter 9: "Women and Food in Tsitsi Dangarembga's *Nervous Conditions*" (Kelli Donovan Wixson)

Bahri, Deepika. "Disembodying the Corpus: Postcolonial Pathology in Tsitsi Dangarembga's *Nervous Conditions.*" *Postmodern Culture: An Electronic Journal of Interdisciplinary Criticism* 5.1 (1994): 26 paras. Online. Internet.

Creamer, Heidi. "An Apple for the Teacher? Femininity, Coloniality, and Food in *Nervous Conditions.*" *Kunapipi* 16.1 (1994): 349-60.

Dangarembga, Tsitsi. *Nervous Conditions.* Seattle, WA: Seal Press, 1989.

Fanon, Frantz. *A Dying Colonialism.* Trans. Haakon Chevalier. NY: Grove Press, 1965.

_____. *The Wretched of the Earth.* Trans. Constance Farrington. NY: Grove Press, 1963.

McClintock, Anne. " 'No Longer in a Future Heaven': Gender, Race and Nationalism." *Dangerous Liaisons: Gender, Nation, and Postcolonial Perspectives.* Eds. Anne McClintock, Aamir Mufti, and Ella Shohat. Minneapolis, MN: Minnesota UP, 1997. 89-112.

Thompson, Becky W. "'A Way Outa No Way': Eating Problems among African-American, Latina, and White Women." *Gender & Society* 6.4 (1992): 546-61.

Vandereycken, Walter and Hans W. Hoek. "Are Eating Disorders Culture-Bound Syndromes?" *Psychobiology and Treatment of Anorexia Nervosa and Bulimia Nervosa.* Ed. Katherine A. Halmi. Washington DC: American Psychopathological Association Series, 1992.

_____ and Ron van Deth. *From Fasting Saints to Anorexic Girls: The History of Self-Starvation.* NY: NY UP, 1994.

Chapter 10: ""Two Disconnected Entities": The Pitfalls of Knowing in Tsitsi Dangarembga's *Nervous Conditions*" (Linda Chown)

Aegerter, Lindsay Pentolfe. "A Dialectic of Autonomy and Community: Tsitsi Dangarembga's *Nervous Conditions*." *Tulsa Studies in Women's Literature* 13.2 (1996) 231-240.

Ashcroft, Bill, Griffiths, Gareth and Helen Tiffin. *The Empire Writes Back: Theory and Practice in Post-Colonial Literature.* NY: Routledge, 1989.

Chown, Linda E. *Narrative Authority and Homeostasis in the Novels of Doris Lessing and Carmen Martín Gaite.* NY: Garland, 1990.

Coetzee, J. M. *Doubling the Point: Essays and Interviews.* Ed. David Attwell. Cambridge: Harvard UP, 1992.

Fanon, Frantz. *The Wretched of the Earth.* Trans. Constance Farrington. 1963. NY: Grove Weidenfeld, 1991.

James, Henry. *The Turn of the Screw and Other Short Fiction.* 1908. NY: Bantam, 1983.

Jolly, Rosemary. "Rehearsals of Liberation: Contemporary Postcolonial Discourse and the New South Africa." *PMLA* 110.1 (1995): 17-29.

Lessing, Doris. *African Laughter: Four Visits to Zimbabwe.* NY: Harper Collins, 1992.

Miles, David H. "The Picaro's Journey to the Confessional: The Changing Image of the Hero in the German

Bildungsroman." *PMLA* 89 (1974): 980-992.

Mohanty, Satya P. Epilogue. "Colonial Legacies, Multicultural Futures: Relativism, Objectivity, and the Challenge of Otherness." *PMLA* 110.1 (1995): 108-118.

Mudge, Bradford K. "Burning Down the House: Sara Coleridge, Virginia Woolf and the Politics of Literary Revision." *Tulsa Studies in Women's Literature* 5 (1986): 229-250.

Nair, Supriya. "Melancholic Women: The Intellectual Hysteric(s) in *Nervous Conditions.*" *Research in African Literatures* 26.2 (1995): 130-139.

Ngugi wa Thiong'o. *Decolonising the Mind: The Politics of Language in African Literature.* London: Currey, 1986.

Rimmon-Kenan, Shlomith. *Narrative Fiction: Contemporary Poetics.* NY: Routledge, 1983.

Ryan, Judith. *The Vanishing Subject. Early Psychology and Literary Modernism.* Chicago: U of Chicago P, 1991.

Sackey, Edward. "Oral Tradition and the African Novel." *Modern Fiction Studies* 37.3 (1991): 389-407.

Savater, Fernando. *Childhood Regained: The Art of the Story Teller.* Trans. Frances M. López Morrillas. NY: Columbia UP, 1982.

Showalter, Elaine. *The Female Malady. Women, Madness, and English Culture, 1830-1980.* NY: Penguin, 1985.

Spivak, Gayatri C. "Can the Subaltern Speak?" *Marxism and the Interpretation of Culture.* Eds. Cary Nelson & Lawrence Grossberg. London: Macmillan, 1988. 271-315.

Thomas, Sue. "Killing the Hysteric in the Colonized's House: Tsitsi Dangarembga's *Nervous Conditions.*" *The Journal of Commonwealth Literature* 7.1 (1992): 26-36.

Villán, Javier. "Carmen Martín Gaite, habitando el tiempo." *La estafeta literaria* 549 (1974): 21-23.

Vygotsky, Lev Semenovich. *Thought and Language.* Trans. Eugenia Haufmann and Gertrude Vakar. Cambridge: MIT, 1965.

Chapter 11: "Trapped and Troping: Allegories of the Transnational Intellectual in Tsitsi Dangarembga's *Nervous Conditions*" (Biman Basu)

Anderson, Benedict. *Imagined Communities; Reflections on the Origin and Spread of Nationalism.* London: Verso, 1993.

Bakhtin, Mikhail. *Rabelais and His World.* Bloomington: Indiana UP, 1984

Creamer, Heidi. "An Apple for the Teacher? Femininity, Coloniality, arid Food in *Nervous Conditions*." *Kunapipi* 16.1 (1994): 349-360.

Dangarembga, Tsitsi. *Nervous Conditions.* Seattle, Washington: Seal Press, 1989.

Deleuze, Gilles and Felix Guattari. *A Thousand Plateaus: Capitalism and Schizophrenia.* Minneapolis: U of Minnesota P, 1987.

Fanon, Frantz. *Black Skin, White Masks.* Trans. Charles Markham. NY: Grove Press, 1967.

———. *The Wretched of the Earth.* Trans. Constance Farrington. NY: Grove Press, 1963.

Foucault, Michel. *Power/Knowledge: Selected Interviews and Other Writings, 1972-1977.* NY: Random House, 1980.

Gates, Henry Louis Jr. "Critical Fanonism." *Critical Inquiry* 17 (1991): 457-70.

Gilroy, Paul. *The Black Atlantic: Modernity and Double Conscious-*

ness. Cambridge, MA: Harvard UP, 1993.

Mbembe, Achille. "The Banality of Power and the Aesthetics of Vulgarity in the PostcoloNY." Trans. Janet Roitman. *Public Culture* 4.2 (1992): 1-30.

McClintock, Anne. "Maid to Order" *Dirty Looks: Women, Pornography, Power.* Eds. Pamela Gibson and Roma Gibson. London: British Film Institute, 1993. 207-31.

Morrison, Toni. "Memory, Creation, and Writing." *Thought* 59.235 (1984): 385-90.

Petersen, Kirsten Holst. "Between Gender, Race and History: Kirsten Holst Petersen Interviews Tsitsi Dangarembga." *Kunapipi* 16.1 (1994): 345-48

Spivak, Gayatri Chakravorty. *The Post-Colonial Critic.* Ed. Sarah Harasym. NY: Routledge, 1990.

Thomas, Sue. "Killing the Hysteric in the Colonized's House: Tsitsi Dangarembga's *Nervous Conditions.*" *Journal of Commonwealth Literature* 27.1 (1992): 26-36

Veit-Wild, Flora. " 'Women Write about the Things That Move Them': Interview with Tsitsi Dangarembga." *Matatu: Journal for African Culture and Society* 3.6 (1989): 101-08

Chapter 12: "Tsitsi Dangarembga's *Nervous Conditions*: An African Woman's Revisionist Narrative" (Mary Jane Androne)

Beverley, John. "The Margin at the Center: On *Testimonio.*" *De/Colonizing the Subject: The Politics of Gender in Women's Autobiography.* Eds. Sidonie Smith and Julia Watson. Minneapolis: U of Minnesota P, 1992. 91-114.

Carr, Robert. Unpublished manuscript (July, 1990), quoted in Sidonie Smith and Julia Watson Eds. *De/Colonizing the*

Subject: The Politics of Gender in Women's Autobiography. Minneapolis: U of Minnesota P, 1992.

Dangarembga, Tsitsi. *Nervous Conditions.* Seattle: The Seal Press, 1988.

Harrow, Kenneth. *Thresholds of Change in African Literature: The Emergence of a Tradition.* London: James Currey and Heinneman, 1993.

Kaplan, Caren. "Resisting Autobiography: Out-Law Genres and Transnational Feminist Subjects." *De/Colonizing the Subject: The Politics of Gender Women's Autobiography.* Minneapolis: U of Minnesota P, 1992. 115-138.

Lazarus, Neil. *Resistance in Postcolonial African Fiction.* New Haven: Yale UP, 1990.

Wilkinson, Jane, Ed. *Talking with African Writers: Interviews with African Poets, Playwrights and Novelists.* London: James Currey and Heinneman, 1992.

Chapter 13: "Reading "The Letter" of a Woman: Narrative Strategies in Dangarembga's Story of Apartheid South Africa" (Jacqueline Wigfall)

Alexander, Meena. "Faultlines: A Memoir." *Written By Herself Volume II: Women's Memoirs from Britain, Africa, Asia and the U.S. An Anthology.* Ed. Jill Ker Conway. NY: Vintage Books, 1996.

The American Heritage Dictionary. Second College Edition. Boston: Houghton Mifflin, 1982.

Asante, Molefi. *The Book of African Names.* Trenton: Africa World Press, 1996.

Childers, Joseph and Gary Hentzi, Eds. *The Columbia Dictionary of Modern Literary and Cultural Criticism*. NY: Columbia UP, 1995.

Conway, Jill Ker. "Introduction." *Written By Herself Volume II: Women's Memoirs from Britain, Africa, Asia and the U.S. An Anthology*. NY: Vintage Books, 1996.

Dangarembga, Tsitsi. "The Letter." *The Sound of Snapping Wires: A Selection of Zimbabwean Short Stories*. Ed. T.O. McLoughlin. Harare: The College Press, 1990.

Davies, Carole Boyce, and Anne Adams Graves, Eds. *Ngambika: Studies of Women in African Literature*. Trenton, NJ: Africa World Press, 1986.

Holloway, Karla. *Moorings & Metaphors: Figures of Culture and Gender in Black Women's Literature*. New Brunswick: Rutgers UP, 1992.

hooks, bell. *Yearning: Race, Gender and Cultural Politics*. Boston: South End Press, 1990.

McLoughlin, T.O. "Introduction." *The Sound of Snapping Wires: A Selection of Zimbabwean Short Stories*. Harare: The College Press, 1990.

Morrison, Toni. "Rootedness: The Ancestor as Foundation." *Black Women Writers 1950-1980: A Critical Evaluation*. Ed. Mari Evans. Garden City: Anchor Press/Doubleday, 1984.

Newell, Stephanie, Ed. "Introduction." *Writing African Women: Gender, Popular Culture and Literature in West Africa*. New Jersey: Zed Books, 1997.

Schipper, Mineke. *Beyond the Boundaries: African Literature and Literary Theory*. London: Allison & Busby, 1989.

Talk, Frank. "I Write What I Like: Fear—An Important Determinant in South African Politics." *Steve Biko: Black Consciousness in South Africa*. Ed. Millard Arnold. NY: Vintage Books, 1979.

Thompson, Leonard. *A History of South Africa.* Revised edition. New Haven: Yale UP, 1995.

Chapter 14: "Embracing the Shadow: Recognizing Liminality in Dangarembga's Jungian Undercurrents" (Kgomotso Masemola)

Armstrong, Nancy & Leonard Tennenhouse Eds. *The Violence of Representation: Literature and the History of Violence.* NY: Routledge, 1989.

Ashcroft, Bill, Gareth Griffiths, Helen Tiffin Eds. *The Empire Writes Back: Theory and Practice in Post-colonial Literatures.* London: Routledge, 1989.

Attwell,David. "Interview with Homi Bhabha." *Current Writing* 5.2 (1993): 100-113.

————. "The Transculturation of English: The Exemplary Case of the Rev. Tiyo Soga." *An inaugural lecture, Occasional Papers in English Studies* No. 1, (October, 1994): 1-43.

Barker, Francis, Peter Hulme, Margaret Iversen, Eds. *Colonial Discourses/Post-colonial Theory.* Manchester: Manchester UP, 1994.

de Beauvoir, Simone. *The Second Sex.* Hammondsworth: Penguin, 1972.

Bhabha, Homi K. "Difference, Discrimination, and the Discourse of Colonialism." *The Politics of Theory.* Francis Barker et. al. Colchester: University of Essex, 1983. 194-211.

————. "DissemiNation: Time, Narrative and the Margins of the Modern Nation." *Nation and Narration.* Ed. Homi K. Bhabha. London: Routledge, 1990. 291-322.

————. "Freedom's Basis in the Indeterminate." *October* 61

(1992): 46-57.

_____. "Of Mimicry and Man: The Ambivalence of Colonial Discourse." *October* 28 (1984): 85-92.

_____. "Remembering Fanon: Self, Psyche and the Colonial Condition." *Colonial Discourse and Post-Colonial Theory: A Reader*. Eds. P. Williams & L. Chrisman. NY: Harvester Wheatsheaf, 1994. 112-123.

_____. "Signs Taken for Wonders: Questions of Ambivalence and Authority Under a Tree Outside Delhi, May 1817." *"Race," Writing, and Difference*. Ed. Henry Louis Gates Jr. Chicago and London: U of Chicago P, 1986. 163-184.

Bosman, Brenda. "A Correspondence without Theory: Tsitsi Dangarembga's *Nervous Conditions*." *Current Writing* 2.1 (1990): 91-100.

Brooke, Roger. *Jung and Phenomenology*. London: Routledge, 1991.

Bryson, Valerie. *Feminist Political Theory: An Introduction*. NY: Paragon House, 1992.

Comaroff, John and Jean. *Ethnography and the Historical Imagination.* Boulder: Westview Press, 1991.

Dangarembga, Tsitsi. *Nervous Conditions*. London: The Women's Press Ltd, 1988.

Deleuze, Gilles and Felix Guattari. *Anti-Oedipus: Capitalism and Schizophrenia*. Trans. R. Hurley, M. Seem and Helen R. Lane. NY: Viking Press, 1977.

Evans, Mari. (ed). *Black Women Writers (1950-1980): Arguments Interviews*. London: Pluto Press, 1985.

Fanon, Frantz. "On National Culture." *The Wretched of the Earth*. (1961). Trans. Constance Farrington. NY: Grove Press, 1977.

Giddens, AnthoNY. *The Consequences of Modernity.* Cambridge: Polity Press, 1990.

Green, Gayle & Coppelia Kahn. *Making a Difference: Feminist Literary Criticism.* London: Methuen, 1985

Greer, Germaine. *Sex and DestiNY: The Politics of Human Fertility.* London: Secker and Warburg, 1984.

Guattari, Felix. *Psychoanalysis and Transversality.* Preface by Gilles Deleuze. Paris: Maspero, 1972.

Hitchcock, Peter. *The Dialogics of the Oppressed.* Minneapolis: University of Minnesota Press, 1993.

Irigaray, Luce. *The Sex Which Is Not One.* Trans. C. Porter. Ithaca: Cornell UP, 1985.

Jung, Carl Gustav. "The Archetypes and the Collective Unconscious."*Collected Works* Vol. 9 pt. I. Trans. R.F.C. Hull. Eds H. Read, M. Fordham , G. Adler. NY: Pantheon Books, 1953.

_____. "The Development of Personality" Vol. 15. H. Read, M. Fordham , G. Adler.

Kandiyoti, Deniz. "Identity and Its Discontents: Women and the Nation." *Colonial Discourse and Post-Colonial Theory: A Reader.* Eds. P. Williams & L. Chrisman. NY: Harvester Wheatsheaf, 1991.

Kock, Leon. "'Civilising Barbarians': Missionary Narrative and African Textual Response in Nineteenth-Century South Africa." PhD Dissertation, University of South Africa, 1993.

Lockett, Cecily. "Feminism(s) and Writing in English in South Africa." *Current Writing* 2.1 (1990): 1-21.

McWilliams, Sally. "Tsitsi Dangarembga's *Nervous Conditions*: At the Crossroads of Feminism and Post-colonialism."

World LiteratureWritten in English 31.1 (1991): 103-112.

Memmi, Albert. *The Colonizer and the Colonized*. Boston: Beacon Press, 1967.

Millett, Kate. *Sexual Politics*. London: Virago, 1985.

Minh-ha, Trinh T. "Not You/Like You: Post-colonial Women and the Interlocking Questions of Identity and Difference." *Inscriptions* 3-4 (1988).

_____. *Woman, Native, Other*. Bloomington: Indiana UP, 1989.

Mohanty, Chandra T. "Under Western Eyes: Feminist Scholarship and Colonial Discourses" *Boundary* 12-13.2 (1984): 333-358.

Montrose, Louis A. "Professing the Renaissance: the Poetics and Politics of Culture." *The New Historicism*. Ed. H. Aram Veeser. NY: Routledge, 1989. 15-29.

Pratt, Mary L. "Transculturation and Autoethnography: Peru 1615-1980." *Colonial Discourse/Post-colonial Theory*. Eds. F. Barker, P. Hulme, M. Iversen. Manchester: Manchester UP, 1994. 24-46.

Radstone, Susannah Ed. *Sweet Dreams: Sexuality, Gender and Popular Fiction*. London: Lawrence and Wishart, 1988.

Said, Edward. *Culture and Imperialism*. London: Chatto & Windus, 1993.

Samuels, Andrew. *Jung and the Post-Jungians*. London: Routledge and Kegan Paul, 1985.

Smith, Barbara. "Towards a Black Feminist Criticism." *New Feminist Criticisms*. Ed. Elaine Showalter. London: Virago, 1986.

Spivak, Gayatri C. "Can the Subaltern Speak?" *Marxism and the Interpretation of Culture*. Eds. Cary Nelson & Lawrence Grossberg. London: Macmillan, 1988. 271-315.

_____. "Three Women's Texts and a Critique of Imperialism" *Critical Inquiry* 12.1 (1985): 43-61.

Stevens, AnthoNY. *Jung*. Oxford: Oxford University Press, 1994.

Thomas, Sue. "Killing the Hysteric in the Colonized's House: Tsitsi Dangarembga's *Nervous Conditions*." *Journal of Commonwealth Literature* 27.1 (1992): 22-36.

Tiffin, Helen. "Post-colonial Literatures and Counter-Discourse." *The Post-colonial Studies Reader*. Eds. B. Ashcroft, G. Griffiths and H. Tiffin. London: Routledge, 1995. 95-98.

Tuttle, Lisa. *Encyclopedia of Feminism*. London: Arrow Books, 1987.

Walby, S. *Theorizing Patriarchy*. Oxford: Basil Blackwell, 1990.

Wilkinson, Jane. *Talking with African Writers*. London: Heinemann, 1992.

Willis, Susan. "Black Women Writers: Taking a Critical Perspective" *Making a Difference: Feminist Literary Criticism*. Eds. G. Green & C. Kahn. London: Methuen, 1985. 211-237.

Contributors

Susan Z. Andrade teaches feminist and postcolonial theory, African and Caribbean literature, and women's writing in the English Department at the University of Pittsburgh. Her book, *The Nation Writ Large: African Fictions and Feminism, 1958-1988*, will be published by Duke University Press.

Mary Jane Androne is Professor of English and Director of Women's Studies at Albright College in Reading, Pennsylvania. Her research and teaching focus on contemporary women writers and global feminism. She is currently working on a book on South African writer Miriam Tlali.

Biman Basu completed his Ph.D. at the University of Minnesota, Minneapolis and is now teaching in the English Department at Hobart and William Smith Colleges. His articles have appeared in *Callaloo*, *College Literature*, *Ariel*, and *MELUS*. An article on W.E.B. Du Bois is forthcoming in *Diaspora*, and he is currently completing a manuscript on African American literature, focussing mainly on African American women's fiction of the twentieth century.

Linda E. Chown is Associate Professor of English and Coordinator of Women and Gender Studies at Grand Valley State University in the State of Michigan. Her research focus is narratology and women writers, both nationally and internationally. Her book, *Narrative Authority and Homeostasis,* on Spanish writer Carmen Martin Gaite and British writer Doris Lessing appeared in 1990. She has published on Clarice Lispector, Willa Cather, Virginia Woolf,

Doris Lessing, as well as conducted a series of interviews in Spain with Spanish women novelists, Ana Maria Matute, Rosa Chacel, Elena Quiroga, Montserrat Roig, Esther Tusquets, among others.

Jeffrey Geller is a professor of philosophy at the University of North Carolina at Pembroke, where he has taught for the past seventeen years. His publications span a wide range of disciplines in addition to philosophy, including psychology, literature, film theory, and cultural studies. His current research interests are primarily in the history of philosophy, including African philosophy, and in the philosophy of science.

Giuliana Lund is Assistant Professor of Interdisciplinary Humanities at Arizona State University. She has published on cinema and AIDS prevention in Southern Africa. She is currently working on a book about plague as an allegory for imperial crises in twentieth century literature.

Kgomotso Masemola attained his degrees from the Universities of the Witwatersrand and Natal, taking his BA and Honours from the former and a Masters in Postcolonial Studies from the latter. He proceeded to teach for five years at the University of Zululand, after a lecturing spell at Vista University. He is currently a Lecturer in the Department of English at the University of Transkei.

Sally-Ann Murray is a South African who lectures in the Programmes of English Studies and Media and Communication at the Durban campus of the University of Natal. She has published on southern African novelists and poets, as well as on areas more unusual in English Studies, among them shopping malls, women's magazines and themed leisure.

Brendon Nicholls is currently completing a PhD in Comparative Literature at the University of Essex. His research focuses on identity, cultural encounters and psychopathology in the fiction of the

Beat Generation, Dambudzo Marechera and Tsitsi Dangarembga. His primary research interests are in American Literature and African Literature, and he has published work on Ngugi wa Thiong'o (in the Association of English University Teachers of South Africa conference proceedings), on Post-Apartheid political violence in universities (in the Australian Humanities Review) and on teaching Robert Frost's poetry in a South African university (forthcoming in *Crossing Boundaries*, edited by Julie Scanlon and Amy Waste).

Jeanette Treiber holds a Ph.D. in Comparative Literature from the University of California, Davis. She has taught Comparative and African Literature as well as African Studies at University of California, Davis and at National University, and has published on Mariama Bâ's *Un Chant Ecarlate*. Since 1997, Treiber has been working as a Program Associate for Freedom from Hunger, a non-governmental organization, which promotes sustainable microenterprise development and education projects for women solidarity groups in the developing world. While stationed in the U.S., her field-work in assessments of women's and children's health and economic status has taken her to Mali and Guinea and Madagascar.

Jacqueline Wigfall is a freelance editor completing a doctoral dissertation on African and Diasporic Literatures at Stanford University. She has taught literature and writing courses at Shaw University, Stanford University, and LaSalle University.

Ann Elizabeth Willey is an Assistant Professor in the Department of English, University of Louisville. Her research focuses on the intersections of rhetorics of national identity and narrative structure in postcolonial Africa. She has published on Yambo Ouologuem, Ousmane Sembene, Ama Ata Aidoo, and Myriam Warner-Vierya. She has also been a Fulbright Lecturer at the Université de Ouagadougou, Burkina Faso.

Kellie Donovan Wixson is a graduate student in English at Tufts University. As part of her work in 19th century British literature, she is interested in the intersection of popular and material culture with the British Empire.

Heather Zwicker is Associate Professor in the Department of English at the University of Alberta. A postcolonialist by training, she locates her work at the crossroads of postcolonialism and cultural studies, with a particular focus on queer theory and feminisms. This essay was supported by funding from the Social Sciences and Humanities Research Council of Canada.

Index